THRILLING TRUE STORIES

ALEXANDER LAKE

Alexander Lake in 1955 Unknown Photographer

THRILLING TRUE STORIES

ALEXANDER LAKE

THE RESNICK LIBRARY
OF AFRICAN ADVENTURE
Mike Resnick, Series Editor

No. 2 in the series

Publisher: Ralph Roberts

Resnick Library of African Adventure
Series Editor: Mike Resnick

Editors: Ralph Roberts, Pat Roberts

Cover Design: ©2001 Storm Alexis Lake
Interior Design & Electronic Page Assembly: **WorldComm**®
Photographs as indicated
Cover Illustration: KUHN

10 9 8 7 6 5 4 3 2

Library of Congress Cataloging-in-Pubication

Lake, Alexander
    Hunter's Choice : thrilling true stories / Alexander Lake
        p.   cm. -- (Resnick's library of African adventure)
    Originally published: 1st ed. Garden City, N.Y. : Doubleday, 1954.
    ISBN 1-57090-026-4   (alk. paper)
    1. Lake, Alexander.   2. Hunters--Africa--Biography.   3. Big game hunting--Africa--Anecdotes.   I. Title.   II. Series.
SK17.L35A3   1995
799.2'092--dc20
[B]   95-49383
                                                        CIP
ISBN 1-57090-026-4   trade paper
ISBN 1-57090-119-8   limited edition hardback

Alexander Books™—a division of Creativity, Inc.—is a full–service publisher located at 65 Macedonia Road, Alexander NC 28701. Phone (828) 252–9515, Fax (828) 255–8719. For orders only: 1-800-472-0438. Visa and MasterCard accepted. Web: **abooks.com**.

Alexander Books™ is distributed to the trade by Midpoint Trade Books, Inc., 27 West 20th Street, New York NY 10011, (212) 727-0190, (212) 727-0195 fax.

Contents

Introduction 7

1 Call For Sixty Monkeys! 11

2 Stand-in for Mussolini 21

3 Buttons for the King 33

4 How to Find Three Emeralds 55

5 A Parade and a Bet 75

6 Don't Spoil the Heads 93

7 Buffalo Pot Roast, etc. 107

8 The Spider and the Quicksand 123

9 Wynken, Blynken, and Nod 139

10 Stuffed Heroes 159

11 Witch Doctor 173

12 Cyril and the Bustard 187

13 Raw Meat in Ethiopia 211

14 Rhino Horns for Romance 225

Alexander Lake in 1922

INTRODUCTION
by Mike Resnick

When we reprinted Alexander Lake's first book, **Killers in Africa**, last spring, we promised you that if it sold at all well, we'd be following it up with his **Hunter's Choice**. The sales figures are in, the readers have spoken, and here it is — another book by that most readable of all authors of Africana.

Encountering an Alexander Lake book is very much like sitting around an African campfire and letting an old pro spin tales of his youth — but while **Killers in Africa** was strictly about hunting, and was divided into chapters about various animals, **Hunter's Choice** is a true potpourri of tales guaranteed to tweak anyone's sense of wonder and adventure.

It even has a chapter unique to African books. Every hunter will happily tell you about the chase and the kill, and then regale you with how wonderful that kudu or impala tasted — but only Alexander Lake tells you, delightfully, *how* to cook that beast once you've killed it.

Ever wonder how to trap sixty monkeys armed with nothing but twenty gallons of bad booze? Trust Lake to supply the hilarious answer.

Could anyone — even Lake's brilliant tracker, Ubusuku — possibly kill six species of large, dangerous game armed only with a hand ax? Lake describes the hunt that was initiated by a two thousand pound bet (the pre-World War I equivalent of a $100,000 wager) between an American hunter and Lake's employer, Nicobar Jones.

Lake even recounts a jungle murder, and the recovery of three of King John's emeralds.

And, of course, he tells these tales within the framework of his life: an American, with American attitudes and an American way of looking at things, who made his way across the African continent as a professional hunter. He recalls his clients, both good and bad, humorous and tragic, with a contagious fondness.

It is amazing to me that this book could have remained out of print for close to forty years, for it is a pure delight from the first page to the last. Still, while Lake was obviously a happy and contented man, true fame eluded him until the last decade of his life.

He was born Alexander James Lake in Chicago, Illinois, on July 29, 1893. His father was a Methodist minister, and the family moved to South Africa in 1908. Lake went to Jeppestown High School in Johannesburg, and then attended the Marist Brothers College, where he captained the rifle team that represented the Transvaal at the All-British Empire Shumaker Cup. His team came in second, but he himself set a record of 11 bull's-eyes in 35 seconds, which brought him to the attention of the famed trader Nicobar Jones, who hired him as a meat hunter, a job that took him to Portuguese East Africa, Tanganyika, Kenya, Uganda, Northern Rhodesia, and German Southwest Africa. Within a couple of years he was a fully-fledged and licensed white hunter.

He took time off from his hunting career to fight for the American forces as a pilot in Europe during World War I, then went back to his beloved Africa for another twelve years, after which he returned to the United States, working as a reporter and editor for a number of newspapers in the Pacific Northwest. Then Africa called to him once again, and he returned there in 1937 for three more years. When he came back to the States in 1940, this time to stay, he met and married his wife, Mildred, and began writing anything that would sell: African reminiscences, business articles, even some pulp fiction.

Says his daughter, Storm Alexis Lake: "He loved being the center of attention, and he was fascinating and fun to be around. He loved life and lived it to its fullest, with a very wild first 40 years. When he met and fell in love with my mother, he became tamed and settled down for the first time in his life. It's amazing what a good woman can do for a man! Once a heavy drinker, after meeting my mother he never touched alcohol again."

After World War II ended, he and Mildred bought a home on the Pacific Coast near the California/Oregon border, and he finally started cracking the major popular magazine markets — *Look, Collier's, Time, Reader's Digest* — with his accounts of Africa and hunting. His main markets, however, were *Field and Stream* and *Argosy*, where he delighted in debunking the myths of African hunting and setting the record straight.

Killers in Africa became a bestseller in 1953, and **Hunter's Choice** also made the bestseller lists a year later. These led Lake to a job as a consultant and writer for Sol Lesser, producer of the Tarzan films. (In fact, Lake may well be the reason that Gordon Scott was allowed to speak in sentences, rather than monosyllables. At least I'd like to think so.)

Finally, in his last few years, Lake began researching his father's missionary work in Africa. This in turn led him to investigate reported answers to prayer, and that led to two more bestsellers, *Your Prayers Are Always Answered* and *You Need Never Walk Alone*. He died on Christmas Day, 1961, while working on a biography of his father.

I discovered Alexander Lake when I was eleven years old. I picked up a copy of **Killers in Africa**, and had read half of it in the bookstore before my mother realized she was either going to have to buy the book or leave me in the store overnight. A few months later I bought **Hunter's Choice** with money I had earned mowing lawns, and from that day forward I knew two things: that someday I would visit the wonderful continent that Lake had made come alive on the printed page (I have, 6 times now, with more trips planned), and that I would find some way to make my living from Africa (that took a little longer, and considering that I became a science fiction writer, it was a lot more difficult—but I managed. I would confidently suggest that no other science fiction writer, dead or alive, has set 13 books and 22 works of short fiction in Africa or African analogs, or received as many major and minor awards for them. And of course, a lot of Lake's reminiscences have been appropriated, thinly-disguised, in my fiction.)

Before we go any further, I want to tell you a little something about the cover to this edition of **Hunter's Choice**. At first glance it appears to be a scene from Chapter 6 ("Don't Spoil the Heads") of this book, but if you'll look at it *closely*, you'll see it's really from **Killers in Africa**'s chapter on elephants. The giveaway is the figure of Lake himself, on the ground beneath the elephant. The African with the ax is, of course, Ubusuku.

So why didn't we run it on **Killers in Africa**? Simple. I didn't know Storm Alexis Lake then. Over the past few months she has graciously gone through her father's old notes and magazine articles as we try to find enough uncollected material to create a brand-new Alexander Lake book. During one of our phone conversations, she mentioned that she and her brother owned this remarkable painting of her father's miraculous escape from a wounded elephant, rendered by an artist named Kuhn. Before she was through describing it, I knew we had the cover for **Hunter's Choice**.

By the way, as the editor of this series, I do try to be thorough, and when it came time to publish **Hunter's Choice**, I thought I would see if I could find a negative opinion, since mine is one of unmitigated praise. Well, I checked every review ever written, and I finally found one, in the September, 1954 issue of *African Wild Life*, published by the South African Wild Life Society, of which less than 2,000 copies were printed. (How's *that* for thorough?)

The reviewer, who uses only his initials — D.E.N. — takes Lake rather severely to task for two misstatements: that lions charge in "forty-foot leaps" and that the lion "is the fastest animal on earth."

Well, they once measured the stride of the great race horse, Swaps, and it turned out to be 33 feet 8 inches, so I have to assume that Lake — who probably did not have a measuring tape handy when charged by lions — was wrong.

As for his statement that the lion is the fastest animal on earth, I'm sure he was as aware of the cheetah's 65-mile-per-hour speed as everyone else. What you have to remember is that we aren't the only creatures who know lions have very little stamina; lions know it too. Hence, unlike the cheetah, who spots his meal a quarter mile away and then runs it down across open territory, the lion rarely charges more than sixty yards. If he hasn't caught his prey by then, he usually gives up. Now, there is no question that the cheetah is the fastest animal on earth, but it takes him a little time to work up to his top speed, whereas the lion is going full speed at his first stride. I've seen them both in action, and I'd be willing to bet Lake was right — *if* you limit it to the length of ground a lion charges (and since Lake was more aware of a lion's limitations than most men, why would he describe a longer race?) So much for D.E.N., whoever he or she was.

Okay. I've gone on long enough, and you've got a wonderful book to read. I think if I were to choose a single word to describe **Hunter's Choice**, it would be *evocative*. Lake's description of his office, or Ubusuku's hunt, or the mystic power of a Zulu witch doctor, or the Sunday baseball games in Johannesburg, or a lonely Christmas Eve in the bush... well, if they don't make you wish you'd been there, then somebody shorted your soul in the areas of Romance and Adventure.

Mike Resnick

CALL FOR SIXTY MONKEYS!

There is more adventure, and far more money, in professional hunting in Africa today than there has ever been. Within one week after landing in any African port a man with initiative can be making a living shooting crocodiles; collecting rare small animals for museums; selling hides and skins to American fur traders; trapping male monkeys for European monkey-gland doctors; shooting meat for mine and road contractors; or working at any of many such jobs.

Unless the man's a smart trader, he won't grow rich, but he'll make a living. He'll work hard, for he'll foot-slog an average of twenty-five miles for each successful shot from his rifle.

Men deficient in imagination are unable to recognize an adventure when they see it. I know a farmer in Kenya who was pestered by lions for thirteen years. He considered them vermin; saw nothing interesting in them. Yet Martin and Osa Johnson, American camera hunters, wrote fascinating books about those same lions.

I know a man who for twenty years has made his living by shooting crocodiles on Congo and Uganda rivers. To him a crocodile is merely a stinking reptile. He doesn't even know to what uses the cured skins are put. Yet my stories about hunting crocs along those very rivers have been published for years in magazines of Europe and America.

An adventure is a happening that involves hazard or danger. The threat is usually to one's life or well-being; but sometimes to one's ego. A deflated ego can be painful... and monkeys are Africa's best ego deflators.

Around 1912 the demand for male monkey sex glands for transplanting into wealthy old roués of Europe and America became so great that the price of a live male monkey jumped from twenty-four cents (one shilling) to almost ten dollars (two pounds). Today gland-transplanting is even bigger business, and although he-goats and rams now share the monkey's burden of supplying "oomph," prices paid for young, healthy male monkeys are still satisfactory.

Orders for male monkeys are usually for lots of fifty—about $500 worth. Using ordinary methods, a man's fortunate if he captures fifty males in a month. But monkey-trapping can be speeded.

I was nineteen, and for two years had been apprentice meat hunter for Nicobar Jones, one of Africa's great traders. We'd just returned to Pretoria from a five-month hunt in the Congo. I'd bagged my first elephant and my first lion on that trip. I really felt like a hunter.

One morning Jones called me into the warehouse and handed me a letter from a monkey buyer. It was an order for sixty live male vervet monkeys, called "gray apes" by hunters. As I handed the letter back Jones said:

"Take two ox wagons and three Kaffirs. Trek up to that abandoned farm of mine near Zeerust and fill this order."

With my head still full of elephants, the idea of catching twenty-pound gray-green vervets was a letdown. I said:

"Apes, for Pete's sake! Why not baboons—they got brains."

"No baboons," Jones said. "Seems some doctors transplanted baboon glands in a New York playboy one time. He married seven women, one after the other. Each woman divorced him 'cause when he wasn't swinging from chandeliers, he was searching for fleas. It'll be good for you to take a try at monkeys. You been throwing your weight about lately."

"Monkeys —"

"There's about $600 in this job, son," Jones interrupted. "Expenses 'll be about $12 a day. If it takes you more than fifty days to catch sixty apes, I'll lose money."

"I'll be back in a week," I said.

"Could be, but I doubt it."

"With any luck at all—"

"Ain't no luck—you know that. Good luck's know-how. Bad luck's ignorance."

"Well, anybody," I said, "could catch sixty apes."

"Sure, if you get 'em drunk," Jones said.

"*Very* funny," I said huffily.

Jones looked at me quizzically, began to speak, shrugged instead, and turned away. I'd a feeling, somehow, that he was laughing at me. It got my dander up.

The rest of that day and part of the night I tried to figure out a way to catch sixty apes in one swoop, so to speak. After midnight an idea struck, and I chuckled.

Early next morning I bought a two-gallon can of ready-mixed cabinetmaker's glue and a package of chloride of lime. When mixed, they'd make a very sticky birdlime. I'd show Jones, the old goat! I'd be back with sixty live monkeys in no time.

We left Pretoria in mid-morning—Masilo, an old Zulu tracker; Jan and Jappie, Basuto boys; and I. We drove the oxen hard and made the 115 miles to Jones's old farm in three days. I put the Basutos to work weaving bamboo cages to fit in the wagon beds, and Masilo and I prowled about looking over the ape situation.

The old orchard was a brush-grown jungle, but it wasn't full of apes. We decided there was only one troop. Masilo, who could read sign as readily as I could read a book, said:

"Maybe seventy-five papas, *Baas.*"

That meant the troop numbered around three hundred; half youngsters, a quarter females, seventy-five papas—and I needed sixty of those papas.

From stores that Jan and Jappie had unloaded from the wagons I got the glue and lime, and mixed them. The resulting mess was as tough and sticky a goo as I'd ever seen.

Next morning, with our hands, Masilo and I began spreading the mixture on the main branches of an orange tree. The mixture worked up our wrists and into my clothes. Not only was it sticky, but it stank. Masilo daubed a branch behind me and I promptly backed my head into it.

Hot, sweaty, and frustrated, I crawled out of the tree and tried rubbing my hands with sand. I succeeded only in producing a sort of stucco. I tried washing in a small stream. Water relaxed the glue a bit and I finally got most of the mess off by using wet sand as a scouring powder. Meanwhile Masilo, still working, was able to coat most of the lower tree limbs before the mixture ran out.

I figured that if we caught only one ape, its cries and struggles would bring the whole troop to see what was up. They in turn would find their feet glued to the tree. Then we'd release females and youngsters, put the males in the wagon cages and take off for Pretoria in triumph.

But for hours apes played all around the "Judas" tree without once touching it. Then just before sundown an adventurous baby got stuck like a fly in tanglefoot. His screeches brought comrades on the run and in no time twenty apes were fighting the tenacious paste, screaming hysterically.

However, only six of the twenty were adults and those six soon jerked loose, leaped to the ground, and high-tailed it into the brush, running clumsily as their birdlimed feet balled up with grass and dirt.

The fourteen little ones still in the tree stopped shrieking, but shivered and chittered in fear. I felt sorry for them. I called Jan and Jappie and the four of us carried baby monkeys to the stream, where we scoured goo off every small black hand and foot and turned the youngsters loose. Then we cut down the tree and burned it.

Next morning I said to Masilo:

"Looks like we went at this job all wrong."

"*Yebo.* A cow does not eat grass with her hind end, O *Baas.* If you would catch apes you must be smarter than the ape."

I said: "You talk too much, Masilo. Show me how you catch monkeys."

Masilo's teeth flashed in a smile. He yelled something to Jan and Jappie. They smiled too, and loped off across the veld. Masilo said:

"The ape that puts his hand in a hole and grasps a *mealie* is caught. The Basutos are gone to bring gourds from the *kopje.*"

I knew, of course, that natives caught vervet and guenon monkeys by drilling a hole in a gourd—a hole large enough to admit an ape's open hand, but too small to permit a clenched fist to withdraw. The gourd was tied to a tree. Once a monkey grasped the corn inside, he was a goner. He'd die before he'd open his fist.

That method caught young and old, females as well as males—a slow process. However, my birdlime idea'd been a flop, so the gourd trick seemed the only alternative.

Jan and Jappie showed up with six gourds about the size of small pumpkins and I sat watching as they cut holes and dropped in *mealie* kernels. It seemed to me that Jones wasn't going to make much profit on this deal.

The Kaffirs each took two gourds, put them on the ground beneath trees, then fastened them to the trunks with rawhide thongs. Squatting like baboons, they then picked up the gourds, shook them, listened to the rattling, pretended to take kernels out. They performed this way until the apes, unable to restrain their curiosity, crowded close, peering from behind an overhead curtain of leaves.

After a while the Kaffirs retired to about fifty feet and lay quietly in the grass. Soon an old female dropped from a branch, ran to a gourd, and hopped up and down beside it. With one hand she made a couple of passes at it, shrieked, and scampered up into the tree. In a minute or so she was down and at the gourd again. She slapped it, then jumped back. With scores of apes above staring in fascination she then picked up the gourd, shook it, put her ear to the hole, listened, and hurriedly set the gourd down. She picked it up again, peered inside the hole, put the gourd on the ground, squatted on her haunches, pushed her hand through the hole, grasped the *mealies,* tried to withdraw her fist—then screamed bloody murder.

She jerked, pulled, tugged, rolled on the ground, bit at the gourd and shook it frantically. She was still screeching when Masilo broke the gourd and turned her loose.

Half an hour later one of Jappie's gourds caught a male and Jappie carried the prize to the wagon cage. That one male was the only adult male trapped for three days although at least fifteen females were snared. On the next day we got four males. The next day one. Ten days had now passed since we'd left Pretoria. With expenses running $12 a day it meant those six male monkeys had already cost Jones $20 each.

I felt pretty low.

I lay long in my blankets that night, staring at the stars. It wasn't fair to Jones to remain on so hopeless a job. I'd decided to leave for Pretoria early next morning, when I recalled Jones's remark the night before we'd left:

"Get 'em drunk."

Suddenly I realized that he'd meant that. It explained the odd look he'd given me, and his shrug.

I didn't know how to go about getting monkeys drunk, but I worked out a plan. I sent Masilo and Jappie to Zeerust next morning—a thirty-five-mile trek—with instructions to buy twenty-five pounds of sugar and four five-gallon paraffin tins. While they were gone Jan and I gathered a couple of bushels of ripe *moopels* (wild dates).

Masilo and Jappie got back in the evening three days later. Early next morning we cut the tops off the paraffin cans and half filled each can with alternate layers of *moopels* and sugar. We filled the rest of each can with water, covered them with a tarp, and left them in the sun.

I figured it'd take at least four days for the brew to develop a decent kick, but when Jan walked up to me three mornings later, burped, and fell on his face, I knew I was all set to contribute to the delinquency of monkeys.

I took the tarp off the cans and with the two sober Kaffirs retired behind the wagons, leaving Jan to sleep off his jag in the grass. From time to time an ape would wander to the brew, sniff, wrinkle his nose, and amble back to the trees. The sun slid lower and lower down the sky. The monkeys showed less and less interest in Demon Rum. I was disgusted. Then, at exactly the moment an old male started for the cans, Jan staggered up from the grass, stumbled to the nearest can, shoved his mouth into the brew, and began gulping.

I grabbed my *sjambok* to give Jan a swipe on the fanny, but stopped in my tracks when I noticed that the ape had sat down about twenty yards behind Jan and was watching him with comical intentness. Jan crawled back to his grass bed on hands and knees. When Jan lay down the ape went to the same can, and without the slightest hesitation began to drink. He spat and sputtered a few times, drank more, leaped to the edge of the can, teetered a moment, fell in. He climbed out, began to run, fell, got up, turned back to the can, jerked at it, and tipped it over. He wobbled around a bit, squawking hoarsely, then swung a sudden punch at the air. He spun like a top, fell on his side, and was instantly asleep.

By this time forty or fifty of the troop had edged up to watch. A young female made for another can, tasted, drank greedily, one hand on the can's edge. Her legs grew limber and she sank slowly to the ground. She sat up, looked at one of her feet, tried to grasp it, failed, and sat chittering weakly.

Abruptly the sun sank behind the *kopje*. As if it were a signal, the whole ape mob wheeled and galloped for their sleeping place. An ape fears nothing more than the dark.

Next morning I rolled from my blankets early to keep Jan away from the liquor. I needn't have worried... the poor lug had a hangover that kept him moaning until noon.

The two captive apes proved to be better drinking men. They guzzled the water we offered, then leaped about happily on the bars of the cage. Masilo freed the female. The moment she was on the ground she made straight for the saloon and in ten minutes was silly drunk—as were about thirty-five other apes.

The orgy started quietly, but soon became hectic. Monkeys stood toe-to-toe and slugged futilely at one another. One ran screaming for a tree, leaped at the trunk, missed by two feet, and went rolling heels over head. Another rushed at Masilo, bit him on the ankle, then scrambled up the Zulu's body, put his arms around his neck, laid his head on his shoulder, and smiled foolishly. A young female chased a staggering male, knocked him down, mounted him. The male screamed in outrage. Another female pulled the rapist off, took a swing at her, missed, fell down, picked herself up, and wobbled back to the cans.

Two old boys who'd each failed to get to the trees under his own power tried helping one another. Time after time one would fall and the other would pull him to his feet, then fall down himself. Repeatedly falling and getting up, they got almost to the grove, became confused, and helped each other get up and fall down again all the way back to where they'd started.

By mid-morning nearly every adult in the troop had had a snootful. Babies and half-grown apes thronged lower limbs of nearby trees staring at their elders in ludicrous unbelief. Several times small groups of young ones, wanting to get to the brew, tried pushing through the melee. They were knocked higgledy-piggledy by milling drunks, and retreated sullenly to protection of the trees.

In the background baboons watched from the slopes of a dark red *kopje*. Practically naked, Masilo and Jappie leaped about among the drinkers, snatching up the more helpless males and carrying them to the wagon cages. The apes, so fearful of humans when sober, seemed now to have no fear at all. Sometimes they shrieked when first picked up, but almost invariably snuggled down in the Kaffirs' arms, apparently content.

Occasionally, however, a tipsy ape would resent the natives and make ridiculous attempts to battle them. One old rascal got his hands in Jappie's hair, sank teeth in the lobe of his ear, shut his eyes, and hung on. Jappie instantly became a leaping, shouting, hysterical ape himself. Baboons on the hillside, as if recognizing a kindred spirit, waughed and barked, leaped up and down in sympathy.

By eleven o'clock there were thirty-five apes in cages and about fifty females sleeping it off in the open. Things grew quiet and I thought the orgy was over for the day. It flared up briefly, though, when seven young males at the cans began fighting. The battle began when one fuddled youngster picked up a short stick and, waving it, accidentally poked a companion in the belly. The victim squealed in rage. All seven apes sailed into one another, biting and clawing. In the struggle they knocked over the three cans that until then had miraculously remained upright. The young fellows seemed to realize what they'd done, for they stopped fighting, grabbed up handfuls of liquor-soaked earth, tasted, spat, and wandered dejectedly back to the orange grove.

The day's orgy was over and I had thirty-five husky male apes. One more big drinking party would fill the order. I'd intended sending Masilo and Jappie to Zeerust for more sugar, but they convinced me that sugar wasn't necessary. They gathered more *moopels* and spent the rest of the day chewing the *moopels* to a pulp. Next morning they chewed handfuls of corn meal until it was wet with saliva, then added it to the date pulp. They half buried the cans this time to keep the monkeys from tipping them.

Five days later the second orgy occurred. In almost every respect it was a repetition of the first, except that this time Masilo, Jappie, and Jan all got drunk too. Masilo, like all Zulus, hated Basutos, so it wasn't long before he was whamming their bare backs with his fighting stick. He chased the Basutos halfway up the *kopje,* came back, and shouted to the apes:

"I kill rhinos with bare hands!" Then he fell down and refused to get up.

The frightened Basutos stayed up on the hill for hours among the baboons. Working alone, I got thirty-one more apes into cages and on the twenty-first day after leaving Pretoria delivered sixty-four healthy males to Jones. Jones said:

"You done good." So I began swanking a bit. My ego deflated quickly, though, when Jones added:

"Next time, put cans of brew in the cages. The apes'll go in after it. All you'll have to do then is to pull the females out."

"Yes, sir," I said.

I said that monkeys feared nothing more than the dark. I should have added, "except snakes." Snakes, poisonous or nonpoisonous, drive monkeys into screaming hysterics. The chief terror of apes in South Africa is the ringhals—the spitting cobra. Its bite is deadly. It can squirt venom six feet with accuracy. In a man's eye the venom causes blindness, and often death. When you attack a ringhals, it pays to wear glasses.

One morning I glanced out through the open top half of the Dutch front door of an Orange River Colony farmhouse. Early sunlight lay golden on the packed-earth *stoep.*

Margie Thoms, an eighteen-year-old blonde English visitor, wearing a green bathing suit, lay on her stomach on the *stoep,* chin cupped in palms, reading a newspaper. And less than six inches from her feet a four-foot ringhals lay outstretched, tongue darting inquisitively toward Margie's bare heels.

Unaware, Margie moved slightly. The ringhals coiled, reared briefly, drew its head back on its coils. I said quietly:

"Don't move, Margie. There's a snake near your feet. Stay perfectly still for a moment—I'll ..."

The girl gasped, drew in her legs, and sat up, facing me. The open newspaper fell across her lap.

Instantly the ringhals reared, hood flaring. But instead of spitting or striking it slithered under the newspaper, pushing its head out close to Margie's breasts. Margie, face white, eyes staring darkly, leaned far back, bracing herself with her hands against the floor. I said:

"Chin up, Margie. He won't hurt you if you don't move. I'll get him, but it'll take a few minutes. I can't shoot while he's coiled close like that and I can't walk across the porch. He'd feel the vibration. Sit absolutely still. I'll be back in a moment."

As I turned from the door Margie's heart began pounding so hard that the newspaper trembled. Immediately nervous shiftings of the ringhals' coils bulged the paper. His head lifted to the level of Margie's breast. The red tongue flickered momentarily, then the snake withdrew entirely underneath the newspaper, where it stirred restlessly. I said:

"I'm sending for Hans, Margie. He's in the orchard and it'll take three or four minutes for him to get here. He'll kill the snake with his whip. Don't speak—and don't move."

I'll never forget that tortured girl's eyes.

I ran through the house into the kitchen. Jim, the big Kaffir cook, was on hands and knees, scrubbing the floor. I said:

"Jim, make quick to the orchard and get *Baas* Hans. Tell him a ringhals— on the front *stoep*—is coiled on Miss Margie's lap. I think he'll have to kill it with his ox whip. Make quick, Jim. Then keep the Kaffirs—everybody—away from the *stoep* until after the snake is dead. Understand, Jim?"

"*Yebo, Baas,*" Jim rumbled, and bounded out the door.

I took my .22 rifle from the gun rack, but stood, breathing deeply to quiet the thumping of my own heart before hurrying back to Margie. If I had to shoot, I'd have to be calm. I wasn't too worried about Hans du Toit's ability to kill the snake with his whip. Like most South African Boers, Hans was an expert with the long-handled, long-lashed ox whip. With a bamboo handle eight feet long, a tapered rawhide lash of thirteen feet, and on the end of the lash, a thin, three-foot, pliable rawhide "stinger," the whip was twenty-four feet in length— and Hans's special delight.

He'd often boasted that he could flick a fly from the ear of an ox with this whip— at twenty feet. I'd seen him, at that distance, cut the neck from a ginger-beer bottle. His favorite trick was to place a silver two-shilling piece on the ground, walk seven long paces away, turn, and send the lash hissing out to flick the coin high into air. As often as not he'd move under the coin and catch it as it fell.

I went back to the open top of the door. Margie seemed in a trance—eyes closed, lips gray. Her heart seemed quiet. Only the tip of the ringhals' tail was visible from beneath the paper.

Young Hans, whip in hands, stepped around the corner of the *stoep.* His face was drawn and white—for he was deeply in love with this beautiful English girl. For a moment he looked the situation over, then said to me:

"We've got to get it out from under the paper. Find Mei-ling, Margie's Peke, and bring him to the door."

I'd noticed the little dog asleep on the sofa in the living room when I'd gone to the kitchen, so I picked him up and held him at the door. Hans said.

"Hold him there a minute."

Margie opened her eyes, then closed them.

Hans was standing in bright sunlight a good twenty-one feet from the newspaper. Slowly, taking a "sighting" shot, he sent the long lash snaking back over his shoulder, then with a flowing motion, drove it forward. The stinger tip settled like a feather at the near edge of the newspaper. Hans stepped back a few inches, withdrew the lash, looked at me and said tightly:

"Put the dog down and push him toward Margie." Then, to her, he said: "It'll be over in a moment, *Hartlum.* Just don't move."

Margie seemed not to have heard him.

I put the Peke down and gave him a push in Margie's direction, but he turned, looked up at me, and then began pawing at the bottom of the door—wanting to go back to his lazy, comfortable nap. Then the newspaper rustled and the Peke walked hesitatingly toward the noise. Suddenly he sensed the snake, rushed close, put his head on his paws, and began to yip.

The ringhals reacted instantly. It reared high, shoving the newspaper aside. Its evil neck arched until the fangs pointed at the dog. Its three white bands below the throat flashed white against the dirty gray of its skin—and Hans's whip struck swiftly.

The snake seemed to leap into the air, then—in two halves—it fell a good five feet way. The tail half writhed and flipped. The head half lay still, but the protruding fangs dripped venom.

Hans picked Margie up in his arms and carried her into the house.

The Peke yipped frantically at the still-living head of the ringhals. I placed the muzzle of my .22 close to one staring eye and pulled the trigger.

STAND-IN FOR MUSSOLINI

In December 1937, I signed an agreement to kill lions in front of the movie camera of Gennaro Boggio, photographer for the Italian Ministry of Education. Later Benito Mussolini was to be dubbed in for me—the idea being to prove to the recently conquered Ethiopians that Il Duce was a mighty Nimrod.

For centuries the lion had been the official symbol of Ethiopia. The headdresses of army officers had been manes of lions they themselves had killed. Mussolini wanted a headdress and it was to be bigger and better than anyone else's. The film was to show him shooting the lion in a roaring, charging close-up.

Boggio had shown up at my hunting camp east of the Lunga River in Northern Rhodesia, with four Bechuana porters, five cameras, and a letter of introduction from someone in the American Consul's office at Johannesburg. I hesitated about taking the job because it's difficult to make lions charge; and next to impossible to find a lion with a mane that's not brush-torn and ragged. When Boggio showed me a draft for £600 on Barclay's Dominion, Colonial and Overseas Bank, however, I signed.

Boggio was a wisp of a man with a big, black soup-strainer mustache, and he never smiled. I got the impression that he believed he'd be shot if he returned to Italy with an unsatisfactory film. At any rate he acted that way.

The very next morning after I'd signed the agreement Boggio was all hot to go after lions, but when I explained I'd first have to prepare three buffalo heads for shipment to a Pretoria taxidermist, he took his hand camera and went off on a hunt of his own. About noon, as Horo, my Bushman top tracker, and I were putting the skinned skulls on an ant heap for the ants to clean, Boggio came a-running, waving his arms and shouting:

"Big lions! Big voices! Hurry!"

"Voices?" I said. "You mean that roaring out there?"

"*Sì*. Hurry, please, signore."

"Those are ostriches booming," I said. "Lions don't roar in daylight."

Boggio didn't seem to believe me, so I told Twak, my second boy, to take him out and show him the big birds. "Be careful, Boggio," I said, "ostriches can be more dangerous than lions."

"Why you make joke?" Boggio asked.

"I'm not joking," I said. "Ostriches have been known to break a lion's back with one kick."

Boggio was astounded. "B-but, the lion! My God, he is the king!"

"Boggio," I said, "instead of going out to look at the ostriches, let's go to camp. We'll have a spot of tea and I'll tell you some of the facts of life."

So while Boggio alternately sipped tea and tongued drippings from his mustache, I also sipped tea as I proceeded to disillusion him.

"Lions seldom live up to the myth that they're creatures of magnificent beauty, courage, and ferocity. Actually they're tick-cursed; and usually cowardly in the face of superior force. In every country in Africa except Kenya and Tanganyika lions are officially classed as *vermin.* That means 'noxious and disgusting' animals. And, as vermin, they may be slaughtered without licenses, in unlimited numbers.

"Normally, lion-shooting's one of the professional hunter's most monotonous jobs. And no experienced white hunter has ever been killed by a lion except through his own foolishness or carelessness.

"Unless pestered beyond endurance, lions attend strictly to their own business, and kill only for food. But they're scavengers, and won't bother game if there are carcasses to feed on. They never kill a large antelope if they can get a small one, nor do they attack a healthy beast if they can get a sick one, or a cripple. Where mice are plentiful, the 'regal' lion makes them his chief item of diet.

"As to being King of the Beasts, the only elephants, rhinos, or hippos a lion will attack are babies that wander away from their herds. Single lions seldom attack large antelope such as kudu, sable, and buffalo. Lions hunt these big fellows in packs. I once watched a buffalo cow rout three lions. She gored one, trampled the second, and chased the third.

"And man-eaters? Well, men eat more lions than lions eat men. Man-eating lions are few, and those few are almost always old, toothless, or sick animals too feeble to run down game. If you can't kill a man-eater, feed him. Leave an antelope or a sheep for him once every ten days or so and you'll no longer have a man-eater.

"Everywhere in Africa, lion country's about the same—sandy or bush-dotted plains—boulder-strewn or grass-carpeted veld. And the habits and characteristics of lions in one part of the country are the same as those in other parts. They live in families of from three to fifteen animals. When food is plentiful they seldom roam more than fifteen miles from their sleeping place. In times of scarcity they follow the game herds.

"Lions are sleepy animals. It's not unusual to come across whole families of them asleep on the open veld. Several times I've stood with rifle ready while Wanda Vik-Persen, of Stockholm, photographed the 'sleeping beauties' from thirty yards. Sometimes I'd have to throw stones at their bellies to make them look interesting. And about all the stones did was to bring the cats to their feet, snarling and switching their tails. Often as not they'd lie down again and begin to snore. Sometimes they'd stalk indignantly for thirty or forty yards before lying down again.

"When not sleeping, lions are usually playing. They act like kittens—mauling, pouncing, wrestling. Occasionally when a half-grown male begins fooling around an older female, the lady's husband will knock the youngster heels over head with a solid cuff. I've teased and pestered family groups many times in an effort to get a lion to charge for the camera. I've succeeded only four times."

Boggio had listened to my discourse with increasing agitation. Now he stood up and began making angry noises in his throat. He said:

"Why you tell lie to me?"

"You're not a big-game photographer, Boggio," I said. "How come the Italian Government gave you this job?"

"Gennaro Boggio is famous with pictures! I photograph every animal in the zoo in Rome. I know about every animal. I know about lions. I read all the books. I see lions in many American cinemas. I know lions bite, charge, charge, charge. Why you tell lie?"

"Sure, Boggio, lions charge, and bite, and claw, and kill—if they're wounded or badgered beyond endurance. A cornered lion will fight for his life as a cornered rat or snake or man will fight for his. It might cheer you up to know that a *desperate* lion can be the most dangerous animal in Africa—for a few minutes. He's the fastest animal on earth. He can charge a hundred yards in four seconds. That's time enough for only two *aimed* shots if you let the first one off when he starts his rush. If you miss that one you'd better drop him with the next, for by the time you let that one off, the lion's only one second—two short jumps—from the gun.

"Fast as he is, a charging lion's duck soup for a cool-nerved, accurate rifleman. The beast's leaps are low and he's coming head on. Let your shot off as his forefeet hit the ground at the end of a jump. Aim at the chest, just below the chin. There's a good chance your bullet will catch heart, lungs, liver, and maybe kidneys. Unless you're sure you can put a bullet between his eyes, don't try a head shot. Men have died because they thought there was some skull beneath that mop of hair. There isn't. Lions have almost no skull above the eyes.

"There's no point in using heavy-calibered rifles on lions. *The big cats can't be killed by shock.* A lion with twenty-three slugs in its body—five of them .450s—killed his man. Anyway, a .270 in a vital spot kills as quickly as a .600 and isn't nearly so messy.

"Because they'd rather run than fight, most lions are killed with a backside shot. That's exactly the reverse of the chest shot; the bullet penetrates the kidneys first, then the liver, lungs, and heart."

By this time Boggio was looking happier and I decided to let him discover any further dope about lions for himself.

"So, Boggio," I said, "what we have to do is to find a lion with a good mane, then drive him half crazy with either fear or pain."

Next morning an hour before dawn we set out. The great valley was good lion country; plenty of game for them to feed on; few hunters. I'd seen lions to the west only a few days before, but hunted to the northeast because the western plain was boggy from recent rains. Northward and eastward the veld was open and parklike. Dry-season fires had burned off the matted grasses and the new grass was short and bright green. The only trees for as far as the eye could see were those that grew on scattered low elevations. It was to the shade of such trees that lions retired after hours of snoozing, frolicking, and rodent-hunting on the flats.

I sent Horo and Twak ahead to locate lions. They were armed with long spears and each carried a small, powerful bow from which he ordinarily shot poisoned arrows. I say "ordinarily," for I'd forbidden them to use, or even to carry, poison while working for me. Bushmen make the stuff by mixing caterpillar guts with milk of the euphorbia tree. It's so deadly that a single drop on a scratched finger will cause death within the hour.

The Bechuana boys carried cameras, tarpaulins, blankets, corn meal, pots, and odds and ends of camp gear. Mokansa, my cook boy, lugged two bandoliers of cartridges and my extra .303. Boggio struggled along with a movie camera and a tripod almost as long as he.

Every step we took was a joy to a hunter's heart. Small herds of zebra, buffalo, sassaby, kudu, and wildebeest turned toward us and stared in mild surprise. A rhino started up from the base of a tree and snorted off in a silly trot, tail up, ears milling. Giraffes, eyes popping with curiosity, watched us until we came within fifty feet, then turned and "floated" away, long necks all slanting at the same angle. Honey birds screamed. Long-tailed songsters started up from the grass. Groups of black-and-white crows squawked insults at us. Secretary birds stalked about like little old stooped bookkeepers with hands beneath long coattails. A lion got to his feet from behind a grass clump, stalked away, looking back over his shoulder until he got behind a bush, then high-tailed it in a most undignified lope, to better cover. Our feet got hot; loads grew heavy. Ants got inside our shirts and chased one another around our belts. The heat mirage slanted listlessly across the ground. Except for birds the veld was silent.

Once in a while Boggio, who scarcely shifted his fascinated eyes from the game, fell into a warthog hole. Toward evening he tumbled into one and broke the tripod. He crawled out cursing, mended the tripod with adhesive tape from the first-aid kit, and twenty minutes later, while trying to sneak up on a buffalo heifer, sprawled into another hole, breaking the tripod again.

Just before we made camp under trees on a bit of wooded rising ground, a herd of zebra that had been watching us suddenly turned to watch a male lion approach them. As if following a command they opened up a passage and let the lion stalk through them.

Boggio, using the back of a kneeling Bechuana boy for a tripod, ground out film, his face almost stupid with amazement. When the lion had disappeared and the zebras were grazing again he said:

"I do not believe!"

"Herds aren't afraid of lions except when lions are on the prowl for food," I said. "Natives say that when a lion's hungry enough to kill, he develops a 'hunger' smell. If that smell isn't present, herds— particularly wildebeest, zebra, and gazelle—permit lions to wander among them at will."

Boggio shook his head and walked away chewing one side of his mustache. Horo said:

"Rain wind come, O Hunter."

Sure enough, the wind had switched to the north, which meant rain before morning. It also meant that lions would be on the prowl. In good weather you won't hear a lion roar from month's end to month's end; but let it storm and they grunt, moan, and roar the night through.

We built two fires, heaped up supplies of extra firewood, made pup tents of our tarps; and because the earth is from ten to fifteen degrees warmer four inches below the surface, we scooped shallow pits to sleep in. We put Boggio's cameras and my spare rifle and ammunition in a hollow tree. We ate broiled haunches of a zebra colt I'd shot in the afternoon; then, with the boys taking turns keeping fires, we rolled in our blankets and slept, feet to the heat.

The rain and the lions came shortly past midnight. I listened to the roaring for a while, but heard no moaning, so went back to sleep —everything was to the good. Lions that don't moan aren't hungry.

Rain continued for three days and nights and Boggio grew increasingly morose. Several times he tried to get flashlight shots when lions came so close to camp that their eyes reflected the firelight, but only one flash was set off— and that by a hyena.

By noon of the fourth day the sun was out and the ground steaming. Horo, Twak, Boggio, and I went looking for a lion with a satisfactory mane. But before we'd gone five miles, mist closed in. Even experienced veld rats sometimes get lost in the pea-soup mists, so we sat down in the open to wait it out. To keep busy, Boggio set up his tripod and camera, wiped the lens, then covered everything with his coat. Horo and Twak slept on the wet grass. Boggio and I sat silent, staring at nothing. Toward mid-afternoon the mist became tinged with lavender and drew away from us until we could see for a couple of hundred yards, but with no perspective. A clump of hooked-thorn bushes a hundred yards away seemed taller than trees.

The sun struggled through the overcast, turning the lavender to gold. Came a roar that seemed to bounce against us from every side. Horo and Twak leaped to their feet, grabbed their bows, and took off at a run as I flipped the safety catch of my rifle and whirled toward the thornbush cluster. There he was—the lion of Boggio's dreams! Five hundred pounds, at least, and a mane so dark it looked black! In the weird light the big cat seemed as tall as the bushes. He was about ninety yards away, facing us, switching his tail.

I glanced at Boggio. No need to worry about Boggio's nerves— he'd removed his coat from the camera and was adjusting the lens as calmly as if about to take a picture of a baby.

Then I saw Horo and Twak. Bows at the ready, they were coming up behind the lion. Horo let fly with a small arrow. I knew he was trying to sting the big cat into a charging rage. He did it. The arrow hit the lion in the behind and the beast rose high in a roaring jump, kicking out his hind legs like a bronco. Then he put his head on the ground, lifted his hindquarters, dropped his tail like a kicked dog, and gave forth with an astonishing mixture of grunts, roars, and coughs.

Boggio, blowing his mustache outward with rapid puffs, ground away at the crank. I checked my back sight for close work, took a look to be sure a cartridge was in the chamber, and lifted my eyes to see the lion coming full tilt. Boggio said:

"Get in the picture, signore, *please!*"

The lion had come fifty yards by the time I'd stepped to a spot satisfactory to Boggio. I lined my sights on the animal's chest, took a deep breath, and firmed the trigger. I'd shoot when the cat's forefeet hit ground on the next jump—figuring that would bring him to a slithering stop at my feet.

But the lion never made that next jump. Even as he sprang, he faltered, stumbled, and buried his nose in the grass. He was up again in an instant, running toward us, then wobbled and sat down, head low.

Boggio, still grinding, turned to me, tears rolling down his cheeks. "Why you shoot?" he asked. "My God, the picture for II Duce, and you shoot!"

"I didn't shoot, Boggio," I said, and walked toward the lion. He was panting, muscles quivering. Horo and Twak ran up, grinning all over their faces. I said:

"I told you damned heathen not to bring poisoned arrows."

Then I put the muzzle of my rifle in the lion's ear and pulled the trigger. The big fellow collapsed, sighed, and lay still.

Boggio stared at the dead lion, shoulders slumped, mustache drooping. I saw his hands trembling. He said:

"A magnificent charge and it go poop! I think at first that you shoot. Why he swoon?"

"The arrow was a poisoned one. Watch." I pulled the arrow from the lion's rump and shoved the tip into a pool of blood that still welled from the head wound. The blood began to foam and bubble. "That's what happens in the veins," I said. "When the foaming blood reaches the heart,—*caput.*"

"He was beautiful, signore," Boggio said.

And I suddenly understood, as I watched the little man pick up his camera and begin walking toward our camp site, how desperately he wanted to get an outstanding sequence. He'd probably been pushed around all of his life. Success with the lions would do something for his soul.

During the next three weeks we must have scouted fifty males. All were hopeless. A couple of females—always more courageous than their consorts, made halfhearted rushes at us. Boggio got some good stuff, but nothing that would suit II Duce's requirements. The weather grew warm. Grass rose from ankle to knee height. Game of all kinds swarmed into the valley, and lions, vultures, and hyenas lived on the fat of the land.

Then one afternoon as we circled a banyan tree we came on a family of five—a big male, two females, and two cubs. The male, except for a lighter-colored mane, seemed a replica of the big one who'd died so ignobly.

We did everything we could think of to anger the lion. Our natives formed a half circle behind him and rushed him, yelling. He deserted his family and went bounding away. Two days later we spotted him on the open veldt I put a bullet into the ground beside him. He raced a hundred yards, got behind a bush, and peeked at us over its top.

In mating season lions often go into frenzy when their lovemaking is interfered with. This wasn't mating time, but I thought maybe the beast might make a show of anger if I killed one of his mates, so as he lay beside one of the females out in the open a few days later, I shot her. At the sound of the gun the male jumped high. All four feet were churning as he hit the ground. He galloped about fifty yards, turned, and came back to the dead female. He sniffed her, pushed her with his paws, got his teeth into the scruff of her neck and tried to pull her. Boggio moved to within thirty yards, then twenty, then fifteen. The lion looked up, stared at Boggio, wheeled, and ran.

Boggio, angered by the lion's refusal to act for the camera, lost his good sense and ran after the beast. At that point Fate took over.

Boggio fell into an old rhino wallow.

The lion, about 150 yards away, turned at the noise of Boggio's cursing— and charged. And Boggio, on his knees, rested the camera on the wallow's edge and began to crank.

Meanwhile I raced for position about twenty feet ahead and a bit to the right of the camera. The lion came grunting—in great, forty-foot leaps. I shot him in midjump, sixty feet from the lens. I heard the thud of the bullet as it hit, but he never faltered. I was pushing the bolt home for a second shot as the big cat flashed past me— straight for Boggio.

He swiped the little man with a forepaw, knocking him at least fifteen yards. Boggio lay still. The lion stood over him, switching his tail and coughing blobs of blood. I fired. The lion dropped, then struggled to his feet and came at me in a sort of jerky wobble. I shot again, between the eyes.

Boggio's shirt was ripped and blood-soaked and I knelt to examine his hurts. Two claws had opened the flesh of his shoulder to the bone. A wrist was broken. Twak came running with the first-aid kit and I opened the bottle of Mercurochrome and began to pour it into Boggio's wounds. Boggio sat up, pushed me aside, and staggered to the rhino wallow. His camera lay on the bottom of the wallow— unhurt. He picked it up, wrapped his arms around it, then looked at me and said: "I cranked until he hit me. His picture is safe in here." Then, for the first time on the trip, he smiled.

Born camera hunters like Boggio seem to have no fear of animals. I've worked with the best—Miki Carter, Wanda Vik-Persen, Martin Johnson, Hsu Punggeh, and Jose Antonio Coimbra. I've seen them within seconds of a crushing or a fanged death and, always, they were smiling.

I once came across an animal artist who'd set up his easel within twenty yards of a water hole patronized by elephants, rhinos, buffaloes, and lions. He worked alone; didn't even have a native camp boy.

On the Zambezi River while acting as gun support for Hollywood's Miki Carter, who was photographing a herd of mating hippos, one of the rampaging males rushed our boat, his open jaws revealing a vast red interior. Miki leaned outboard, trying, it seemed, to get a close-up of the beast's tonsils. He yelled to me:

"Don't shoot. This is wonderful color."

"Then stop rocking the boat," I said. But Miki kept right on exposing film.

Another male surfaced behind us and the swell from his rising pushed us nearer to Miki's bellowing subject. The boat swung around, taking Miki and his clicking camera within eight feet of the gaping, big-tusked mouth. My bullet went down the animal's throat and he sank without a struggle. Then I started the outboard motor and zigzagged out of the herd.

Several frames of that particular film of Miki's were completely filled with nothing but a close-up of the hippo's eye.

Yes, professional camera hunters are a race apart. With most of them, however, the gun support holds the key to life and death. Not so with the Cantonese naturalist, Hsu Punggeh, who specialized in close-ups of deadly snakes. I was with him once when from six feet he photographed a high-rearing, hissing, eleven-foot black mamba—the deadliest serpent in Africa. For several nerve-tightening moments "Pung" was within a half second of death.

The black mamba is fast. During the Zulu War one chased and killed an Imperial army officer fleeing on horseback. When Oom Paul Kruger, first President of the Transvaal, was leading a patrol against the British, a twelve-foot black mamba leaped among his men, killing three of them, and, for good measure, also killing two dogs. Zulus call the black mamba "The Snake That Walks on His Tail" because it travels on the lower half of its body, the upper half reared so that the head seems to glide swiftly along above four-foot grass. Zulus also call the mamba *Muriti-Wa-Lesu* (The Shadow of Death).

Men bitten by a black mamba sometimes die within ten minutes. Few live longer than an hour. At mating time the mamba is the most vicious and dangerous of the cobras. His attack is like a lightning stroke. When he bites, he chews—squirting venom with each chew. He flashes down hills like a dark streak, sailing over seven- and eight-foot bushes in his path. He is so powerful that he occasionally knocks down the men he strikes.

It was a balmy afternoon, with the four-foot veld grass golden in sunlight. Pung and I sat under a thorn tree to smoke our pipes, having first trampled the grass flat for several yards around. Puffing reflectively, Pung quoted from Li Po:

> Gently I stir a white feather fan,
> With open shirt sitting in a green wood.
> I take off my cap and hang it on a jutting stone;
> A wind from the pine-trees trickles on my bare head."

Homesick Pung began another verse:

> "I sat drinking and did not notice the dusk,
> Till falling petals filled the folds of my dress.
> Drunken I rose and walked to ...

His voice ceased as a yard-long bright red snake, striped with white down the length of the back, wriggled toward us over the trodden grass. Pung reached for his camera, and the snake, frightened, writhed past us and up into the thorn tree. Pung said:

"That snake has no business here. His habitat is the Cameroons. Only two have ever been captured. I must have this fellow."

It wasn't too difficult to follow the snake's progress among the dusty-gray limbs of the tree. We'd lose sight of it for minutes, then sunlight would flash on its red hide. The snake climbed awkwardly, making short forays on side limbs, seeking a way to the treetop. When it disappeared into an abandoned secretary bird's nest, Pung said:

"We've got to get up to that nest."

"Those curved thorns are like a million great fishhooks," I said. "They'd tear us to pieces."

"We can trim branches—make a sort of tunnel through the boughs."

"Or wait down here until the snake descends."

Pung shook his head. "No," he said, "if that snake's eaten recently he may stay in the nest for days. Anyway, he's more apt to come down at night than in daylight. We've got to climb the tree."

That wasn't easy. We'd left our natives in camp, and we had only skinning knives to work with. We hacked away, getting snared and snagged until we bled from scores of tiny wounds. It took over an hour to clear a thornless area ten feet up the trunk. We needed a platform from which to work higher into the tree, so we crisscrossed cut branches until we had a "floor" strong enough to bear our weight. On this, about eight feet above the ground, we sat and rested.

Pung kept his eyes on the nest above us, but mine strayed out over the veld. About fifty feet from our tree was a large, flat red rock, perhaps sixteen feet square. About twelve inches of its top rose above the four-foot grass. A faint trail darkened the grass from the base of the rock to a long, low native hut about three hundred yards away. The trail had evidently been made by someone from the hut who came out to the rock occasionally.

I noticed movement in the tall grass about a hundred feet down the trail and watched it idly. What appeared to be a black knob on the end of a thick stick raised abruptly out of the grass—a black mamba. It seemed nervous, for it turned its head this way and that. I nudged Pung:

"It senses us," I said. "It's his mating season—he's probably pretty touchy."

Pung grabbed his camera and dropped to the ground. I said:

"Don't be a fool, Pung."

Pung made no reply, but angled off, putting the rock between himself and the mamba. Grumbling, I, too, dropped from the tree, picked up my shotgun from where it leaned against the trunk, and followed Pung. I felt silly, for shotgun support for snake hunters isn't worth much—not if the hunters are close-up fiends—like Pung. When a camera's only feet away from an angry, threatening snake, the cameraman's apt to get as many scattering pellets as the serpent. I've had it happen.

With me at his heels Pung, crouching low, moved around the rock to a point where he could see the spot where the mamba had reared. The big snake had disappeared.

"That mamba's somewhere close by," I said as I scrambled to the rock's top and reached down a hand to pull Pung up beside me. He shook off my hand, and standing perfectly still, with camera ready, searched the grass around him.

"*Cave!* Watch out!" I said as the mamba's head, looking like a small bulldog's, popped over the grass tops less than ten feet away. It was a male, and I knew he was angry by the way he kept puffing out his neck. Mambas haven't the flaring cobra hood, but their necks swell a little when they're furious.

Pung raised his camera to look through the finder. The mamba darted to within six feet of the lens, reared higher, hissed, turned his head to one side, and glared at Pung with one unblinking, metallic-black eye.

For a few moments Pung, the mamba, and I stood absolutely motionless. My shotgun was in my hands, but I didn't dare lift it to aim; the snake was so close its fangs would have been in Pung's flesh before I could squeeze the trigger.

The snake glared coldly, darting its tongue. I thought: That *tongue looks red, then it's black, then red again.* And I noticed the mamba's skin was not black in the sunlight, but brownish-green.

The mamba hissed, which, at close quarters, usually means a strike. Pung moved his camera to the left. The mamba swayed in the same direction. Pung moved the camera across his front to the right. The snake swayed with it. Slowly left and right the camera swung, and slowly left and right the mamba swung the upper part of its body. It was "The Dance of Death."

"I'm going to shoot, Pung," I said.

As I raised my gun, the camera clicked. Within a fraction of a second the mamba had disappeared in the grass. I dropped my shotgun, got hold of Pung's shoulders, and jerked him up on the rock. I said:

"Let's get back into the thorn tree, Pung. If we don't, you'll lose your red snake." Pung said:

"I have obedient ears."

Back in the tree, we hacked our way to the nest and tore it apart, but the red snake was gone.

BUTTONS FOR THE KING

Ubusuku, my Zulu tracker, used to say: "Courage makes its home in the heart of the kind man."

It's true. I have never seen a truly kind man, white or black, who was a coward.

George Vossos was a kindly man. He was an Armenian Greek who hired me to take him after antelope in Nyasaland. He was big and fat, and underneath the fat were mighty muscles. Most fat men become lean after a few weeks on the veld. Not George. We were out for more than five months and although he foot-slogged it with me mile for mile, he never lost a pound.

We started hunting west of Nyasaland's red dust country. George bagged a few antelope and was proud of his trophies. He'd look at them and say:

"Good man, Vossos. With one mouth I saying it."

Our hunt would probably have been only ordinary had George not tried to shoot an ostrich. When he saw the big male bird with its magnificent white plumes, his eyes sparkled as he said:

"Such feathers I must having for I discerning that they putting yeast in my wife."

When we first spotted the big cock he was with two hens. I could tell by their actions that they had chicks. That meant that when the cock saw us he'd try to draw us away. Had we been in bushless country, he'd have started off with a limp, leading us on and on, the limp becoming less evident the farther we got from his family. Here among the bushes the wise old bird played a different game.

The females disappeared. I knew, of course, that they were squatting, necks low, and that the cute little gray-brown pullet-size chicks were also lying doggo, pretending to be rocks or grass clumps. George and I walked slowly toward the beautiful black and white male, who stood watching us with neck stiff and straight, feet shuffling impatiently.

George knelt and aimed his .256. The ostrich ducked behind a large bush. George chuckled and tiptoed slowly forward, skirted the bush like a stalking Indian, then stood staring with slack jaw. The ostrich had vanished.

George didn't think to look for the bird's spoor, and I didn't remind him. He glanced at me from the corners of his eyes and asked:

"What you theenk?"

I pointed to the male ostrich about a hundred yards away. He was staring at us exactly as before. This time George didn't kneel, but threw up his rifle only to have the ostrich scurry behind another bush.

George said "Hah!", pulled his old felt hat down to his ears, and charged across space as if he meant to bayonet the bird. He peered through the bush, then began circling on hands and knees. When the bush hid him from me, I listened for curses, but all was still. When I caught up with him, he glared:

"Why you no tell me he is mirage?"

I pointed to the bird's spoor. "He's putting bushes between him and us and running like hell when we can't see him," I said. "He's leading us away from his babies back there."

"Babies?"

"Yes—little pullet-size chicks."

"No mamma?"

"Two mammas. I saw them."

George burst out angrily: "Why you tell me about thees babies? I now cannot shooting the papa."

"Good man, George," I smiled. "Someday I'll show you a papa ostrich that has no babies. Then you can get feathers to put that yeast in your wife."

George laughed. "That wife!" he said proudly. Thereafter, before he'd shoot at anything, he'd ask:

"He got babies?"

I never quite understood his philosophy, but it had something to do with his wartime experiences. He once said:

"Soldiers going that day to shooting papas and papas and papas. What those papas' babies do, huh? So I having tears and going away from that war."

We hunted another week, but George had lost interest in Nyasaland. One night as we gnawed at roasted duikerbok haunches, he said:

"I having a feeling to go far. Maybe to other ocean." He pointed west. "What is the end of there?"

"Angola. Portuguese West Africa."

"They having ostriches?"

"Sure. We can cut straight across Northern Rhodesia. Across swamps, mountains, plain, forest, desert, and bush. We'll probably see ostriches all the way."

"We go," George said.

I thought he was fooling, but he wasn't. Next morning he sent his Kaffirs to Blantyre with his trophies. About noon we set off due west—George, my two Kaffirs, myself, and our ox wagon. George's clothes were identical with mine—a strong shirt, tough pants, heavy-soled boots, and an old felt hat. We each had a rubberized sheet for sleeping on wet ground, four blankets, two rifles, a 12-gauge shotgun, a skinning knife, a hatchet, and lots of ammunition. When we made camp, one Kaffir scouted wood for the fire, the other took the oxen to graze. Both natives slept beside their fire. George and I slept under the wagon and when it rained, hung a tarp on the windward side.

Where snakes were numerous, each of us—Kaffirs and whites— slept snuggled up to the belly of an ox. The big beasts sensed snakes that came close, and waked us with their shivering, moaning, and snorting. Even then we threw off our blankets only after ascertaining that no snakes had crawled in with us.

Nothing, not even snakes, seemed to faze George. Nothing, that is, but chameleons. The first one he saw—crouching on a branch— cocked one eye forward and the other eye backward. George quavered:

"They loose—the eyes of him."

While I was explaining that chameleons can move each eye independently, the little reptile flicked out its six-inch tongue and a blue moth vanished down its gullet. George grunted in unbelief. The chameleon brought its big, round, protruding, backward-looking eye to bear on George, while the other eye swiveled upward to watch a hovering butterfly. George gasped and backed away.

"The chameleon," I said, "has two nervous systems—one for each side. Sometimes one half is asleep while the other's awake. Walk close to him, George, and shade him with your hand."

"No. I not liking he look at me."

I said: "Then stand where you are, and watch."

I walked slowly to the side from which the sun shone, held up my open hand until its shade fell on the chameleon. At once the reptile's shaded side turned almost black. The other side remained a sort of lavender-gray. George said:

"They is loose too—the colors."

The chameleon's eyes swiveled about; legs on one side behaved as if they wanted to run. The birdlike claws of the feet on the other side clung to the branch. I withdrew my hand and the side of the little beast on which the sun now shone brightly turned almost white. George grunted. The chameleon stood erect, feet clutching the twig. It curled its long, tapering tail downward, lifted one front foot, and rolled one eye at George. George took two steps backward. The chameleon vanished among the leaves. George muttered. I said:

"What?"

"Why he hating me?"

I laughed. "He doesn't hate you, George. If you'd catch and feed him, he'd become a cute pet."

"In that loose eyes of him I seeing he hating me like hell," George replied.

The farther we trekked the more plentiful the game. Small herds of antelope were everywhere. All except the springboks were easy to approach even in short grass, and we seldom had to take a shot at more than seventy-five yards. George was good with a rifle, but by the time we got into the country north of Lukanga Swamp, he was missing almost every shot. One morning when I accused him of missing a duikerbok deliberately, he looked embarrassed and said:

"He making his ears at me and I thinking he liking me. So my bullet, he missing him."

"George," I said, "maybe we'd better call this trip off."

"No," he said. "It is for me the winds and the nice smells and the little birds. And also the bugs."

A day or two later during the early afternoon heat, as I dozed in the shade of the wagon, I heard George laugh, and looked up to see him standing under an acacia tree watching a Tommy gazelle sporting in the knee-high grass. The little antelope, not much bigger than a large hare, was dancing stiff-legged, his small tail flicking and flirting joyously.

George was beaming like the morning sun. Our two Kaffirs lay on their bellies nearby, chins in hands, watching George with amusement. I thought idly how remarkable that a gazelle, usually terrified at the sound of a human voice, sensed that in George there was nothing to fear.

After several minutes the Tommy bounded away, stopping twice to dance again in the sunlight.

Toward evening I walked out across the veld, spotted a Tommy, and shot it. The Kaffirs roasted it; took the forelegs and went to their own fire. I cut a slice from a haunch, speared it on the point of my knife, and handed it to George. He shook his head.

"I am having tears in the middle of me. I thinking you killing my Tommy."

"No," I said. "This is a different one."

"I thinking maybe it being the wife of my Tommy."

"No. This is a male."

"Maybe he being papa."

"Look, George," I said. "You're carrying things too far. It's all right to be softhearted. It's all right for you to quit killing animals. But remember that this antelope died quickly and painlessly. If he'd lived, he'd certainly have died violently, later. Few African animals die natural deaths. Before his heart stops beating, the lordly lion, lying down to die of old age, is torn to bits by hyenas and vultures. The dying rhino becomes the harvest of ants. The elephant in the mud and water of a swamp to cool his last, fevered moments becomes food for crocodiles and fish. A man's got to have meat—eat up, now."

George got up to walk away, but paused to say:

"He was gold in the sun on him, the Tommy. Then the wind coming under his hair and he making like white under the gold. He was happy on the inside of him and he cannot stop it—the dancing in his legs."

"Yeah," I said.

Our trek became a slow and happier one. The sound of a rifle was seldom heard. George didn't stop eating meat, but ate more of other things. He was particularly fond of big white mushrooms that grew on abandoned ant hills. Those mushrooms weigh up to four pounds and are a delicacy when lightly fried in hippo lard. Large red mushrooms were plentiful too, but were poisonous.

The abdomens of some species of black ants contain an acid that gives an intriguing tang to salads, especially to the somewhat harsh tasting greens gathered from the dry veld. George liked the ant flavor and once when no black ants were available, he tried red ants. He might as well have used red pepper.

Animals—particularly the zebra, antelope, and wildebeest— seemed to know they were safe with us, for they permitted us to go close—sometimes to within fifty yards. On the few occasions when we came upon lions sleeping or lolling in the shade of scattered trees we sometimes moved within fifteen yards before they became alarmed and loped away.

George got pleasure from small things that most hunters miss. He studied the activities of bugs, beetles, spiders, tarantulas, lizards, frogs, turtles, bees, and ants. He'd sit for hours on a hummock watching scavenger beetles roll dung into balls as large as golf balls, then lower their heads, raise their hind feet, and propel the balls backward to suitable soil and bury them. When a ball's progress was stopped by a pebble or stick, George would watch the beetle's struggles for a time, then say:

"Stop having a troubles, little bugs," and remove the obstruction, smiling as the beetle resumed its task.

"Why thees bugs hiding the balls?" he asked the first time he watched them.

"When the ball's buried," I told him, "the mamma beetle eats a hole in it and lays eggs in the hole. When the eggs hatch the babies eat the ball."

"Thees babies liking that food?"

"Sure! They love it."

"Such a eating!" George said.

One day when stinging gnats were annoying, George said to them reproachfully:

"Favor and kind I do to letting you eating me. Why you biting me to hurting?"

Of the wars between the black ants and the red ants George remarked:

"Such a crazy ants and peoples. Killing papas and papas and papas not having the same colors. Why red ants killing black ants? Why white peoples killing black peoples? It is full of happy, the world, and ants and peoples making it the tears."

We did the first five hundred miles of the trek at an average speed of eight miles a day. We reached the highlands below Kambove in the middle of May. Nights and early mornings were so cold that our Nyasaland Kaffirs were miserable, so I paid them off and sent them home. Shortly thereafter we met two Alala hunters and hired them as ox drivers and camp boys. They were brothers, with names so difficult for George to pronounce that he began calling them Long-One and Thick-One. Long-One was the elder, quick to smile and to let Thick-One do the harder jobs. Thick-One didn't seem to mind. Both were excellent trackers. They carried knobkerries and six-foot spears with eighteen-inch blades.

Although the rains had ended, each morning clouds hung low until almost noon. The first half of each day was depressing with penetrating cold. When the sun came out, however, its warmth quickly drove the chill from our bones. Winter floods had left deep slime in many places and the oxen had hard going.

To add to discomfort, pools and water holes were alive with tiny worms, the larvae of flies.

We crossed into Portuguese territory the afternoon of July 17, and made camp in a brush-ringed glade that was as neat and trim as a German park.

Next morning George strolled toward the bush while the boys were cooking breakfast. He came back muttering angrily and said:

"I walking into a bush and flies biting me like hell. I do such a slapping and jumping, but thees flies eating me like a stabbing."

"Tsetse," I said, and called Long-One. "Let the oxen graze in a bunch today," I said, "we're going to need the manure."

Long-One wrinkled his nose and said: "Ow!"

"*Cheechee* flies?" George yelped. "But, I am bite!"

"Itchy," I said.

George refused supper that night, explaining that he was "having a bunching in the middle of him." I assumed he had a touch of indigestion, suggested a drink of hot, salted water, but he shook his head and sat leaning back against the wagon wheel.

After Thick-One had been set to herding the oxen so their manure wouldn't be too scattered next morning, I rolled up in my blanket and fell asleep. I wakened about midnight because George was walking around the wagon, mumbling:

"No shutting the eyes of you, George Vossos. No having the sleep."

I thought: *The poor lug has a bellyache,* and fell asleep again. I wakened about two in the morning. George was still plodding around the wagon.

"Stir up the fire, heat some water, and drink it hot. That'll fix your stomachache."

Wearily George said:

"The eyes of me are shutting and shutting. In the middle of me I am afraid."

"Pain?"

"No having a pains. I having the sleep sick."

"The what?"

"Those *cheechee* biting of me."

"For Pete's sake, George," I said, "are you trying to say you've got sleeping sickness?"

"I am sad to saying."

"Look, George. The tsetse flies in this area can't infect a man. Cattle, yes. The flies pick up the bug from the game and pass it on to the oxen. But before a tsetse can infect a man it must bite a man who has the sickness. There are no humans living in this particular area, therefore, there can be no men with sleeping sickness. Therefore, the fly can't infect men."

"But I walking and walking and the sleeping is in the eyes and in the all of me."

"Listen, George. Every night shortly after sundown you roll in and sleep like a log, so why shouldn't you be sleepy? Stop this nonsense and get some rest. Sleep late in the morning if you like. We'll stay outspanned tomorrow so we can accumulate enough manure to rub the oxen with it before we push through the tsetse area."

"Manure is being a medicine for *cheechee?*"

"Tsetse won't come near manure," I said.

"I am now having a happy inside of me a little. Tomorrow I rubbing manures on the skin of me." He reached for his blanket.

"Okay," I grinned. "Now tuck yourself in, George, and go to sleep. You know, sleeping sickness doesn't make you sleepy, it makes you weak—dries up the blood. Anyway, it's days after being bitten before you have any ..."

But George was already snoring.

It was noon next day before we'd got the last of the oxen well rubbed with manure. We skirted the tsetse area, but occasionally a fly swarmed out of the bushes, settled on a manure-plastered ox momentarily, then buzzed off in disgust. When George saw that the boys and I did not mind the flies biting us, he lost his fear.

We crossed the Zambezi four days later and outspanned in a triangular flat at a juncture of the river and a rush-bordered creek. This was familiar territory and I loved every square foot of it. The creek was abundant with fish, skeeter bugs, water spiders, and small crocodiles. Islands of lily pads floated close to the reeds. A hundred-foot-wide strip of the flat back of the rushes was carpeted with tiny, bright yellow flowers. Scattered trees and bushes broke the clearing into fascinating vistas. At the far end, where green grass met dark brush, a long, low ridge of broken rocks lay bare. At the base of the ridge no grass grew.

Although there seemed to be plenty of water in the ground, the surface of the rock ridge was hot and dry. One evening it rained. Not much, but enough to dampen and cool. The rain stopped about nine o'clock and a bright full moon rose swiftly above the trees. The moonlight was so intense that George read old letters by its light. Finally he arose, said he was going for a walk, and ambled toward the ridge of rocks. A few minutes later his startled yell hushed the night noises.

I grabbed my rifle and ran toward him. He stood at the edge of the bare strip at the base of the rocks. In the white moonlight highlights of his face seemed luminous.

He pointed to the grassless strip beside the ridge. It was heaving, shifting, spreading, and contracting as hundreds of scorpions, claws outstretched, tails straight up, danced weirdly.

"They hide in holes while it's dry," I said. "The rain brought them out."

"My God! They holding the hands of them and dancing!"

"They're about to mate."

"Mate?"

"Yes. About to get married."

"You meaning they making it the babies?"

"Well, right now the papas are getting the mammas hot and bothered."

George said, "Such a crazy!"

"Scorpions, George," I said, "are even meaner than crocodiles. Each lives alone. When they meet, they usually battle to the death. The winner eats the loser."

"But they now being happy together."

"It won't last. Watch."

These scorpions were about six inches long, and of a particularly poisonous species. The males were more slender than the females, with longer tails. We concentrated on a pair close to our feet. The female seemed unwilling, so the male lifted his tail with its nasty sting at the tip and did a jerky dance before her. She raised and lowered her eight legs one by one. He held out a claw. She reached for it with hers, drew back, reached again, put her claw in his, and joined in the dance. For a time their tails swayed above their bodies, then met and locked just below the stings.

George said: "They stabbing everyone to death with the tails of them."

"No, they're mating now," I said.

"You meaning thees being the way thees...?"

"Yes."

"By the tails of them?"

"Yes."

"Such a crazy!"

"Watch, George," I said.

The females, still clutching the males by their claws, began backing and sidling toward the rocks. When a male resisted, the female tugged gently. Slowly but surely the males were coaxed into holes and crevices.

"They still liking each the other," George said.

"In a few minutes, George, every female will kill her husband and eat him. Tomorrow I'll show you what happens to male scorpions after their weddings."

At dawn we returned to the scene of the love festival. Hundreds of scorpion shells, the big dead claws looking grotesquely large, lay at the base of the rocks. George turned one over with a stick and said:

"He is empty the shell of him. How the mamma getting the meat?"

I picked up a carapace and showed George the base of the claws near the mouth opening. "See those little pinchers there? The female bites and tears with them. She wounds the male, chews around the wound, and shoves front feet inside him. Her legs contain digestive fluids that turn her husband's meat to liquid. When his insides are nice and fluid, she puts her mouth over the wound and *pumps* with her throat. When the shell is empty, she drags it to the opening of her cave and pushes it outside."

George looked dejected. I said:

"Don't take it so hard, George. That's the way scorpions are. The husbands don't seem to mind."

"I used to thinking bugs being kind. Now I seeing bugs being hurting in the heart of them like peoples. Do thees bugs killing me when they biting me with the tails of them?"

"Their venom's about like that of the cobra. But don't worry, George, we've anti-scorpion serum in the first-aid kit."

"How she having the babies, the wife?"

"The eggs hatch inside her. The babies are born alive—about one hundred at a time. Soon as they're born they crawl up on the mamma's back and stay there until they molt. The mamma carries so many babies that all you can see of her is tail and claws."

"What is the molt?"

"Shed their shells—like snakes shed their skins. The babies don't eat for weeks because their insides are packed with egg yolk. Scorpions don't eat often—these mammas probably won't eat again for more than a year. And if they can't eat another scorpion, they'll eat insects. I've seen —"

A shrill, choking yell rose from the bush. I turned toward the sound, flipped back the bolt of my rifle and stood waiting. Long-One and Thick-One came running, their assagais flashing in the morning sun. Long-One said:

"A man is hurt."

"Might be a leopard," I said, but I knew it wasn't.

We moved toward the trees, but before we'd taken many steps the bushes parted and a naked, brown-skinned native shuffled stiff-legged into the open. He moved with head down, hands grasping something in front of him. Behind him stuck out what looked like a tufted tail. It was an arrow. Its head stuck through the man's belly and he was holding it with his hands.

I had my arms around him as his legs buckled, and I put him on the ground on his side. In a mixture of Luchazi and Portuguese he said:

"I am Pepeca. I have come."

Long-One touched me and pointed to the brush. I nodded and he and Thick-One bounded into the trees to look for the killer. George said:

"Better we pulling out the arrow."

"No. He's dying. Run to the wagon and get the morphine pills from the first-aid kit, George. Hurry."

Pepeca shook with spasms. I waited for them to pass, then asked:

"Who shot you, Pepeca?"

He gasped: "They have broken the fingers of *Senhor* Coelho, but he will not tell them about the buttons. Therefore, they will break more fingers and he will die."

"Who are they?"

"I was tied with a rope, but I loosed myself and ran away. I ran in the dark. Then the sun came and I smelled your fire. I came, but one, Hohe, who followed me, killed me with his arrow."

The rest of his words were lost in a gurgle. George handed me the morphine. I placed a pill between Pepeca's purple lips and gave him a mouthful of water from my canteen. He relaxed, smiled briefly, and fell asleep.

He never wakened.

I broke the arrow off close and pulled it from his body. Then George helped me carry him to camp, lay him on the wagon bed, and roll him in a blanket.

"We'll have to bury him right away," I said to George. "The sun's getting hot."

George said: "Ants and scorpions and peoples! Killing, killing, killing. What we doing now?"

"When Long-One and Thick-One get back we'll send them to the *chefe do posto* at Cangamba. He'll send police."

"But they is keeping break the fingers of *Senhor* Coelho!"

"Yeah," I said. "Sounds like white men. That arrow was made by an Ambuella. I know the Ambuellas well and I can't imagine them breaking fingers."

Long-One loped into the clearing. He said:

"Spoor. Three white men. Six, maybe seven, black men. Two days ago, maybe, they go to the river." He pointed southwest toward the Kwando. "Thick-One follow spoor. I come to tell. Thick-One come back maybe one day."

"Go fill your belly with mush," I said. "Then take my letter to the *chefe do posto* at Cangamba. If he's not there, give the letter to the magistrate. You come back quick."

Cangamba was almost a hundred miles southwest, but Long-One was back in six days with the *chefe do posto,* a sad-looking, fever-ridden man named Bernardino Silva.

Meanwhile Thick-One had shown up with news that the natives of the party he'd been trailing were indeed Ambuellas. He'd followed them to a branch of the Kwando, watched them embark in canoes and land on an island in the river.

"Two white men are Arabs," he'd said, and spat.

"The third white man?"

"He is sick. Sometimes he falls down."

Silva had four Bihe policemen with him. "I am glad you are here, *Senhor,*" he said to me as George stood by listening. "I was in the hospital when your tracker arrived. My feet are in great pain, for I have a severe infection between my toes from sand fleas. I must ask you, in the name of the Presidente of Portugal, to assist me in the capture of the black-bearded Aliche Fazai and his partner, the one-eyed one, Ahmed Rashid. If it be God's will we will also rescue the coat with the buttons and we may even rescue that poor man *Senhor* Jose d'Andrade Hermenigildo Coelho."

"But first being the buttons?" George asked sarcastically.

"But, certainly, the buttons. You have buried Pepeca?"

"Yes," I said.

"The buttons—" Silva continued.

"Never mind the buttons," I said. "How about Coelho? Who is he? Why is Fazai breaking his fingers?"

"*Senhor* Jose d'Andrade—"

"Coelho," I said.

"Yes. *Senhor* Coelho is the special messenger of *Presidente* Teixeira Gomes, who is the *Presidente* of Portugal and—"

"I know."

"For *Senhor* Coelho's rescue you will be paid well. For the rescue of the buttons you will be rewarded magnificently. I must trust you. Within the buttons, which are round and of brass, are hidden the three emeralds of King John II." Silva looked as if he expected me to gape. I said:

"What's so special about the King John emeralds?"

"My God!" Silva said. "You do not know?"

"No."

"Know, then, that King John's emeralds are worth great sums. They were purchased as a present for the King by Dom Vasco da Gama in 1497 from an Arab in Malindi. That was almost 550 years ago, and the emeralds have not yet arrived in Portugal, for Dom Vasco took the emeralds with him to Calicut when he discovered India. Mohammedan traders turned the Indian zamorin against Dom Vasco, raided his post, and stole the emeralds. Many years later a captain of a Portuguese slave ship found them on a slave who said he had taken them from an Arab he had killed in French Dahomey. That captain died of fever and the emeralds disappeared. In 1888 they were found in possession of a native chief in southeast Angola by Major Serpa Pinto. Pinto sent them under guard to King Luiz I. En route they were stolen. Only recently the emeralds were found on an Arab in the District of Moxico. They were taken from the Arab because they rightfully belonged to Portugal. *Senhor* Jose d'Andrade Herm—"

"Coelho," I said.

"Yes. He was sent from Lisbon to conduct the emeralds safely. He brought with him a coat with brass buttons, three of which were prepared so that the emeralds could be placed within them. The emeralds are now within those buttons and —"

"Well, Silva, I'll try to help you get Coelho. The emeralds are something else again."

"But you do not understand, *Senhor*. The emeralds are beyond price. They were engraved in Crete five hundred years before Christ was born. They were engraved by the greatest"—Silva stopped for a moment to glare at George, who'd grunted scornfully—"the greatest artist of the world," he continued. "His name was Epimenes and on one emerald he engraved the head of a horse. On another the head of a lion. On the third two warriors, fighting. The emeralds are flat and are the size of the thumbnail."

"Well, if we get Coelho, he'll probably be wearing the coat. One of my trackers says that Fazai has holed up in the *kraal* of an old friend of mine— an Ambuella chief named Kaputo. I'll go with you, but I can't just take off in a cloud of dust. I'm working for George, here. He'll have to give me some days off."

"This Kaputo," Silva said. "It may be we will have to kill him as well as Fazai."

"I'm not killing anybody, Silva," I said. "How about it, George? Will you give me a few days off to go get Coelho?"

George said: "Talking, talking, talking. No one is feel sad for Pepeca. Such a bastards. I am burn in the insides of me. Why you no sad for Pepeca?" He clenched a fist and patted the knuckles. "That Fazai!" he said. "I finding and punching him with all my hands. We starting now. Yes?"

"Not until morning," I said. But by morning one of Silva's toes was so badly infected that I had to amputate it. He couldn't go with us, which was just as well. He'd probably complicate things and I figured that without him I'd have little trouble getting Kaputo to back me up when I demanded Coelho from the Arabs. Coelho was all I cared about. Fazai and his partner could go their way. After all, I wasn't a cop.

George, Long-One, Thick-One, and I took off the next morning.

We left the four Bihe policemen to care for Silva. Bihes hate Ambuellas— they'd have pushed Kaputo's people around.

We traveled light. I had my Lee-Enfield and twenty cartridges. George left his rifle in camp "because I no shooting peoples." The Kaffirs carried stabbing spears and knobkerries. At the last minute Silva had given me a letter of authority to act for him and I'd tucked it into a back pants pocket.

The going was fine the first two days. We passed through bits of forest and across wide parklike clearings. We forded numerous small, clear streams. Antelope and hares were so plentiful and so easy to approach that Long-One, with his spear, had no trouble bagging all we needed to eat. The third day, as we approached the Kwando, we encountered marsh so spongy that, what with falling down and getting up, we were soon covered with mud from ears to ankles. We cut back to higher land, skirted the sloughs, and on the fourth day hit the branch of the river on which Kaputo's *kraal* was built. We struggled through bog and got involved in a belt of reeds that slowed our advance to less than a mile an hour. We were bedraggled and pooped when we finally came out on a sand and mud flat on the river's edge and saw Kaputo's island squatting in the afternoon sun.

Several dugout canoes were moored to the bank. We took one and poled it through shallow water into the main stream. Hippos sported among the lily pads. Birds of all sizes and colors swooped screaming above us. The swift current caught us, whirled us about like a cork, then shot us into still water. Watched by about forty Ambuellas, we drew up to the island.

In the past these people had smiled or laughed a welcome when they met me. Now they greeted us in sullen silence. I spotted Kaputo, stepped ashore, and held out my thumb to be shaken. He said:

"When I saw you come I ordered a hut prepared for you. Do you come in peace?"

"Sure," I said.

"It is good. A fire is lighted at your hut. Eggs and a chicken are laid by the door. Follow me."

His people, faces blank, opened a passage for us. We followed Kaputo to a dome-shaped, thatched hut on the opposite side of the island. On packed earth before the low opening that served as a door a fire burned in a five-gallon paraffin tin that had been converted into a stove. Atop the tin a cast-iron pot steamed listlessly. A plucked hen, covered with black ants, lay on the ground. Six eggs, dirty with manure, lay beside the fowl. I said:

"Are we pigs that you give us filthy food?"

Kaputo said: "Tomorrow you go."

"Are you no longer my friend, then?"

For a moment I thought Kaputo was going to weep. His face worked as if restraining tears. He stepped close and said through nauseating breath:

"Why you come?"

"To take the sick white man back with us."

"No white man here."

"Don't lie, Kaputo."

"No white man here. Better you go." He looked over his shoulder nervously. "Better you go," he said again, and left.

George followed me into the hut. The interior was gloomy, and stank. Lizards scurried over the walls. A string of ants marched across the mud and dung floor. I drew my skinning knife and cut a square window in the wall opposite the entrance. Light streamed in, and a different stink. I looked out and saw an old male ostrich scratching for grubs in a big manure pile. I said:

"George, Kaputo is terrified. Probably by Fazai. Could be that we're in for trouble." I leaned my rifle against the wall, hung my bandolier on it, and went outside to look around. There were twenty huts in the village. Kaputo's, I remembered, was the large one in the center.

"I'm going to visit Kaputo, George," I said. "You wait here."

As I walked toward Kaputo's hut, natives retreated before me in brooding silence. Kaputo was not in. He wasn't on the riverbank. No one would answer my questions. I returned to our hut.

Back of the hut stood George, feeding the ostrich. Long-One and Thick One were gone. I went inside the hut.

My rifle and ammunition were gone.

I stuck my head through the window and asked George if he'd taken them.

"No," George said. "You leaving it, the rifle in—"

"I know. Who's been here, George?"

"One black mans. He comma behind here and saying where is you. I saying you walking. He going away."

"Did he come in the hut?"

"I not knowing. You thinking he stealing the rifle?"

"I'm damn sure of it," I said, and sat down to think.

Nicobar Jones, my old hunting boss, used to say: "When you're in a jam, dig into your brains."

Loss of the rifle worried me. I was pretty sure that Fazai, lying doggo in one of the huts, had ordered it stolen. And I was pretty sure that he'd ordered Kaputo to horse us out of the village next morning. Everything pointed to a fight coming up. I didn't want a fight.

Dusk fell and I still sat. I heard Long-One and Thick-One arguing about who should cook the chicken. I heard George asking them to hurry supper. Still I sat, unable to decide on a plan.

I remembered Jones telling me once that whenever I didn't know what to do, to go ahead and do something, anyway.

It was dark by the time I decided to have one more talk with Kaputo. I got up and went out just as six spear-armed natives squatted on their haunches at the edge of our firelight. I said:

"What do you want?"

None answered. They just sat, whites of their eyes gleaming. I said:

"Get the hell out of here."

One made a threatening gesture with his spear. Long-One picked up a burning brand. I said:

"No fighting, Long-One. George, keep our boys here. I'll be back."

I went into the hut, climbed through the window I'd cut, slipped into shadow of the next hut, then inched my way through darkness to the center of the village. It was soon evident that the village was deserted. I went to the river.

All canoes were gone. I cut back through the village, thought I saw a glimmer of light in one hut, went down on my belly, and wriggled close to the hut's wall. I heard a low moan.

I moved part way around the hut, paused, and listened. Again I heard a moan. Slowly and carefully I crawled near the entrance. Something white filled it. At first I thought it a curtain, but as my eyes adjusted, I saw it was the skirt of a white chamma, and that the man who wore it was bending over, his back to me.

I heard the moan more clearly. I felt certain that the two Arabs were giving Coelho the works again. I acted fast—perhaps this nightgown-clad guy's position inspired me, but anyway I knelt close behind him, put the palms of my hands flat together as if in prayer, drew my hands down, and still holding them like a wedge, drove them with all of my strength, upward between the man's buttocks. I scored a bull's-eye. He froze—paralyzed, hunched as motionless as a statue.

I knew he was in agony. That wedge-like thrust to the most tender part of the fanny is one of the cruelest blows I know. The victim can't yell. He can't even breathe. The paralysis doesn't last long, but long enough for you to slit his throat, bang his head, or tie him up. I did none of these.

Instead, I struck a wax Vesta (match) and set fire to the hem of his robe. Flames shot up his back, caught the grass walls beside the door and in seconds the whole side of the hut was ablaze. The man still stood hunched, but was suddenly knocked backward as another Arab, screaming, came into the open.

I went into the hut, grabbed a white man under the armpits, and dragged him out. It was Coelho.

For one brief moment I saw a dancing, yelping figure tearing off blazing clothes and throwing them right and left. Then the second Arab, knife in hand, jumped at me. I ducked the knife and drove my heel into his instep. As he hopped on one foot I clipped him hard on the side of his neck with the edge of my hand. He tipped toward me. I grabbed him by the beard, jerked his chin up, and socked him on the Adam's apple—again with the side of my hand. Then I let him drop.

I picked up the Arab's knife and threw it into the burning hut just as the roof caught fire with a roar, blazed high, and sent flames against the next hut. The guy whose clothes I'd set afire was stark naked now and still yowling. He was clean-shaven so I knew he was Ahmed.

I bent to drag Coelho clear of the heat and he jabbered something to me in Portuguese. His feet were tied. I cut the thongs, slung him across my shoulders, and trotted with him toward our hut.

When I got within about fifty feet I saw that George, Long-One, and Thick-One were in a close huddle, the six Ambuellas holding them there at spear points. I laid Coelho on the ground, jerked a center pole from the nearest hut, and rushed the warriors.

Most African natives can take it on the head, but bang their leg bones and they fold. I swung the pole hard against a black, mangled ankle. The fellow's yell of pain coincided with a new flare of light as yet another hut caught fire. I belted the next warrior across the shins. He dropped his spear, doubled up, and rolled on the ground beside the lad with the busted ankle.

The other four Ambuellas turned toward me, and George, Long-One, and Thick-One hit them in a bunch. It seemed a grotesque dance I watched as the seven mixed it up. Then a rifle cracked and a bullet ricocheted into the outer side of my right thigh. I went down, got to my knees, and crawled to Coelho. With my knife I cut all buttons from his coat, then dragged myself back and into the hut with the idea of hiding them.

Shrill shrieks took me to the entrance. In the light of leaping flames I saw the two Arabs running toward the melee. Fazai's white robe was tucked up around his waist. He carried a rifle. Ahmed, still naked, waved a long, curved knife.

Inside my pants leg, blood was pumping. I felt no pain, but was growing dizzy. I started to rip the leg of my trousers with my knife. I glanced out and saw the ostrich hopping around, bewildered by noises and flames. I rolled the brass buttons in front of him. Their shiny surfaces twinkled like stars in the light of the growing holocaust. True to his instincts, the old ostrich gobbled the buttons down his long throat.

I tried to get to my feet, wobbled, and sat down. I saw Long-One and Thick-One go down with spear thrusts. Four of the Ambuellas were dead. Later I learned that one of the four was Hohe.

The two surviving Ambuellas jumped George. There was a brief struggle and one native went flying through the air, landed hard, and lay still. The other turned to run, took a roundhouse right on the side of the jaw, rolled over several times, then he too lay quiet.

Fazai leveled his rifle at George. I tried to yell a warning, but my voice was only a croak. I crawled out of the hut, but my arms collapsed and my face pushed into the sand. Something brushed past me. It was the ostrich bouncing around in terror. A spread-winged jump landed him between George and Fazai as the Arab's rifle barked. The ostrich toppled over and lay kicking.

George's yell ripped the night. He rushed Fazai, staggered as the rifle exploded, then grabbed the gun, jerked it from Fazai's hand, and jabbed as with a bayonet. Fazai shuffled backward. George followed and pushed the toe of the butt upward against Fazai's jaw, then brought the barrel down on top of the Arab's head. I heard the skull crack. Fazai was dead.

George took after Ahmed. That poor devil moved so fast that he was six jumps away before George got fairly started. George hurled the rifle. It wrapped around Ahmed's legs and he went down in a heap. Instantly George was on top of him. One punch and Ahmed was all through. Four months later he was hanged.

I blacked out. When I came to, George had bandaged my thigh and was working on Long-One and Thick-One. Both were in bad shape.

"Did you bring in Coelho, George?" I asked.

George grinned. "I bringing him in the hut. He is paining, but only in his fingers."

One by one all the huts caught fire, but ours was the last to go. George helped us to the river and made us comfortable on the sand. Kaputo and his followers showed up toward dawn and took over our care. When certain that Fazai was dead, Kaputo was so happy that he started to cry. It was one of the few times I've seen a native in tears.

I slept until afternoon, and when I wakened, was told that men had been sent to get Silva and that Long-One and Thick-One would live. I said to George:

"You were putting up a good battle all along, George, but suddenly you seemed to go nuts. What happened?"

"I get burning up on the insides of me."

"Yeah. But why?"

"Because that man shooting the ostrich. That ostrich liking me."

I said: "You look peaked, George. You sick?"

"No sick. A bullet shooting me at the side but not going inside of me. No making me sick. Only hurting. Kaputo fixing just now."

"You're quite a guy, George, in case you don't know it," I said.

"What saying?"

"Never mind," I said.

Eight days later Silva who'd left two of his four Bihes to guard our wagons, arrived on a litter. By that time Kaputa's people had almost rebuilt their village, the ostrich's crop had been opened and the brass buttons sewed again on Coelho's coat. Long-One and Thick-One were having the time of their lives being waited on by big-bottomed women. My wound was healing with no sign of infection and I'd begun to get around on improvised crutches.

George seemed to have no regrets for having killed Fazai. I asked him why. He said:

"He is being dead, the Arab. I no feeling bad. I seeing the papa scorpions being dead and I feeling sad a little, but not for him, the Arab. Maybe I can't explaining, but ..."

"I understand," I said.

A few days after his arrival Silva held a hearing for Kaputo, who said that Fazai had terrified him by threatening to inform authorities that he'd sold some children into slavery several months before. "They were girl children," the chief said, "and they went to become wives for sultans in Saudi Arabia."

"You were paid a 'dowry'?" Silva asked.

"It is so."

"And the girls were told that if questioned by authorities en route they were to say that they went willingly?"

"That also is true."

Silva shrugged. He said to me: "The League of Nations has done much to suppress slave trade, but when victims announce that they go with the slavers of their own will as 'wives,' or as 'legally adopted children,' there is nothing that officials can do. The slave blocks of Saudi Arabia are still much in use."

George said: "I have seeing many slaves in Saudi Arabia. They is being happy. They is better as here maybe."

"True," Silva agreed. "Slaves are not badly treated these days, but these ugly black girls who think they will be wives have been lied to. Harems of sultans are filled with beautiful girls, many with white skins. Kaputo has done wrong and he knows it. He must go with me to the magistrate. He will be fined to the amount of the 'dowries.'"

Silva then ordered Coelho to open the buttons so that he might report that the emeralds had actually been recovered. Coelho's fingers were in splints, so Silva himself opened the buttons. George and I watched intently as the *chefe do posto* separated the two halves of the first button, exposing a small wad of cotton wool. His fingers trembled as he picked the cotton apart.

No emerald.

Coelho gasped. Silva seemed stunned. George said:

"He is going away, the emerald!"

Silva hastily opened the other buttons. Two contained wads of cotton wool. No emeralds.

Coelho burst into tears. In Silva's cheek, muscles twitched, and he stared at me strangely. I looked at George. George said:

"Such a crazy!"

A lion crouches watchfully on a rock.

Baby African elephant napping with mother guarding.

HOW TO FIND THREE EMERALDS

We were sitting on the ground in front of one of the new huts—a perplexed and frustrated group as we watched Silva handling the empty half shells of the buttons. It was as if he were playing some melancholy game. Coelho's sobbing had stopped, but tears still trickled down his black beard. George had picked up one of the wads of cotton wool and was tearing it into tiny tufts. Kaputo, when able to understand about the loss of the emeralds, mumbled:

"Ow!" and made tongue noises like corks being drawn.

Silva said to me: "You are the only one, *Senhor*, who had possession of the buttons except *Senhor* Coelho."

"You forget the ostrich," I grinned.

"It is no matter for joking, *Senhor*. You perhaps would not have opened the buttons and taken the emeralds, but the magistrate and the officials do not know that. You must come with me to Cangamba. There we will tell the story to the magistrate."

"You're dreaming, Silva," I said, and took one of the half buttons from his hand. It seemed part of an ordinary brass button such as are worn on many military tunics, except that the halves screwed together with small-gauge spiral thread. On the last turn of the thread a small spring barb slipped into an indentation in the other half of the shell, locking the halves together. The halves could be unthreaded when pressure on top of the button cleared the spring barb. It was a clever little gadget. I handed the button shell back. Silva said:

"The magistrate will ask why, in the midst of battle, you cut the buttons from *Senhor* Coelho's coat."

"Now, Silva," I said, "don't make me peeved. Why weren't such valuable gems put under heavy guard? Why was Coelho prowling through the back country with emeralds hidden in brass buttons— like a cloak-and-dagger character?"

"You do not understand, *Senhor*," Silva said. "For a guard we had only native policemen. They would have been at the mercy of Fazai had he attacked. *Senhor* Coelho has long been the trusted messenger of the Government."

I turned to Coelho. "Did you, yourself, Coelho, put the emeralds in the buttons?"

"I, myself watched as they were put in the buttons," Coelho said.

"And from then on they never left your possession until I cut them from your coat?"

"Not for even one moment," he said. He put his bandaged hands over his face and blubbered.

"For Pete's sake, Coelho! Stop weeping," I said, and struggled up on my crutches.

"It's a mess," I said, "and I'm through with it. And I'm certainly not going to Cangamba, Silva."

Silva got to his feet, looked at his two Bihe policemen, glanced speculatively at Kaputo, shrugged, and said:

"We shall see, *Senhor*."

I hobbled to my hut.

That afternoon the two Bihes started for Cangamba leading Ahmed by a rope around his neck. I felt sure they'd return with reinforcements.

Coelho had crying spells all day. Toward evening I began to suspect that he was delirious. I took a medical thermometer to his hut, pushed his protesting hands aside, and put the thermometer in his mouth. His temperature was 104. I called Silva.

"This man's sick," I said, "very sick." Leaning on my crutches, I watched Silva strip Coelho bare. Coelho was literally skin and bones. I called George and sent him for Kaputo, and when the chief arrived I asked for meat—lots of it— any kind of meat. Twenty minutes later a couple of women arrived with two plucked chickens, a skinned ground squirrel, and a three-foot snake.

I told them to take the insides out of the chickens—Ambuellas eat chicken entrails and all. I cleaned the ground squirrel, skinned, cleaned, and cut the snake into three-inch pieces, and dropped squirrel and snake into a pot of water. The women pulled the chickens to pieces and dropped them in with the snake and squirrel. I motioned the women to keep the fire going and went back to Coelho. He was shaking with chill. I said:

"It's a long time since you've eaten, Coelho. Didn't Fazai and Ahmed feed you?"

"Only water, *Senhor*."

"Well, I'm cooking broth. I want you to drink it until you think you'll pop."

"I am not hungry, *Senhor*. But my bones are sore. I wish to die."

"Don't be an ass," I said. "Eat, and get well."

Coelho sat up with a jerk, gasped, and fell back panting. A louse crawled from his beard, walked out on his chest, turned, and scurried back into the whiskers.

George brought me the first-aid kit; I got scissors from it and began cutting Coelho's beard close to the skin. He tossed and turned, cursing in Portuguese. One of the women came in with a half gourd filled with broth. George sat on the ground beside Coelho, lifted his shoulders, and held him against his chest. I placed the gourd to Coelho's lips. He turned away his face. I said:

"Drink, Coelho."

He sipped rebelliously at first, then eagerly—gulpingly. I tipped the gourd until he got the last drop.

"More, please," he said, and immediately fell asleep. He slept like a dead man, not even wincing as I shaved him with an old-fashioned razor. His shock of black hair was speckled with nits. I shaved his head, too. Then I had George gather blankets, and we piled them on our patient. We sat beside him and when it grew dark George lighted a candle stub. And Coelho still slept.

George finally went to his hut and I had the women bring the broth and meat into Coelho's hut, then told them to go home.

About three in the morning Coelho opened his eyes. I held a chicken leg to his mouth and he chewed it clean. Then I pushed bits of white snake meat between his lips. He ate all of the snake. I filled the gourd with broth. He gulped several mouthfuls, then fell asleep again. The candle flickered, and the wick drowned in melted wax.

I lit another candle, looked at Coelho, and noticed he was sweating. I tucked the blankets around him securely, stretched myself out on the floor, and slept without dreams.

A pencil of sunlight streaming through a hole in the thatch wandered across my face early next morning and wakened me. I looked at Coelho and chuckled aloud. His shaven head was knobby; his face, sickly-white where the beard had been, was thin and lantern jawed; his nose—a long, brown, narrow wedge against the white skin—reminded me of a picture I'd once seen of *Pinocchio*...Coelho's ears were brown, and against his shaven pate and looked like leather flaps. His eyes were brown, large and sad. I said:

"Excuse me for laughing, Coelho, but you look so damned funny."

"I am hungry, *Senhor*," he said, "and my broken fingers feel like sticks."

"First, your temperature," I said. "And keep the thermometer under your tongue."

I looked at the reading. "Back to normal, Coelho," I said.

"You fed me, *Senhor*. The doctors never feed me when I have the fever attacks."

"Well, long ago," I said, "I learned to feed a fever. Want your meat cold, or warm?"

"Cold," he said, and wouldn't let me feed him. He grabbed squirrel and chicken chunks awkwardly with his bandaged hands and began wolfing. Silva came in and said to me:

"There's a witch doctor at Kaputo's hut, *Senhor*. He wants to talk to you." Then he noticed the mess Coelho was making of his bandages, called him a pig, and left. Coelho finished the last scrap of meat and promptly slept again. And while he slept I rebandaged his hands. The broken fingers seemed to be coming along fine, so I left off the splints.

In front of Kaputo's hut the witch doctor squatted on his haunches. On his head he wore a large pompon of chicken feathers.

He smiled a jagged-tooth greeting, held up his hand palm outward, and said:

"You were a boy. Now you are a man."

"Batu!" I said. "You old goat! How are you?" and held out my thumb. Batu shook it heartily.

"I have come," he said.

"But, Batu, you're of the Mucassequere tribe," I said. "You've always hated Ambuellas. Why are you here?"

"Kaputo."

"Kaputo?"

"He send."

"Kaputo sent for you to come here?"

"*Ai.*"

"Why?"

"To make magic to find thief."

I shouted for Kaputo and he came from his hut, wiping his mouth with the heel of his hand. I pointed to Batu. Kaputo said:

"The emeralds were lost because I was in fear of the Arab. Batu will find the thief."

I said: "One time Batu took me into his cave, made the smoke, and cast the bones. In the smoke I visioned an elephant charging me with trunk curled back. Two weeks later, when many miles from Batu's village, that very elephant charged me, his trunk curled back."

Batu said: "I have come. Now I go." He picked up some pebbles, placed them in a row, and said: "That day you come and I make the smoke."

"Sixteen pebbles," I said. "You want us to come to your cave in sixteen days. Right?"

Batu picked up the pebbles, then tossed them at my feet. "That many suns, you come," he said. He spat on my boot, got up, and stalked from the village.

"Kaputo," I said, "when did you become friendly with the Mucassequeres? You used to call them dogs, and always beat them when you met them in the forest."

"It is true that the Mucassequeres are curs. But, in the smoke, Batu sees the future. One of *Senhor* Silva's Bihes told the woman who slept with him last night that men are coming to carry you to the post at Cangamba. You are my friend. You came, and the Arab is dead. I sent for Batu, who will find the thief. Thus you will remain free."

"I'm not going to Cangamba, Kaputo," I said.

"It came to me, O Hunter, that if Batu finds the thief perhaps you would tell *Senhor* Silva that he is not to take me to Cangamba to stand trial before the magistrate for having sold girls to slavers.

"Chief," I said, "the *Senhor*s Silva and Coelho will have nothing to do with Batu and his magic. Furthermore, you sold those girls, knowing it was against the law."

"You are not my friend, then?"

"Yes, Kaputo, I am your friend. I am your father. But slavery—"

I heard Coelho yelling and limped to his hut. One of the women who'd prepared the chickens for last night's broth was trying to get under the blankets with him. I pushed her out of the hut, tucked the blankets around Coelho again, and said:

"There's a Mucassequere witch doctor, Batu, who thinks he can make magic and find out who stole the emeralds."

Coelho pushed the blankets off and sat up, saying excitedly:

"If this is true I am no longer a ruined man." He got to his feet, skinny shanks trembling. I put him down and covered him again, then said:

"You want the witch doctor to make the smoke? You believe in magic, Coelho?"

"Of the utmost certainty, *Senhor.*"

"Well, Batu won't do anything for sixteen days. He's waiting for the full moon, I think. Stay warm, and eat all the meat you can."

Days passed. My leg grew stronger. One morning I visited Long-One and Thick-One. I examined their wounds and said:

"You fellows are well enough to be up and about. I'll tell the women they don't have to nurse you any longer."

Long-One said: "Do not tell this to the women, O My Father, for the nights are cold, and because we are sick the women come in the darkness and being full of fat they warm our bones beneath the blankets. Hunters must always in time return home, for the unmarried women of the *kraals* have need of being filled with babies. The need of these Ambuella women is greater than the need of the women of the Alala, O My Father. Therefore, my brother and I will become Ambuellas. Here we will remain."

"Remain peacefully, then," I said, "but name me two of Kaputo's men to replace you."

"Moera and Cahinga," Thick-One said.

Moera and Cahinga were in the thirties, very black, and scarred from fighting. Kaputo gave me permission to hire them and they left that afternoon to take charge of our camp and relieve the Bihes. After they'd gone, Silva called me to his hut.

"I have heard, *Senhor,*" he said, "that *Senhor* Coelho would consult that Mucassequere sorcerer regarding the emeralds."

"He seems to have faith in magic."

"That Batu is a lawbreaker and a troublemaker."

"I know Batu's an old rascal," I said, "but it could be he *just* might be able to give Coelho a clue to the thief."

Silva's eyes flashed. He said: "Let it be understood, *Senhor.* Neither *Senhor* Coelho nor yourself will consult the witch doctor."

"I'll tell Coelho," I said.

I went to Coelho's hut, took his temperature, propped him up comfortably, and said:

"Coelho, when did you first hear about the emeralds?"

"I was in Lisbon, *Senhor*, and—"

"When?"

"Four months ago."

"What were you told?"

"I was ordered to leave at once for Cangamba, and there receive the emeralds from the *chefe do posto.*"

"From Silva?"

"*Sim, Senhor.*"

"How did he get possession of them?"

"The emeralds were found on an Arab in Moxico who'd been taken as a thief. A second Arab escaped. It must have been that second Arab who informed Fazai about the matter."

"Did the authorities suggest that you put the emeralds in the buttons?"

"*Não, senhor.* It is my own very clever, secret method."

"Not so secret, Coelho. Pepeca mentioned the buttons as he was dying."

"I had told Pepeca. Pepeca was a good man."

"Who else knew about the buttons?"

"The magistrate at Cangamba, *Senhor*. Also the big Bihe sergeant who is in charge of military stores at the post. Also *Senhor* Silva. Also—"

"Who put the emeralds inside the buttons?"

"It was I."

"With your own hands?"

"No. The big sergeant, he who is called Mote, put the emeralds in the buttons at my order. I watched him like an eagle, *Senhor*. He put the emeralds in the buttons as he sat at a table. He screwed the buttons together and immediately put them in my hand."

"Why did you let Mote do it?"

"This black sergeant, *Senhor*, had the cotton wool on the shelf of the supply room. This cotton wool was rolled in blue paper and on the paper was printed, 'From American Red Cross.' It was for the purpose of the hospital and it was a big roll. May I have water to drink, please, *Senhor*?"

I handed him the water gourd and asked:

"It was you, Coelho, who sewed the buttons on your coat?"

"*Sim.* But, *Senhor*, I am of the opinion that Fazai stole the emeralds while they were breaking my fingers."

"Then why did they continue torturing you, Coelho?"

"I do not know, *Senhor*. I was sick with pain and with hunger. And then you came, and —"

"Fazai didn't steal the emeralds, Coelho. Neither did I. I don't believe the emeralds were ever in the buttons."

"But, *Senhor*! I myself saw —"

"Were you and this Sergeant Mote alone when he was supposed to be putting the emeralds in the buttons?"

"*Sim.* We were alone, and *Senhor* Silva, also."

"Silva was there?"

"But certainly, *Senhor*. He handed the emeralds to Mote, who put them in the buttons with the cotton wool and then placed the buttons in my open hand. I held them in one hand while with the other I signed the release for the emeralds."

"Release?"

"A receipt stating that *Senhor* Silva had delivered the emeralds to me."

"And then you sewed the buttons on your coat. Where did you do that, Coelho?"

"At Mote's table. I sewed them on while Mote and *Senhor* Silva watched me. Then I put the coat on and I never took it off—night or day—not even while Fazai and that one-eyed one broke my fingers."

"What I can't understand, Coelho, is why you didn't send the emeralds to Portugal by post. The government mails ..."

"The mails from Cangamba, *Senhor*, are carried by natives. It was thought best for me to take them."

"Why didn't you head for Benguela? Why did you travel south?"

"We thought it best that —"

"Who is 'we'?"

"*Senhor* Silva and I. We—"

"Silva? He advised you to go south?"

"*Sim, senhor.* We thought it best to go to the southern border and thence into British territory. I would then proceed to Walvis Bay and there take passage on a vessel."

"George was right when he said that the whole thing's crazy," I said. "Where did Fazai capture you? How the hell did he know you carried the emeralds?"

"I have explained to you, *Senhor*," Coelho said wearily, "that a second Arab escaped when—"

"Yes, I remember. How long were you out of Cangamba when Fazai caught up with you?"

"He and the one-eyed one, and seven of Kaputo's natives, were waiting for me at the first camping place. They beat me with sticks, tied my feet, and carried me in the darkness until the sun came. Pepeca they tied by the hands while we walked, but at night they tied his feet also. Then they broke my finger. Fazai put his thumbs on the joint and the bone cracked with a noise ..."

"Did Fazai ask about the emeralds, Coelho?"

"He did not speak, *Senhor*. But after they had carried me one more night he grasped another of my fingers and said: 'Where are the emeralds?' I said: 'I know nothing of emeralds.' Then he broke that finger. The pain made everything red before my eyes and I wept, *Senhor*. That night they tied Pepeca again, but that night he escaped."

"Well, Coelho," I said, "Fazai knew you were coming. Someone tipped him off."

"The Arab who escaped —"

"He didn't know anything about your proposed route. I wouldn't be surprised if that guy Mote—"

"Mote did not know of the way I would go, *Senhor*."

"Mote didn't know?"

"*Nāo, Senhor*.

"Silva and you and Pepeca, then, were the only ones who knew your route?"

"That is true, *Senhor*."

I said: "Rest for a while, now, Coelho. I'll be back."

I went out into the sunlight and limped among the huts. I now felt certain that Silva was behind the theft. But where were the emeralds? They'd probably never even been put in the buttons. Yet Coelho had seen them put in the buttons. I sat on the ground and pretended that I was Mote and that I intended to hide the emeralds. I went about the business in every possible way. Then I hobbled back to Coelho's hut and said:

"Let me tell you how Mote put the emeralds in the buttons, Coelho. Don't interrupt. If I'm right —"

"Please, *Senhor*, I am worn with questions."

"Listen, Coelho," I said. "Mote was sitting at a table in the supply room. Right?"

"It is so."

"And the roll of cotton batting—wool—was on the table at one side of Mote?"

"It was in front of him, *Senhor.*"

"He held half of a button in one hand?"

"No. He held an emerald in one hand."

"He picked cotton wool from the roll and wrapped it around the emerald?"

"*Sim, senhor.* Then he put the emerald in the bottom half of a button and reached for the top half of the button. He then —"

"Wait, Coelho. He wrapped cotton wool around the emerald, placed it in the button, but it didn't fit snugly, so he reached into the roll of cotton wool and got a bit more. Right?"

"Let me think of that, *senhor. Sim.* That is what he did. He wrapped the emerald in insufficient wool each time, so he took more wool from the roll and pushed it into the button so that there would be no movement of the emerald. He then screwed the top on and handed each button to me. I then—"

"I know. Let's go over it again, Coelho. First Mote wrapped a bit of cotton wool about an emerald."

"*Sim.*"

"But it wasn't enough wool."

"It is as I told you, *Senhor.*"

"Mote held the partially-wrapped emerald in the hand with which he reached into the roll for more wool?"

"*Senhor,* I—I am not certain. It may have been so."

"It was so, Coelho," I said.

"Please, *Senhor,* will you now talk no more? Talk makes nothing."

"Only one more thing, Coelho, and then I'll let you sleep. What happened to the roll of cotton wool?"

"Nothing happened, *Senhor. Senhor* Silva gave me the release to sign. Mote handed me a pen. I dipped the pen in an ink bottle and I signed the release. That is all."

"But the roll of cotton wool?"

"It was returned to the shelf."

"By Mote?"

"No. *Senhor* Silva put it back."

"You're sure of that, Coelho?"

"Sim, senhor. I then sewed the buttons on the coat and we left that room. I then called Pepeca, who was to hunt food—for we carried no supplies—and—"

"Well, get some rest now, Coelho," I said.

Outside the hut I felt in my back pants pocket for the "authority" Silva had given me when Long-One, Thick-One, George, and I had started out to find Coelho. I'd not thought of the paper since. It was there all right, jammed down deep. It was soiled and wrinkled, but when I opened it to read, the written side was clean. It said:

> To all whom this may concern: The bearer is empowered by me to act in my behalf in matters of every nature. His authority is that of my own.
>
> (signed): Bernardino Silva.

I went to my hut, sent for George, and as we put fresh dressings on each other's wounds, I said:

"Silva's going to arrest me, George, for stealing the emeralds."

"But you no stealing the emeralds!"

"No, of course not. But I know who did steal them."

"Why Silva thinking you stealing? What saying you? You knowing it the stealing?"

"I'm pretty certain."

"Then why you no telling Silva so he no putting you in it, the jail?"

"Because it was Silva who stole the emeralds."

"What saying?"

"Silva's the thief. He also set Fazai on Coelho."

"But that cannot being. He being police, Silva. He knowing about them, the buttons?"

"Yes."

"Why he letting the fingers of Coelho being breaking by him, the Arab?"

"Could be, George, that the finger-breaking was just an act to make the theft look right when an investigation took place. If Fazai had really wanted to make Coelho talk, he knew a score of ways to do it. Broken fingers aren't so painful. Do you feel strong enough to go to Cangamba for me, George?"

"How far that being?"

"About a hundred fifty miles, there and back."

"I getting lost, maybe?"

"No. I'd send one of Kaputo's trackers with you."

"The journeying, it is nothing. I am being well only with a tight and sore in the side a little. What I doing in Cangabble?"

"Cangamba, George. You take a message from me to a black sergeant named Mote. You'll find him in the military supply store there. You will ask him for a roll of cotton wool. He will give it to you, and you will bring it back to me. Be careful of it, for I think the emeralds are in it, the roll. Damn it, George—you've got me talking like you talk! I'm a bit excited."

George grinned. "Me too am exciting. I going now at the once. Thees Mote he knowing the emeralds being... ?"

"Yes, he knows. He may not want to give you the cotton wool, but you will have a letter from Silva. You will say to Mote that Silva gave you the letter. Then Mote will give you the cotton wool."

I went over the program again and again with George. Then I asked Kaputo for the loan of his best tracker. The chief sent an old fellow who looked like a bundle of tendons held together by brown skin. His name was Someka. I said:

"Take your bow and arrows, Someka, for you will have to shoot the food you eat. You must travel slowly, for the white man is sick with a bullet."

"I have joy in the fat white man, O Hunter. He is a mighty warrior. Ow!"

"Go courageously," I said.

In eight days George and Someka were back—and they had the roll of cotton wool. George took it into my hut and I began to unwrap it, but my hands shook so that I had to pause. I said:

"George, I've faced every sort of wild animal in Africa, but I've never felt so nervous as now. Did you have trouble with Mote?"

"When I asking for the cotton wool his eyes getting big and white. He jumping up and saying, 'No, no, no, no!' I saying, 'Yes, Mote, for I being *Senhor* Silva,' and giving Mote the letter. He reading it, the letter, then he laughing with all his teeth and giving me the rolling of cotton wool. I wrapping it in much paper and coming away. Why you no opening it, the paper?"

I tore off the wrapping. An emerald peeped from the whiteness. I handed it to George, and put my questing fingers into the wool. Nothing. I shook the wool gently and two emeralds fell to the floor. George picked them up and said:

"They not being pretty, the emeralds. Why peoples stealing such ugly?"

"They're dripping with blood, George," I said.

"I no thinking about thees emeralds when I killing Fazai. I thinking of ostrich."

"You're a character, George."

"What is thees being, the character?"

"A character's a guy who thinks more of an ostrich than he does of a hundred thousand bucks."

"But that ostrich liking me."

"I know, George. Now put these emeralds in your tobacco pouch and keep them there until I want them. I'm going to try to figure how to get back at Silva without getting involved in a lot of legal stuff."

Shouting and the padding of running feet took me to the hut's door. Twelve Bihe warriors wearing police belts were standing at attention before Silva's hut. Silva saw me watching and limped over to me. He said:

"Tomorrow at dawn, *Senhor*, you will accompany me to Cangamba."

"Do you really believe, Silva," I said, "that I stole the emeralds?"

"You took the buttons from the coat, *Senhor*."

"Are you certain that the emeralds were in the buttons?"

"Let us not have words, *Senhor*. I do not say that you stole the emeralds. I say that you must come with me to the magistrate."

"Consider carefully, Silva," I said.

"Tomorrow at dawn, *Senhor*," he said, pointing to his Bihes. Then he shrugged and limped away.

I called to Kaputo. He came scowling, and said: "I have thirty warriors— and you are my friend."

"No, no fighting, Kaputo," I said. "Come into my hut."

Inside I gave him a handful of coarse tobacco. He put it in his mouth, chewed noisily, and swallowed it. Then I talked, and Kaputo listened, grinning.

Toward evening Kaputo returned to my hut with Batu. We went into a huddle. After Batu understood my plan, he cackled like an old hen. But in the midst of the cackling Silva appeared at the door, face dark with anger. He said:

"The witch doctor must leave this *kraal* at once. If he returns he will be beaten with sticks by my policemen." He glared at me and added: "Do not make it necessary for me to restrain you, *Senhor*. It is not fitting that black policemen should be called upon to —"

"You've twelve warriors, Silva," I said. "Kaputo has thirty."

Silva whirled on Kaputo. "You ..."

"He is my friend," Kaputo said.

"You haven't a chance, Silva," I said, "if it comes to a fight. Let's make a deal."

"I do not understand, *Senhor.*"

"Let's bargain," I said.

"You must come with me to Cangamba, *Senhor.*"

"There's a chance, Silva," I said, "that if we let Batu make the smoke, he'll be able to locate the emeralds. If he does locate them, you go your way, and I go mine. If he fails, I go with you willingly."

"You mean this, *Senhor?*" Silva asked incredulously.

"I mean it."

"But, *Senhor,* a witch doctor cannot— This is insanity! Do you mean this, *Senhor?*"

"You have my word."

Silva stared at Batu for a long minute, then laughed abruptly. "Make the smoke. Make it immediately, tonight," he said. "We shall leave at sunrise in the morning."

Batu croaked like a frog. I said:

"Silva, you will come to see the magic?"

"In this hut?"

"Yes."

"I will come, *Senhor,* and when the 'smoke' is finished, I will have Batu whipped from this *kraal* like a dog."

Batu smirked.

After Silva was gone, Batu dug a hole about the size of a cup in the floor of my hut near the door. About a foot away he bored a half-inch hole at an angle so it entered the larger hole near the bottom. In the angle hole he shoved a four-foot hollow reed. Thus he'd made a smoking pipe. From a smelly skin bag that hung from his waist Batu took a handful of powdered Indian hemp, known variously as dakka, bhang, hashish, and marijuana. He mixed the hemp fifty-fifty with tobacco and packed the mixture snugly into the "bowl" of the "pipe." He lit a long taper of twisted grass, held it to the hemp and sucked on the end of the reed. He closed his eyes, inhaled deeply, and snorted smoke from his nostrils. Then he said:

"*Eeyo-eeeee!*"

Kaputo bent and took a deep drag. He too shut his eyes as he inhaled. He said:

"Ow!" and coughed.

Batu dipped into his skin bag again, came up with a small green bottle, uncorked, and tipped it into a half gourd the size of a muskmelon. Thick, resinous juice of the hemp plant *(churras)* poured like cold syrup. He added water, stirred the liquid with his finger, took a swallow, and said:

"*Eeee-ak*!"

He offered the gourd to Kaputo, but the chief refused. "Makes everything go too quick," he said.

At the other side of the hut Batu drew a four-foot circle in the dirt with his big toe. Then he dumped the contents of another bag into the circle. I recognized the skull of a baby monkey, snakes' vertebrae, human finger bones, pebbles, leopard claws, and crocodile teeth.

Squatting on his heels, sipping occasionally from the gourd, Batu studied the way the "bones" had fallen. At last he looked up, then leered and said:

"The spirits come on the saddle of the wind. Go now until the moon is tree-high above the hill." He wrapped his head in his blanket, and then he lay back and began to snore. George said:

"He being drunk, the *drole.*"

"Only high, George," I said as we went outside.

Moonlight was silvering the roof of the forest when Silva arrived with six of his Bihes. Kaputo slipped away into darkness and returned in a few minutes with fifteen spear-armed warriors. Silva cursed, and sent his men away. Kaputo, grinning, dismissed his.

Inside the hut Batu raised a weird chant interspersed with short whinings like those of hyena cubs. I went in. The hut, pitch-dark, was hot and airless. Batu heard me and his yelpings grew shrill. I said:

"Stop the noise, Batu. It's only me."

He cackled, then whispered: "Put the emeralds in the gourd."

I struck a match, dropped the emeralds in the dregs of hemp and water, and said:

"We are waiting, Batu."

Batu croaked: "The hut is filled with demons. They will ride astride the policeman's neck." He struck a match and lit a small fire in a hollowed-out stone, then he put the stone on the floor just outside the magic circle. He dropped punk on the flames, waited until there was only a deep red glow, then sprinkled powdered hemp on the coals. Smoke that rose straight up wavered and spread through the shadows. I coughed. Batu squatted beside the brazier, his face an orange mask. He said:

"The demons are hungry."

I called: "Bring in the guests, George."

They came in one by one—Kaputo, Silva, Coelho, then George. They hesitated just inside the entrance. Batu said:

"Smoke," and pointed to the reed sticking from the ground. Kaputo took a drag, walked to the edge of the circle opposite Batu, and squatted on his heels. Silva looked at the pipe and shook his head in refusal. Batu said:

"Smoke."

Silva put his lips to the reed, puffed distastefully, then seated himself beside Kaputo. George said:

"Such a stinking," drew on the reed, inhaled, coughed and said "Hashish!" and took several quick puffs. "I now having bubbles on the insides of me. Soon I singing," he said, and laughed as he took his place next to Silva.

Coelho refused the pipe. I sat beside George.

Batu sprinkled more hemp on the glowing punk. The sharp, sweetish smoke scratched at my throat and I began to feel light-headed. Batu gathered the bones from the circle, shook them in his palms, then dropped them to the ground. All fell within the circle except a crocodile's tooth that came to rest in front of Silva. Batu screeched.

My heart thumped. Drops of sweat stood on Silva's upper lip. Kaputo's eyes seemed all whites. Batu chanted. His voice, low and rasping at first, rose to a crowlike cawing. Movements began in the shadows above Batu's head. I knew I was a bit hopped up, but the movements seemed real. Silva cursed under his breath, his eyes fixed on a point beyond Batu's shoulder. His lips were loose.

George joined his deep bass to Batu's chant. I said: "Quiet, George." He stopped. Batu gathered the bones and threw them again. The monkey's skull lay upside down. Eyes wild, Batu foamed at the corners of his mouth. His face muscles twitched; his hands wove back and forth. The narcotic fumes filled my head with whirlpools and I grew fearful that my plan might collapse. Batu, seating himself to the left of Kaputo, seemed to read my thoughts, for he looked at me, and for a brief moment his eyes were sane.

Again he threw the bones. Again a crocodile tooth rolled toward Silva. It was hard for me to believe that Batu could cause those bones to do what he willed. Silva said:

"I'm choking. Let me out of here." He got to his knees. I restrained him with a hand. Kaputo moaned. George said:

"I hearing drums."

Silva crossed himself.

Coelho made noises in his throat.

Batu picked up the gourd, quaffed deeply, picked up the brazier, and held it under his chin. He looked like a devil. With pink-rimmed eyes holding Silva's, he picked up the monkey skull, held it to his mouth, spat into it, then shook the skull as if it were a dice box.

It rattled.

Batu swept the bones from the circle with a palm, smoothed the earth, and upended the skull.

Three emeralds fell to the ground and glowed dully in the dirt.

Silva clutched his throat.

Coelho shouted.

Kaputo laughed.

I grabbed up the emeralds and put them in my pocket.

Silva staggered from the hut, still clutching his throat.

George began singing again.

I lit a candle and blinked in the sudden light. Batu gathered his paraphernalia, cackling all the while. He said:

"I came. Now I go," and disappeared into the night.

I took the emeralds from my pocket and stared at them. It didn't seem possible that the rabbit had been pulled from the hat. I said:

"George, flap a blanket around and see if we can get some of this smoke cleared out."

He didn't answer. I looked to see why. He was sucking on the reed pipestem. I jerked it away and broke it, and then pushed him through the door.

Coelho was so shaken that he had to be helped to his hut. He kept saying:

"I must tell the priest. I must tell the priest."

"Tell the priest what?" I said.

"The priest does not believe, *Senhor*, that witch doctors work true magic."

"You still don't seem to know who stole the emeralds, Coelho."

"It was Fazai, *Senhor*. That now is assured. Fazai opened the buttons while I was sick with pain. I have thought much about it. It was all confusion, but I have intelligence in such matters."

"You're feeling pretty cocky now," I said.

"I should have ordered a search of Fazai's clothing. It is plain that the witch doctor dug up the body and found the emeralds. But I was very sick, *Senhor.*"

When I returned to my hut, Silva was waiting for me. He looked whipped. My ideas of revenge evaporated. I said:

"Coelho still thinks that Fazai stole the emeralds. Let him continue to think that."

Silva licked his lips, tried to speak, swallowed, turned abruptly, and left without saying a word.

To get away from the stale hemp smoke, I took my blankets outside and lay down close to the hut. As I dropped off to sleep I heard George bellowing a song.

The sun was peeping over the eastern hills when Coelho wakened me by shaking my shoulder. I sat up, still fuzzy from the hemp smoke. He said:

"We go now to Cangamba, *Senhor* Silva and I. May I have the emeralds, *Senhor*, please?"

I looked to where Silva stood beside a hut watching his Bihes filing toward the river. Beside another hut a young Ambuella poured water over George's tousled head. I took the emeralds from my pocket, put them in Coelho's bandaged hand, and said:

"Stick close to Silva, Coelho. He'll protect the emeralds with his life."

Coelho smiled. "I have admiration for you, *Senhor*, for you are a friendly man. But you have not had experience in these things. I have lived a life of great peril and my wits consequently have been sharpened. *Senhor* Silva will indeed guard me, but there will be little need. The emeralds will be well hidden. You see, *Senhor*, I have still the buttons."

"Coelho," I said, "you're a genius."

"That is true, *Senhor*, and I am also grateful to you. That is why I advise you to continue as a hunter. One must be of a certain intelligence to circumvent knaves. I go now to Portugal. Do not feel sad at the parting. I go to great honors."

"Good luck," I said.

George and I stuck around recuperating in Kaputo's *kraal* for another eight days, then took off for our camp. For about two hours I led the way along the trail, George plodding at my heels. My leg grew weak. I said over my shoulder:

"We'll have to rest pretty soon, George. My leg ain't so hot."

He didn't answer. I glanced behind. No George. I went back along the trail and spotted George on his hands and knees talking to something on the ground. He looked up when he heard me, shushed me, and said softly:

"Do not making the noise, please. He praying, the bug."

I looked over George's shoulder. A praying mantis clung to a weed pod, its "hands" folded, its eyes turned upward as if in devotion. I said:

"He's a mantis. He *acts* as if he were praying. He *looks* as if he were praying, but he's one of the worst killers in the insect kingdom. He kills and eats anything he can get hold of with those spiny forelegs."

George got to his feet, sighed, and said:

"Peoples and scorpions and ants and mantises. I thinking I going home to that wife. She not eating her husbands. She got kind and good in the heart of her."

King John's emeralds didn't stay long in Portugal. Shortly after Coelho arrived there with them, they were sold by the Government to King Fuad of Egypt. When Fuad's son, Farouk, fled Egypt in 1952 to escape revolutionists, King John's emeralds fell into the hands of the present Egyptian Government.

African antelope: Grant's Gazelle.

A PARADE AND A BET

Back at the wagons George and I discussed the best and quickest way for him to return to Greece and "that wife." Practically all of his gear was stored at Blantyre on the other side of Africa. We'd almost decided to push down through Southwest Africa to Walvis Bay, sell our wagon outfit and take ship to Cape Town, when I remembered we'd left instructions at Balantyre to forward our mail to Livingstone.

"You've been gone from home for seven months, George," I said. "There should be some mail for you."

George, who'd been sitting on the *disselboom* (tongue) of the wagon, jumped to his feet, pulled his battered hat down on his ears, and said:

"We go. We go now. I having the bubble in the middle of me. That wife, maybe being writing the letters." Then, as if inspired, he said: "We can cablegramming in thees Livingstone?"

"Send cablegrams?"

"That is what I saying."

"Sure."

"That is where we going—thees Livingstone. I cablegramming that wife to meeting me in Johannesburg. Come, we go now."

Moera and Cahinga agreed to stay with us until we found others to take their places. We loaded everything shipshape and backtracked to where we'd first crossed the Zambezi, then more or less followed that river through Barotseland. Near Senanga we met a party of zoologists that was breaking up, and one of them, a redhead named Rory O'Rorke, who wanted to go to Johannesburg, joined us.

O'Rorke was a Western American who'd been educated in Europe. I gathered he was a top-hole animal sociologist who specialized in organization of vertebrate groups. Most of the time he'd talk with an exaggerated American twang, but occasionally, when on a binge of scientific jargon, his voice was that of a cultured Irishman.

He was tall, lean, and hungry-looking. His mouth was wide, nose sharp, and, when angry, his blue eyes turned gray. The three of us had been out for a long time, and looked like veld rats.

A few days before we reached the border between Bechuanaland and Southern Rhodesia we picked up a couple of Hottentots to replace Moera and Cahinga. This proved a mistake, for soon the new men were joined by their families and we had an additional four women and eight or nine children to feed. We made camp inside Rhodesia with the intention of staying a couple of days to rest and clean up before going on into Livingstone.

Next morning O'Rorke and I started out to shoot meat, and George, too nervous to stick around camp, decided to go with us. We stayed out all day and returned with a buffalo calf at sundown to find our Hottentots throwing a family beer party. They had five big gourds of it left—about four gallons, and admitted they'd traded an ox yoke and my favorite long-handled ox whip for their beer. I asked:

"Where is this *kraal* where you got the beer?"

"Not far," they said, and pointed southwest.

"Fine," I said. "Now, all of you get the hell out of here and don't come back." And, as punishment for the theft of the yoke and whip, I kept their beer.

Early next morning a man rode into camp, beckoned O'Rorke to him, said: "Mind my horse, my man," and tossed him the reins.

O'Rorke took the reins, and with cold gray eyes watched the stranger dismount. The man said:

"I say, chaps, you mustn't come through right here. Push up north a bit. I'm taking animal pictures. Name's Mills—deputy game warden, y'know. Bit of a name with animal pictures, y'know. Doing a great job for the fauna of Rhodesia. Mustn't be disturbed in my work, so push north."

"What being thees fauna?" George asked.

Mills looked at George as if George were dirt, ignored him, said to me:

"There's sable over there behind those bushes. Don't move around. I hope to get photographs. Color, y'know. Delicate work." He tossed a shilling to O'Rorke and said:

"Water my horse. I've another bob for you when I return."

We watched him strut off after the sable, and laughed. O'Rorke said:

"Jumping Jesus!"

George said: "He no liking me."

O'Rorke patted the horse's neck, led him under the tree where the five gourds of Kaffir beer were, emptied one gourd into a washbasin, and held the basin under the horse's nose. The horse sniffed, and then drank.

O'Rorke emptied another gourd, held the basin again, but the horse snorted and backed away. O'Rorke set the full basin down, tied the horse to the tree, and we all went about our business for an hour or so. The sound of the horse pawing the basin with a front foot brought us back to him. He'd drunk the beer and was asking for more. O'Rorke gave him two more gourdfuls.

A little later Mills showed up, puffing and angry because he'd got no pictures. He threw sixpence at O'Rorke, jerked the reins from the tree, adjusted them over the horse's head, stood with one hand on the pommel, and said:

"Be on your way at once."

"Yes, sir," I said.

He scowled at me suspiciously, and then he leaped into the saddle and slid back over the horse's tail as the beast sat down, forelegs braced. Purple with humiliation, Mills kicked the horse on the rump, got him to his feet and remounted. The horse wobbled, took a few staggering steps, then spread his front legs like a giraffe does when drinking, and hung his head.

I thought Mills would have a stroke. He sat leaning back awkwardly, stirruped feet sticking out at an angle. Veins on his neck and temples knotted. The horse slowly lowered his rear end as if borne down by a too heavy weight.

Mills got off, kicked the beast in the belly, and the horse broke wind. George said:

"You kicking thees horse again and I busting you with both my hands."

"Shut up, George," I said.

"I no shutting the up," George said angrily. "Thees horse being drunk. For why thees son of a bitching being kicking him, the horse?"

Mills roared a curse and swung at George. He missed, and George's roundhouse right caught the picture taker on the side of the jaw. He fell beside his horse—out.

I emptied the last gourd of beer on Mills's head and Mills sat up. The horse got to its feet, and Mills mounted. The horse moved forward uncertainly, then took off in a sideways shuffle.

We watched them out of sight, inspanned the oxen, and headed for Livingstone *without* "pushing up north." After a while O'Rorke, walking beside the wagon, reached in a pocket, withdrew the shilling and the sixpence Mills had given him, looked at them, then laughed.

At Livingstone, O'Rorke bought a railroad ticket for Johannesburg, where he was to meet with university scientists. George and I went to the post office. My mail was run-of-the-mill. George got letters from his wife. He sorted them according to postmark dates, and read the first one as we stood at a street corner. He smiled and put it in his pocket. He opened the next, read a few lines, and walked rapidly away. I watched him turn into a pub, figured he'd got bad news, and, deciding he'd rather sweat it out by himself, went into a barbershop, got a haircut and shave, then followed into the saloon.

George stood leaning on the far end of the bar, head in his hands. I put my hand on his shoulder and said:

"George."

He turned, tears dripping from the sides of his nose. I said:

"Can I help, George?"

"No can helping." He wiped his eyes with the heels of his hands. He looked like a big, heartbroken kid. I felt a lump in my throat. And then I noticed he was smiling. I said:

"That's better—I thought you'd had bad news."

He opened his lips to speak, but started to cry again. I looked at the bartender. The bartender shook his head and indicated by motions that he thought George was crazy. I said:

"For the love of Pete, George, what's eating you?"

George put his hands on his stomach and said:

"I am being dancing all over the insides of me. I am being having it— the baby."

"Look, George," I said. "It's been months since you've had a drink—that's why it's gone to your head. Let's get out of here."

"The baby!" he said, and banged the bar with the side of his fist. "You must drinking it with me—the bottle. For the first time I having it—the baby."

"Oh," I said, "the letters—your wife?"

"Now that wife she can having it the babies and babies. Long she telling her arms being hurting to holding him—the babies, because she having plenty of him—the babies, in the heart of her."

I bought a couple of drinks, toasted George, then, taking his arm, started him toward the door. Suddenly he jerked away and stood holding a hand hard against his chest. Then, smiling all the way to his ears, he spoke softly in Greek. I said:

"What's that?"

"I am being nice and loose on the all of me. Thees me, George Vossos, is now being it—the papa!"

For an hour or so I stayed with George while he wandered around town looking up Greeks and announcing his big news. At first I'd thought the baby'd been born, but it gradually dawned on me that the event wasn't expected for almost two months. I finally left George in the kitchen of a Greek restaurant with a bottle in one hand and a ham bone in the other.

I found a buyer for the oxen and wagon, sent a few telegrams, ate my first restaurant meal in more than five months, then went looking for George. I found him in the same kitchen, surrounded by a half-dozen countrymen, all seemingly as thrilled about the baby as George was.

We stayed that night at the home of an old friend of mine, and next morning went out to book George's passage to Greece. He bought tickets by way of Johannesburg and Cape Town, then announced he had shopping to do. I arranged to meet him at the station shortly before train time.

Arms filled with packages, George was on the platform when I arrived. For the next ten minutes I admired babies' sunbonnets— blue ones, pink ones, yellow ones. Then, almost before I realized it, George was gone.

He wrote me a few times during the years. They'd named the baby Paul, and he admitted sadly in one letter that his wife "no liking them—the sunbonnets."

What I called my office and warehouse in Johannesburg was really a sort of catchall for freak trophies, unusual skins, unique native weapons, odds and ends. On one wall hung a kudu head with one spiral horn and one straight one, a giraffe head with five unusually developed horns, a forty inch hippo tooth, and a baboon head with incisors almost eleven inches long.

Tucked away on shelves along another wall were several black leopard skins I was saving until I got enough of them to make a kaross. Scattered about were Pygmy bows and arrows, some deadly blowguns, disks for stretching lips of the duck-billed women of the Mangbettus, copper bangles, shell and stone necklaces, Zulu shields, Masai spears, and about a dozen worn-out rifles.

This "office" was in shantytown between the horse market and the Indian bazaar. An old Zulu called Voetsak took care of the place. I often slept in the office although I had a comfortable house on Isipingo Street in Bellevue East.

In a corner closet hung a Johannesburg baseball-team uniform, on a hook beside it a well-worn fielder's glove and a pair of spiked shoes tied together by their laces. In a rack beside the uniform were three Lee-Enfield military rifles, one supplied by the Transvaal Cadets, one by the Witwatersrand Rifles, and the third by the Transvaal Medical Corps; I was on rifle teams of all three outfits.

While in town I seldom missed a morning on the rifle range out beyond Turfontein, and Sundays found me cavorting in left field at the Wanderers' Grounds. Shooting and baseball were my two loves.

Johannesburg had a four-team baseball league. Players were of all ages and from many occupations. There was sixty-year-old Jim Northrup, a successful businessman who played first base for Johannesburg, and my fifteen-year-old brother Joe, who played left field for the Wanderers' nine—both top hands when it came to playing ball. The league roster listed about sixty names, and almost every name belonged to a "character." The majority had played ball in the United States—in high school, college, semipro or minor-league outfits. For a while we had a former major-leaguer with us. I can't remember his name, but we called him Silver Jack.

Among the players were two Englishmen, Woods and Hutchinson, who refused to wear regulation-colored uniforms, and played their positions in suits of brilliant red. The baseball field at the Wanderers' was larger than Yankee Stadium. The ground was hard-packed red earth, as smooth and fast as concrete. When a ball bounced at the Wanderers', it really bounced.

Fans were from all nations—Yankees, Canucks, Britons, Germans, French, Russian—and all liked to cut loose in the manner of Brooklyn enthusiasts. It was a sort of compensation for the necessity of restrained dignity imposed by custom at cricket matches in an adjoining playing field.

The race for the flag was always hot, and most games were tightly played. Occasionally, however, games became a circus. One Fourth of July the proprietor of Johannesburg's famous Old England Bar placed a keg of beer at third base. His idea was that any man reaching third got a drink. That worked fine for about three innings; then it was decided to make third base first base. So the rest of the game was played in reverse. Third basemen were ordered to move over to first base, and first basemen, to third base. The third basemen refused to leave the keg, so for the rest of that game we had four "first" basemen. It didn't matter, though, for rules were changed so that any batter who got to the beer barrel was credited with a run. I think the final score was Johannesburg 137—Crescents 141.

Then someone got an idea for a Fourth of July parade. We moved downtown, hired fifty rickshaws, and bought fifty small kegs of beer. Two men and one beer keg were assigned to each rickshaw. Someone dug up fifty small American flags, and the parade moved off down Eloff Street with the Stars and Stripes waving gloriously among beer fumes.

Nicest thing about Americans in Johannesburg during the first decade of the century was pride in being Americans. There was little of the loudmouthed, boastful, overbearing attitudes of many Americans abroad today. Of course there were a few ignoramuses who, after a few drinks, noisily proclaimed that "England is a ten-cent island," and "We licked the British in '76, and we can do it again." When such vermin showed up in Johannesburg in the old days, the decent Americans soon found ways to give them the bum's rush.

Well, the parade went on for a couple of hours. It was noisy, but good-humored. Johannesburgers lined sidewalks and smiled at the antics of the celebrating Yanks. There were no fights among the paraders, just plenty of cheering, singing, and burping—and a few beery tears of homesickness.

The parade ended at the Rand Bar—the classiest in the city. It was owned by an American, an understanding guy. The bar was packed and hilarity was at its height when someone, probably from west of the Rockies, pulled a .45 and began shooting bottles off the shelves. All in fun, of course.

But British Law is British Law, and such goings-on couldn't be condoned. Police came—lots of them. A conference was held with leaders of the paraders, then the bobbies herded the whole gang into an empty second floor of a downtown building and asked them to stay until morning. They stayed.

Next day a committee waited on the owner of the Rand Bar, and gave him a check to cover damages.

I said that most of the Americans who played baseball were characters. I've forgotten many names, but I'll never forget Hungry Wilson, whose quaint Americanisms kept British listeners in stitches; Hairless Roach, catcher for the Crescents, who rubbed castor oil and kerosene into his bald pate for more than a year in an effort to grow hair, and who was as astonished as others when his hair grew back with a rush; Jim Brady, of Detroit; Jim Raby, of York, Pennsylvania; McKeogh; McBride; Big Jones; Frank Mitchell of Sault Sainte Marie, Michigan, whose father once owned a half interest in the fabulously rich Simmer and Jack gold mine; young Northrup, son of old Jim Northrup; "Johnny" Crabbe, a Canadian, who kept the league record books; and Doc Brennan, another Canadian, who played a good game of ball despite one of the biggest bellies in the Transvaal. Millionaires, miners, businessmen, mechanics—an assorted lot who succeeded in showing the best side of Americans to their hosts—the South Africans.

A number of Americans were members of the Union Club, among them, Nicobar Jones. One evening, as we sat around sipping drinks while waiting for the dining room to open, a member introduced a guest named William R. Carrie, a wealthy American of the Me-and-God school. He was a husky man in good physical shape who'd just returned from a nine-month shooting trip that covered most of Africa. He was introduced around, and greeted each of us heartily until he came to Nicobar Jones, when he said sarcastically:

"Oh, the big-shot hunter!"

"Sort of," Jones said.

Carrie drank three fast whiskies and began boasting about his trophies. His friend tried to switch subjects, but Carrie wasn't having any. He'd run giraffes down with a truck, shot lions from a tree platform, bagged elephants from the rear, shot rhinos from trees, and even bragged about getting a hippo with a sub-machine gun.

Jones, who always tried to give animals an even break, walked out and sat in another lounge. Carrie followed and said:

"I shot 617 animals in 290 days."

"What for?" Jones asked.

"What for?" Carrie shouted. "Because I'm a sportsman—that's what for. I'm a sportsman."

"Of a kind."

"Is that a crack?"

"Go away, mister," Jones said.

Carrie's friend took him by the arm and dragged him off.

At dinner Jones and I sat at a table near the kitchen. Carrie and his friend ate at the far side of the dining room. Nothing out of the way happened until Carrie started in on a bottle of sherry during dessert. After two or three glasses he began glaring at Jones.

We went to the billiard room and were racking the balls for a game of snooker when Carrie entered, grabbed Jones by the shoulder, and said:

"I'm a sportsman. Got lions, elephants, buffalo. I've the finest guns in Africa."

Jones said: "You didn't really need guns. You could have got all those animals without so much noise."

Carrie said: "You can't kill animals without guns."

"How do you think natives killed big game before guns were invented?" Jones asked.

Carrie glared. Before he could say anything, his friend pulled him roughly from the room. In five minutes he was back. He said:

"No guns, huh?"

Jones said: "Listen, fellow. I'm an old man, but even now, without a gun, I could get all the animals you bagged. I know a native tracker who could start out right now with only a hand ax, and within sixty days return with heads of elephant, lion, croc, buffalo, rhino, and hippo. He wouldn't use guns or poisons. Now go away, please, before I lose my patience."

By this time there was quite a group around us, and two husky club stewards were approaching to be on hand if things got rough. Carrie's friend had disappeared. Carrie shouted:

"I got $10,000 that says you're a liar, Jones. No man ever born could do what you claim." He pulled a billfold from a back trouser pocket and waved bank notes in Jones's face.

Jones said: "Wait here." He went to the club office, got £2000 from the cashier, came back, and laid them on the billiard table. He turned to me, said: "Take over," and left the room.

I said: "Carrie, the tracker's name is Ubusuku. He'll leave Kindu, Congo, wearing only shorts, his only weapon, a hand ax. He'll return to Kindu within sixty days with the heads of an elephant, a lion, a croc, a buffalo, a rhino, and a hippo. He'll use any additional weapons that he can fashion himself. No guns. No poisons. Jones has left this £2000 on the table. Lay yours alongside, and it's a bet."

Carrie threw his money down. Witnesses formed a committee to hold stakes and to work out details of the hunt. I slipped away, found Jones playing a slot machine in Raby's Arcade on President Street, and told him the bet was on. Jones said:

"Well, Carrie's got lots of money, and can afford to lose. But in the morning, if he wants out, we'll call the bet off."

Carrie didn't want out the next morning. In fact he put up another four or five thousand dollars that was covered by club members. Details were simple. Carrie and

I were to go with Ubusuku. Two Englishmen, D. C. Davis and Arthur Aylcough, whose integrity couldn't be doubted, were to accompany us as referees. Both were wealthy, retired, and tickled pink to share the novel hunt.

I sent for Ubusuku, who'd been home at his *kraal* in Natal for a year getting families started among three new wives. He was a Zulu, 26, chocolate brown, six feet four, and weighed 205 pounds. He'd been my tracker since we were kids. His father, Umgugundhlova, had been Jones's tracker for thirty years. Both killed all big game with spear, knife, or hatchet, and thought nothing of it.

Two weeks later Ubusuku showed up and our party left next day. Carrie acted as if we were out to rook him, but he had guts, and all of us, including Ubusuku, developed a sneaking liking for him.

Davis and Aylcough were fine types of men. They never complained and were always considerate. Both could outshoot Carrie, but not once did they humiliate him by doing so. I've met many Englishmen like them—good men to be with when going is tough.

Nicobar Jones had selected the Kindu area for Ubusuku's hunt because in 1909 he'd taken an elephant census there for the newly formed Belgian Congo Government and so could tell Ubusuku exactly where to find the easiest hunting for each animal on the list. However, we never got to Kindu.

Fifty miles or so above Kasongo our boat smashed up on a hidden rock as we drifted close inshore. The water came only to our waists. We had little trouble saving our gear, but the boat was hopeless. We abandoned it, and on foot pushed northeast through heavily wooded country. Our plan was to find a native village and buy another boat.

Late on the first afternoon we entered an area of smaller, more scattered trees interspersed with tremendous baobabs. As darkness fell we emerged into an almost treeless plain.

It was early December, and even in the shade the day had been hot, but as night grew deeper the temperature dropped and within an hour we were glad to hug our roaring fire. We traveled unusually light. Each of us had an army haversack containing necessities such as snakebite serums, antiseptics, bandages, tourniquets, small splints, morphine pills, candles, waterproof matches, extra skinning knives, pocketknives, binoculars, spare rifle parts, and folding cups.

Ubusuku's pack contained our screw drivers, pliers, copper wire, extra cartridges, and a large can of castor oil to be used in preserving the heads. Each of us had two blankets rolled in green waterproof canvas, and a canvas water bag.

We carried no plates, table knives, forks, or spoons; no tents, mosquito nettings, liquor or cooking utensils except one small billy with a folding handle. Each had one full bandolier over a shoulder, and a filled cartridge belt around the waist. All carried holstered choppers, and Aylcough and I lugged heavy-calibered revolvers.

Ubusuku had started out with only his favorite weapon, an American hand ax with a specially-made twenty-seven-inch handle, but he now sported a seven-foot teakwood spear, and an eighteen-inch dagger. He'd made both from a sapling, tapering and hardening them by holding them in fire. The spear looked like an immense thorn; the dagger like a butcher's steel.

When I awoke at dawn, Ubusuku was squatting beside me waiting for my eyes to open. He flashed his white teeth and said softly:

"*Saku bona, Baas.*"

"I see you too," I said, and sat up.

Ubusuku motioned to the others still sleeping, and whispered:

"This is the place, *Baas.* Come without disturbing *Baas* Carrie, and I will show you."

We walked northeast across new grass glistening with millions of minute water droplets. Here and there spiders had spread webs among branches of low bushes, and the webs were strung with tiny water pearls. Birds seemed everywhere—some flew in formation, others hovered. Starlings rose in a mob, fluttered, and settled again. We'd gone about a mile when Ubusuku pointed as a spur-winged plover volplaned out of sight.

"Where did he go, *Baas?*"

"Into grass," I said.

"No. He has gone to a riverbank to visit crocodiles."

I looked across the plain. It was as flat and smooth as a table. "There's no river here," I said.

"A little one, *Baas.* It is hidden. I saw it this morning when I walked in the darkness."

We moved forward a couple of hundred yards and the ground dipped abruptly into a swale. It was boggy, and grass grew tall and coarse. Through the swale's center a rivulet ran between low sand and-mud banks that bordered the stream like a wide ribbon. Instead of being smoothly flat, however, the sand at this point swelled and sank in a series of shallow billows.

Ubusuku moved slowly through the grass, and parallel with the sand strip. He stopped to follow the flight of another plover, then motioned me toward him, and pointed. A medium-size crocodile lay just out of the water. The plover roosted on the croc's head.

"It is a sign, *Baas*, "Ubusuku said. "Here I will slay the crocodile for Old *Baas* Jones. Here also I will slay the elephant. They are nearby."

"No elephants here, Ubusuku," I said. "This time of year they're high in the cool mountains." I pointed eastward to distant peaks now outlined by the rising sun.

Ubusuku moved back to a dip in the swale and said:

"*Figa lapa, Baas.*"

I went to him. He stood beside a deep impression of an elephant's foot. Water lay three inches deep in the bottom of it.

"Old spoor," I said. "It was made at least a month ago before the rains ended."

"Not so, O Hunter. The water is from below." He followed the low point of the dip, pointing to other elephant-foot "wells" here and there. He said:

"The dung is not spaced far part, so they are not traveling. The dung is scattered, and fresh dung overlays the older in some places. They drink from this river and stand dreaming among the bushes when their bellies are cooled. I will find the herd."

As we headed back toward camp, a distant rifle shot told us someone had bagged breakfast. When we arrived, Aylcough had just finished skinning a hartebeest heifer. He handed me the liver. I sliced it and told Ubusuku to broil the slices on a stick. I walked back toward the trees, gathered leaves from a species of orchillas (archil) weed and brewed a fair-tasting tea in the common billy.

Through a mouthful of liver Carrie mumbled: "We goin' to live on nothing but meat?"

"There's plenty of edible tubers, berries, greens, mushrooms, and wild grain for the finding," I said, "but there's nothing wrong with a strictly meat diet. Incidentally, we can save a lot of time by starting the hunt right here. Ubusuku and I saw crocs in a little river this morning, and there's elephant sign."

Carrie scowled. I expected him to protest. Instead he said:

"Looks to me like we're making a sucker out of Ubusuku. He takes all the risks, and Jones or I get all the money. I don't want to see the brown boy killed."

"What about the bet?"

"Hell. Let Jones collect."

"Let's get straight on this thing, Carrie," I said. "If you were to give Ubusuku a gun to go after the animals, he'd be almost certain to get killed. He's a smart

Kaffir, but he can't get over the idea that the harder you pull a trigger the faster a bullet goes. I doubt he could hit an elephant from ten yards. But give him a spear, a knife, and his 'little hatchet,' and with any luck at all he'll win the bet without getting even a scratch."

Aylcough said: "Here's something," and rummaged through his haversack and came up with a letter. He handed it to Carrie and said:

"Jones told me to give that to you when we arrived at Kindu. But if the hunt's to start here, you'd better have it now."

Carrie tore open the envelope, read the letter, swore softly and handed the letter to me. I read it aloud:

> *"If you've cooled' off, Carrie, you probably realize you've made a bum bet. Ubusuku won't fail. Go through with the hunt, if you wish, but forget the bet—and no hard feelings.—Jones."*

"Could be," Carrie said as I finished, "that Jones has cold feet."

I laughed.

"Well," he said firmly, "the bet stands, and the hunt starts here, if that's the way you want it."

Ubusuku spent the rest of the morning practicing with his spear —that from a heavy three-inch butt, tapered to a sharp point. He hung the skin of the hartebeest from a low branch, stepped back about fifty feet, and, grabbing the spear by its point, hurled it somewhat after the manner of a knife thrower. On the first throw the spear hit the skin broadside. Ubusuku stepped back five or six paces and threw again. The spear revolved once, end over end, and passed through the hide point first.

After a few more throws—all successful—he hung the dismembered carcass of the hartebeest against the hide, then, grasping the spear's point with both hands, the butt far back over a shoulder, whipped it forward, through carcass and skin.

Davis said: "My word!"

Aylcough said: "That could go clean through a rhino."

Carrie said: "No guns! Damn it, that thing's as powerful as a cannon!"

Ubusuku buried hide and carcass, went off with his spear and came back in less than an hour with a 125-pound bush pig. The spear had buried half its length in the beast's body back of the ribs. I skinned the animal and cut chunks from the hams for each of us. We broiled them on sticks, ate, then followed Ubusuku toward the little river.

We took positions behind bushes at the lip of the swale, adjusted our field glasses so that the river bank seventy-five yards away seemed only a few paces. Carrie stretched out on his belly, his .450 beside him. He was nervous, although he tried hard to hide it. Twice within minutes he checked to be sure there was a cartridge in the rifle breech.

Aylcough adjusted his camera. Davis sat cross-legged, puffing an empty tobacco pipe in a manner that showed he was nervous too.

Ubusuku angled downwind, dagger hanging from the left side of his belt, hatchet from the right. Halfway to the river he leaned his spear against a bush and went on without it.

Carrie cursed, fidgeted a few minutes, then whispered:

"If he's going to try to kill a croc with that dagger, he's nuts!"

I smiled inwardly—I knew Ubusuku. He could have drilled a croc with the spear from a safe distance, but he loved to put on a show. This should be good.

The Zulu stepped into the river, submerged quietly, and began swimming slowly upstream. In imagination I saw crocs speeding toward him from all directions. Instinctively I readied my rifle.

Carrie loosed a deep sigh. Davis chewed the side of a finger. Aylcough ran the tip of his tongue back and forth across his upper lip.

Ubusuku crawled out of the water opposite us, bellied across the sand for about fifteen feet, then lay on his side, his back to the sun, one arm across his face.

"What th' hell!" Carrie said.

"Bait," I said nonchalantly. But my nerves were twitching. I'd seen this trick before, and didn't like it. Watching a man lie motionless while a hungry croc sneaks up close is almost unendurable. Carrie, eyes dismayed, edged over to me.

"Bait?" he said. "You mean... ?"

"Ubusuku's seen a croc along there. Now he's pretending he's dead so the croc will attempt to drag him into the water. Not many men can remain motionless long enough to allay a croc's suspicions. This may take hours."

Carrie thought a little, then asked:

"Would you say Ubusuku's sixty-five yards away?"

"Sixty-five or seventy."

Carrie adjusted his back sight. I said:

"Don't do any shooting, Carrie—you'd horse things up. Give the guy a chance."

"But —"

"If it gets tough, I'll do the shooting," I said. "Get back to your glasses. Somewhere along there you'll probably see two black knobs—crocodile's eyes. And please don't talk any more."

I put up my own glasses, searched the edge of the stream, found the croc, and said:

"One finger right from Ubusuku. Edge of water. Black rock about the size of small pumpkin. See it?"

All three men nodded.

"Croc," I said. "Watch."

Ubusuku lay like a dead man, but I knew he was watching the croc from under his arm. I suffered with him, for I knew he was being bitten by sand fleas, pestered by gnats, nipped by flies, chewed on by ants. I looked at the croc. The head seemed slightly larger, but I wasn't sure. I couldn't tell if it'd seen Ubusuku yet or not.

If it didn't see him, it'd drag itself into sunshine after a long look around. If it did see him, it'd move as slowly as the hour hand on a clock—so slowly that the only way you could know it moved was to turn your eyes away for a time, then back again.

It took at least thirty minutes for that croc to drag its full length out of the water. It was a big fellow, probably twelve feet from nose tip to tail tip. For a while it lay head toward us and we saw white fangs in a mouth that seemed to grin perpetually. Thinking to give Carrie an additional thrill, I said:

"If the croc gets Ubusuku, he'll drag him into the water and drown him, but won't eat him for probably a week. Crocs can't chew, so they let corpses rot until they can tear them into chunks small enough to swallow. If they're very hungry and can't wait for a corpse to really soften, they'll drag it to the surface, grip it in their teeth, dig a hind foot into it and pull it apart. Sometimes they just shake a corpse like a dog shakes a rabbit. And sometimes —"

"Shut up, damn it!" Carrie said. "I've had about enough. I never figured on any such —"

"Quiet," Davis said. We looked at the croc. He'd made a little rush and had put a sand billow between himself and Ubusuku, and between himself and us.

"Now it starts all over again," I said. "Watch the top of that mound that hides the croc from us and from Ubusuku."

I stared at the ridge of sand so hard and so long that it seemed to dance. Several times I saw two black knobs that I thought might be the croc's eyes as they peeked over the ridge, but when I blinked my eyes, the knobs disappeared and I knew them to be only spots caused by eyestrain.

I rested my eyes, looked again, and blinked. This time the knobs didn't vanish.

Little by little the croc's head lifted above the sand ridge, first appearing to be a small rock, then a larger one. Slowly the entire head was visible, teeth flashing their demoniac grin.

Ubusuku still seemed to sleep.

I judged the croc's mouth was twenty feet from him, and nervous sweat ran down my sides. I wiped the palms of my hands on my thighs.

Carrie was white about the mouth, and breathed irregularly. Davis and Aylcough were as still as hiding antelope calves.

I figured the croc had eight feet or so to go before he'd make his rush to kill. He might stand on his toes, scurry forward and try to grab Ubusuku with his teeth; or he might whirl and slap the Zulu a crushing tail blow. I checked the cartridge in my rifle chamber, pushed the bolt home carefully, and sat, elbows on knees, finger on trigger.

The croc slid forward, stopped, slid forward again. Carrie said, "Christ!" and fired. His bullet thudded into the croc's side. The reptile reared, roared, fell sideways, stood on its tail, opened its jaws wide, roared again, whirled half around, and smacked the ground with its belly, head toward the river.

Ubusuku leaped on the wounded beast's back, knelt just behind the head, bent forward, and wrapped his powerful fingers around the croc's closed snout.

Only the top jaw of a croc moves—the lower jaw is joined solidly to the skeleton. A croc can crush a thighbone by closing his jaws on it, but once the jaws are closed, any pair of strong hands can hold them shut.

I knew what Ubusuku was trying to do—keep a strain on the jaws so that when he loosed his grip suddenly, the jaws would open wide enough for him to push his dagger down its throat.

Closely followed by Davis, Aylcough, and Carrie, I ran toward the battle. Too late. The croc whirled end for end, throwing Ubusuku clear. The Zulu leaped erect, and the croc's slashing tail banged against his ankles, cutting him down like a scythe lays grain.

Carrie's heavy bullet seemed to be taking its toll, for the croc passed up Ubusuku and headed jerkily for the water. I drilled him through the neck. He shuddered and tried to get to his feet. I stepped close and put a bullet into an ear. And that was it.

Ubusuku said: "I heard the voice of the big gun, and it came to me that a man who blows much wind from his mouth also blows it from his other end."

"Ubusuku," I said, "*Baas* Carrie was —"

"Leave the boy alone," Carrie said. "I spoiled his game. I concede the crocodile's head."

Ubusuku stalked away. Aylcough watched him out of sight, then jumped as if stung, and said:

"Dammit—I forgot all about having a camera!"

Aggressive hippo.

DON'T SPOIL THE HEADS

With bullets through their hearts duikerbok will sometimes run a hundred yards, elephants a half mile, lions fifty feet. A crocodile, however, can live for an hour after the heart has been pierced. A croc's heart, cut from the body and wrapped in a damp towel, will palpitate a long time if kept warm.

The only shot that will instantly kill a crocodile is the one through an ear into the brain. The ears are about two inches behind the eyes and are fitted with horny flaps that are lowered when the croc is in water. Body shots don't pay off, for a wounded croc makes for the river, and, if it dies, sinks. Neck shots usually pin a croc down, but it requires three or four of them to kill him.

Ubusuku's problem was to kill his croc on land so he could get the head. If he drove his big spear through the reptile anywhere except the neck, the croc would take off, spear and all.

There was no use telling Ubusuku to play it sensibly and safely —for once in his life he was the center of interest and, an actor at heart, he was going to make the most of it. I wasn't much worried about his getting hurt—he was an experienced hunter and knew what each animal would do under any conditions. He had the strength of two men, astonishing stamina, and perfect muscular coordination.

The sun rose hot the morning after Carrie's shot had spoiled Ubusuku's first attempt to get a croc. The pink-and-copper dawn sky soon blanched to a reluctant gray. As the day advanced, even the birds fled the heat of the open savannah.

Davis, Aylcough, Carrie, and I were ready to watch the crocodile chase by midmorning, but Ubusuku dawdled, polishing his spear, rubbing oil on his dagger, whetting his hatchet on a stone. After a half hour of this I said impatiently:

"Make quick, Ubusuku."

In Zulu he said: "That man who shakes the trees with his wind must leave his gun in camp."

"*Baas* Carrie was nervous," I said. "He didn't want to see you killed."

"If a man's bowels quake when he sees a crocodile, O Hunter, they will turn to liquid at sight of a lion or an elephant. The windy one is more dangerous than is *ngonyama* or *indhlova.*"

I said to Carrie: "This big lug's turned stubborn. He won't play if you take your rifle. Mind leaving it in camp?"

Carrie began an angry reply, broke off abruptly, and tucked his .450 under folded blankets. He said:

"I'd about as soon go hunting naked as without that gun, but if Brown Boy wants it that way—that's the way it'll be."

At Carrie's words a look of surprise flitted across Ubusuku's face —for a white man to accede to a native's wishes was almost unheard of. Ubusuku said:

"I have heard the voice of my *e/hose* [guardian spirit], and it comes to me that the gun with the big voice will not hurt me." He got Carrie's rifle, handed it to him, and said:

"It is not you, *Baas,* that is the *umfagozan* [rascal], but I." Then, shouldering his spear, he headed for the river.

Carrie had won a friend.

Ubusuku walked upstream. We followed a little way behind. Twice crocs slid into the water as Ubusuku neared them, but the big Zulu went on as if he hadn't seen them—they weren't large enough to interest him.

After two miles the flat banks of the river grew less sandy, more muddy. Large, dead, leafless bushes now lined the water's edge. Ubusuku stopped, held up a hand in warning, walked away from the river, then he circled, regained the bank a hundred yards downstream, laid his spear on the ground, and slipped quietly into the water. He pushed out from the shore and turned on his back; he floated a moment and turned over and sank with barely a ripple.

I focused my field glasses and searched the muddy bank where Ubusuku had held up his hand in warning. At one point straggling brush opened a little, giving a view of the water as through a large picture frame.

I examined the river edge inch by inch, saw nothing. I asked the others to train their glasses on the same area. After several minutes Davis said:

"Nothing but mud."

Carrie, who'd not lowered his glasses, said:

"God Almighty!"

I looked again, and this time saw two rows of white fangs. Nothing else—just white fangs that vanished momentarily, then appeared again with a small bird picking at them. Then we saw the croc, the front half of its body out on the mud, tail and back legs in the water. Its dark, scaly skin was so like the color of the mud that had it not moved slightly we'd probably never have seen it.

"That's the baby he's after," I said.

Carrie said: "What the hell's Brown Boy doing in the river with hungry crocs?"

"He'd as soon fight them in the water as on land," I said. "Once in the Okavango swamp country I watched him battle a croc in a deep slough. He got the croc by a foreleg, hung on, and with a short-handled assagai stabbed—stabbed—stabbed. The croc swam in a circle like a steamboat gone mad, Ubusuku clinging to the leg and stabbing all the while. He killed that croc to demonstrate to me that shooting crocs *with guns* was, as he said, 'work for fat women.'"

Davis, still peering through his field glasses, asked:

"Why does Ubusuku go into the water?"

"You can't crawl through mud silently," I said. "It sucks at you. Ubusuku'll approach this croc from behind—under water. That way he can move silently, and the water will prevent the croc getting his scent."

Aylcough adjusted the telescopic lens on his camera with trembling fingers, pushed his hat back off his forehead, loosened the neck of his shirt, and said:

"He's been in the river for at least ten minutes. Do you think —"

"The croc's ears!" I said. "Look!" The ear flaps were fluttering like shirttails in a wind. The bird flew out of the croc's mouth, settled on the reptile's back momentarily, then darted away. I said:

"Crocs' ear flaps flutter when the beasts are excited. He probably senses Ubusuku." Then Ubusuku's head, a dark round ball, appeared at the river's brink. The croc twisted its body as if to start back into water. Ubusuku popped out on the mud beside the croc, his long-handled hatchet held high. Down it came on the small of the croc's back with all of Ubusuku's strength behind it.

The front half of the croc's body threshed from side to side. The tail end didn't move. Ubusuku had severed the backbone. The croc roared and lifted its foreparts, pointed its snout to the sky, opened its mouth wide, and bellowed, remaining in that position for several seconds. Then the body fell, splashing mud.

The hatchet was still buried in the croc's back. Ubusuku grabbed it, tugged, couldn't get it out, jerked his dagger from his belt, leaped to the croc's back, knelt, pushed the dagger point into an earhole, and drove it home with a blow of his other hand. The thrust brought instantaneous death.

Leaving his dagger in the ear, Ubusuku went to his hatchet, wrestled it without loosing it, bent his back, and jerked violently. The hand ax, evidently caught under the backbone it had severed, came out suddenly and Ubusuku sat down hard.

Not for one moment during his attack on the croc had Ubusuku forgotten he was the top performer in an exciting show. Now, fanny-down in the mud, heels raised, he got to his feet, gave us a sheepish glance, and retired behind some brush.

Chuckling, we walked to the croc. It still grinned, but its eyes were fogged in death. It was a big male—between thirteen and fourteen feet long, I guessed. Aylcough photographed it.

I pulled Ubusuku's dagger from the ear, made a cut through the heavy skin at the shoulders. When I'd cut all the way around the base of the neck, I yelled for Ubusuku, and with knife and hatchet the two of us severed the head from the body.

A croc's head is difficult to skin, particularly around the ears, eyes, and nostrils, but we did a fair job and Ubusuku lugged the messy skull to an ant heap. We'd seen no hyena or jackal sign, so left the skull unprotected while we went looking for greens, tubers, and young plant shoots as a change from a meat diet.

At sundown Ubusuku brought the skull to camp. It was as clean as a newly washed dish. We let it dry for a few days, then rubbed it well with castor oil to discourage bone-boring insects. We dried the head skin in shade and fleshed it with a blunt knife, rubbing in salt as a preservative.

When the job was done, Carrie said with a grin:

"Elephant, rhino, hippo, buffalo, lion, and crocodile. Six animals. I've bet about $15,000. That means that this head'll cost me 2500 bucks."

"And jolly well worth it, I'd say," Aylcough said. "I've faced two or three wild animals in one place or another, but I don't think I was ever quite so near funking it as I was when watching Ubusuku. Don't know if I want to watch him do in an elephant or not."

"The elephant shouldn't give Ubusuku much trouble," I said. "There're several safe ways to kill elephants, and Ubusuku knows all of them."

"I got one in Nigeria," Carrie said, "coming at me ears out, trunk up, and squealing. Old Jones doesn't seem to think much of heavy rifles, but if I hadn't had a .510 that day I wouldn't be here now."

"Sure," I said, "elephants can be dangerous, but that doesn't mean they're difficult to kill. Pygmies get them with poisoned arrows. Mangbettus sometimes sneak up on an elephant, shove a spear into its belly from below, then get behind it and yell. Elephants always face toward the point of danger. When they turn in a hurry, they lower their rear ends. If a spear's dangling from the belly when the elephant squats to turn, the ground pushes the spear deep into the guts."

"To hear you talk," Carrie said, "you'd think that elephants are blind and deaf."

"Not deaf," I said. "With those big ears spread they can hear sounds a mile or more away when the wind blows toward them. And they aren't blind, but I doubt they can recognize a man fifty yards away even by evening light. In bright sunlight they can't spot a man, as a man, at thirty yards. If a man comes from downwind, he can approach within fifty yards of almost any elephant. It's not until they get your smell that they get really panicky.

"With the exception of some of the antelopes, most wild animals let a man come within fifty or sixty yards before taking off. And even the antelopes will often let you come right up to them if you're riding a horse. I don't know how Ubusuku plans to kill his elephant, but I told him I didn't want any more of the Hollywood stunt-man stuff he pulled with the crocs."

While Ubusuku was away scouting up an elephant herd, the rest of us did a bit of hunting. Carrie bagged a wildebeest and a buffalo cow. Davis got a roan antelope with good horns, and Alycough got pictures of drinking buffalo that made him happy.

I watched Carrie and Davis prepare to take the heads from their animals, stopped them, and said:

"For some reason, most men come to Africa to hunt without first learning anything about skinning and preserving trophies. Both of you've started your neck cuts too near the heads. Nothing looks sillier than a mounted head with a too short neck." I took Carrie's skinning knife and said: "Watch."

I cut the mask of Davis's roan around the base of the neck close to the shoulders, cut *around* each horn, then across *between* the horns. Next cut was down the *back* of the neck to the mask cut at the body. Skinning ears, eyes, and nose is work for a careful man. Natives are invariably careless and slash away happily with long-bladed knives. Truth is, the best skinning blade is never more than two inches long, and that's long enough to do a skinning job on rhino or elephant, too.

There are several ways of taking off a body hide, but, in my opinion, only one correct way. Lay the animal on its back and cut from the lower jaw to the base of the tail. Don't cut *through* the testicle bag. Cut around it. Make leg cuts on the *inside.*

Dry skins in the shade. In wet weather dry them slowly beside or over fires. Skins to be mounted *must not* be stretched. Shrinkage will occur, but normal size can later be regained by soaking and stretching. Stretch and peg out skins that are to be used as rugs.

Flesh skins with a dull knife. Thin thick places on heavy skins by scraping. Do *not* use wood ashes for curing. Ashes cause the hair to fall out. Do *not* use alum and saltpeter, either. Alum on a fresh hide makes it so stiff it will be almost impossible to wet back for proper dressing. For curing use salt alone; or just dry the hide in the shade, and *keep it* dry.

Skulls are easiest fleshed by putting them on an ant hill. However, be sure to have a reliable native guard them from prowling scavengers. Also remember that there are millions of beetles and borers eager to get at your trophies. The only way I know of keeping them out is to have all skins and skulls absolutely free of flesh and cartilage.

Rub all bones, skulls, and horns well with castor oil. Do a good job of rubbing it in, for if you don't, you'll find that boring beetles have made sieves of them.

Most countries to which you may ship trophies demand some form of fumigation. Best bet is to check with authorities at shipping points.

If you're the type who doesn't like skinning, let your natives do it, but *make all first cuts yourself.* I've never known a really good native skinner.

Lastly, measure your beasts. Measure accurately, particularly around the neck back of the horns, around the chest, belly, in front of the back legs, around the legs, and from tip of nose to base of tail. Too few measurements put your taxidermist in a tough spot.

Early next morning, as we plodded through dew-wet grass, a small herd of impala dashed from behind bushes and raced toward us. We froze, hoping they'd come close enough for Aylcough to get pictures, but they saw us at about three hundred yards, veered at right angles, and went bounding and jumping away. I said:

"Something frightened them back there in the brush—probably natives. Let's go see. We need porters."

But it was a white man who'd scared the herd. He stepped into the open, looked a long time at the impala, now specks in the distance, then tossed his rifle on the ground, took off a white cork helmet, threw it beside the rifle, and lay face down, head on his arms.

When we got close, he heard us, sat up, and said, with a Spanish accent:

"You found me, thank the Mother of God!"

His eyes were sunken, face blotchy white. Muscles twitched at the corners of his lips. I said:

"You're sick."

"Hungry," he said. "Perhaps sick also. Four days ago I sent my two white assistants to hospital downriver. Fever. My porters deserted. I have been alone. I have tried to shoot meat, but with a gun I am not good."

I gave him bush tea from my canteen, and *biltong* from my haversack. He chewed hungrily on the hard, dry meat. He said:

"I was never alone before. The porters took my canned foods." He rubbed a shoulder and said: "My shoulder is very sore. I shot many times and always missed." He held out a hand, and I pulled him to his feet. He said:

"Gentlemen, I am Salvador Montano."

I introduced Carrie, Davis, Aylcough, and myself. Montano said:

"I am *the* Montano."

"Your camp," I said, "where is it?"

"You do not know of Salvador Montano?" he asked wonderingly.

"No."

"Montano, the friend of Hideyo Noguchi? Montano, who is of the University of Mexico? You have not heard?"

Aylcough said: "You study animals, don't you? I heard of you in Cochin China."

Montano beamed. "That is Montano," he said, "who has measured, weighed, and compared the organs of birds and animals all over the world. You have found me. Now you will come to my camp and help me to carry on my great work. You will shoot the elephants and the river horses for me. Yes?"

"Well," I said, "we'll help you line up some porters. We need some ourselves. And I know of a white hunter near Kama, not far from here. Where's your camp?"

"I am not certain, senor. I walked for two days, shooting— shooting. Not once did I wound an animal. The camp is on the river, Ulindi, and not far from this Kama of which you speak. I am in great worry, senor, for in the tents I have many specimens in bottles."

Davis and Aylcough volunteered to find Montano's camp and to stay there until the rest of us arrived. Carrie, Montano, and I waited for Ubusuku. Two days later he arrived with news of a small elephant herd less than ten miles from where I judged Montano's camp to be.

En route to Montano's we heard singing in the brush to our left. Ubusuku went to investigate and returned shortly to say:

"Wagenias. Many of them. They go to Stanleyville to spend shillings. They wait for you to talk your wishes."

Anatole, the Wagenia headman, told me he had sixty-two men with him. They'd been working as porters and hunters for an American motion-picture outfit and had been discharged when they'd refused to go into the cold of high mountains in the Kivu district. They were willing to work for us, but not for long, as they had money to spend.

Ubusuku refused to have anything to do with the Wagenias. He said they smelled of fish, and to a Zulu fish are loathsome. Nor did the Wagenias like Ubusuku. Anatole told me privately that it was plain to him that Ubusuku was the result of a love match with a female baboon. I had to order Ubusuku to stay away from the porters because by scowlings and mutterings he indicated he'd like nothing better than to battle all sixty-three of them.

Montano's camp was a mess. The expedition had spent lots of money, but almost everything was wrong. Tents were of poor quality, and so large and complicated that engineering knowledge was almost required to manipulate them. None of the cartridge and film cases were waterproof, so, of course, all film was ruined and cartridges liable to misfire. Kerosene had spilled over many things. Instead of hard tropical candles, they'd bought soft ones which had melted into flat cakes. Food boxes had no locks—an invitation to natives to help themselves— which they'd done. Furthermore, all boxes were of wood, and had been set on the ground instead of on stones or blocks. Result: bottoms had rotted.

The camp stank, and we finally traced the smell to piles of skins that had been improperly fleshed and then rolled up. The only things in really good condition were Montano's specimens, kept in airtight glass jars.

Two days were required to put things shipshape. Davis proved a good man with natives and had them cooperating cheerfully in no time. It became evident that both Davis and Aylcough knew a lot more about hunting safaris than they'd let on.

When I briefed Anatole one morning on how to find the white hunter near Kama, Carrie said:

"Seems to me we could go on with Ubusuku's show and at the same time stick with Montano."

"We could," I said, "but I don't want to get tied up. There's work waiting for me as soon as we get back to Johannesburg. We can stick around, though, until this white hunter shows up."

"I've been talking to Montano," Carrie said. "He's willing to let me be his hunter."

"You?"

"Why not? We've lots of good natives now. All I'd have to do is point a gun and pull the trigger. I'd rather be a professional hunter than to make another *million*. Ever since I was a boy, I've ..."   ;

My heart went out to the guy. "Carrie," I said, "natives will take you to the game, but when you're ready to shoot, you're on your own. You can't depend on natives to stick when things go bad. There aren't many natives like Ubusuku, you know."

"I think I can stand up to anything that might happen," he said.

"Well," I said, "it's okay with me. Bear in mind, though, that it isn't how *hard* you hit animals, but *where* you hit 'em."

"Elephants," Carrie said, "are what Montano wants next."

"Well, elephants' skulls are filled with air cells. Doesn't do much damage to blast their big heads, but there's a soft spot about two inches above an elephant's eye. A bullet there will shatter the brain. Trouble is that that spot isn't exactly in the same place on every elephant. Head shots will likely get you into trouble. It's better to put four or five slugs in the muscular part of either shoulder—destroy the big concentration of blood vessels there and the elephant will die before he's gone fifty yards. A heart shot's good, but the animal may travel a half mile before it drops. If an elephant charges, remember that you can outrun him, and that if you get forty or fifty yards away, he can't see you."

"What do I do next?"

"Take over," I said. "You're Montano's white hunter now."

Carrie turned away, trying to hide the exaltation in his eyes. He seemed like a little kid who'd unexpectedly found himself sitting on Santa Claus's knee.

Next morning Davis and Montano stayed in camp with the porters while Carrie, Aylcough, and I went elephant-hunting with Ubusuku.

Ever since I'd asked him to lay off the Hollywood stuff, Ubusuku had acted like a spoiled brat. He'd refused the help of the Wagenias in bringing our gear from our own camp, and had eaten alone by his own fire. Now, as he stalked ahead of us across the brush-studded plain, I called to him in Zulu: "The bird that is silent too long forgets how to sing, Ubusuku." He paused and said:

"That is true, *Baas.* Also, the raven that squawks too much gets a sore throat. You have told me to kill, not as the lion, but as the snake. Therefore, I will kill like a snake; and Umgugundhlova, my father, will be told of this and he will feed me mice when I return to his *kraal.*"

"Okay, be a snake," I said, "just don't spoil the heads."

"The head of the elephant will receive no hurt that cannot be mended with needle and thread, O *Umganaam* [friend of mine]," he rumbled, and stalked on again.

So, that was the way he planned to kill the elephant! Bleed it to death! I didn't like the method, although it's painless. Ubusuku would make a deep cut in the trunk, probably with his hatchet. The wounded beast would fuss, fidget, blow, rumble, and cough at first. Then it would smell the blood, grow panicky, and lumber off to collapse and die.

It was a method of killing used by several Central and West African tribes, a method more humane than the use of poisoned arrows or a multitude of spears, yet I hated to see it used.

Ubusuku led us through a boscage of sparsely leafed small trees and out into a long, narrow field rank with a five-foot growth of broomlike weeds covered with fuzzy, pale lavender blossoms. The breeze blew strongly toward us, bringing barely perceptible elephant-herd noises. Aylcough said:

"I'll not be able to get a picture in these weeds—they're too high."

"Don't talk," I cautioned. "The wind may change direction."

Ubusuku picked his way among the lower bushes. We followed, trying not to stir up little clouds of fluff from the blossoms. Upon Ubusuku's signal we stopped beside an isolated thorn tree. The big Zulu took off his shorts—he wore nothing else—walked a few yards to a pile of fresh elephant dung, and rubbed himself liberally with it. Carrie whispered:

"Where's the elephant?"

Ubusuku pointed.

We moved out to one side of the tree, and there it was! A male, about fifty yards away, facing us, ears spread wide, the rimples at their edges appearing in relief because of a peculiarity of the light. Through my glasses the beast's eyes showed only mild curiosity. The great trunk, partly hidden by a tall, leafless shoot, hung relaxed. The tusks were not particularly large—about forty pounds each— but they were well matched, with perfect tips.

When he'd taken his shorts off, Ubusuku'd placed spear, dagger, and hatchet on the ground. Now he took the hatchet from its holster , felt the edge, said softly to me:

"*Indhlova* knows we are here, but he thinks we are baboons. I will go now. Do not let the red-necked *umlungu* [white man] shoot the big gun."

I nodded. Ubusuku dropped to hands and knees and crept away at right angles to the elephant.

Ubusuku took his time stalking. I couldn't see him, but knew he was circling so as to close in on the elephant from behind, trusting to the manure on him to hide his own smell when he arrived upwind. Although I'd seen no other members of the herd, I knew they were close, and that Ubusuku was being careful not to alert them.

Twice while we waited the elephant turned and faced the opposite direction, raising its trunk, testing the air, cocking and fanning the big ears. He turned to face us again each time without signs of unusual agitation. In turning he'd turned to the right, and I knew Ubusuku would be watching for that maneuver. Elephants habitually turn in only one direction—some to the right, some to the left. Seldom, even under stress, will one turn in the opposite direction.

If startled, they turn toward the point of danger, thrusting trunks straight out as they turn. It was Ubusuku's plan to cause this elephant to turn, and to be close to the outthrust trunk when the turn started.

The elephant, fears lulled, was slowly flapping its ears against its withers when Ubusuku, who'd bellied through the broom as soundlessly as an adder, stood erect beside the beast's right flank, moved quickly toward the shoulder, raised his hatchet, and said: "*Ai.*" The elephant's ears opened like wings, its trunk shot straight out, and it almost sat down as it turned frantically toward Ubusuku. The hatchet flashed, almost severing the trunk about a foot from the tip. The elephant screamed, blew what looked like a cloud of black smoke from the wound, whipped its trunk straight up, smelled and tasted the blood, then shrieked in fear and rage.

When the hatchet bit into its leg, the elephant seemed to shrink into itself.

Trumpetings, mixed with the squeals of totos, rose from the herd. The wounded elephant swung end for end. His screaming ceased abruptly as Ubusuku dodged behind him. I knew that with one blow of the hatchet Ubusuku had severed the tendons of a hind leg about a foot above the ground—I'd seen him do that before.

When the hatchet bit into its leg, the elephant seemed to shrink into itself. Ears hung limp; bleeding trunk dangled listlessly. Rumbling deep in its chest, the elephant then did something I'd never before seen an elephant do—it sank to its rear end, flopped over on its side, and lay still. Noises of the frightened herd faded into the distance.

Carrie, beside me, asked in a puzzled voice:

"What happened? I saw the ax raised, then what?"

"He almost cut the beast's trunk off, then severed a tendon in a back leg," I said. "Most animals can get along for a while on only three legs, but not the elephant—he needs four. Apparently this poor fellow sensed he was all through, and lay down to die."

"Trunk?" Carrie said wonderingly.

"Large arteries and veins," I said. "When they are severed, the animal quickly bleeds to death. Ubusuku's won this part of the bet, too, Carrie. Why don't you walk up and end that beast's misery?"

"Yes," Carrie said doubtfully. "What'll I do?"

"Put three or four slugs through the heart," I said.

And Carrie did.

While Ubusuku and Carrie went back to camp to get Montano, Aylcough and I waited beside the dead elephant. Montano came with all of the porters. They set up an immense wooden tripod, and from its apex, they hung a weigh master's scale. On level ground they placed small bullion and platform scales. Montano rolled up his sleeves, made first cuts through the elephant's hide, motioned the skinners to start work, stood back, rubbed his hands together, and smiled.

Four hours later, Montano, porters, and scales dripping blood, and sections of elephant piled all over the place, Montano handed me the following tabulation:

> Length: tip of tail to tip of trunk, 23 feet, 1 inch. Height at shoulder, 10 feet, 2 inches. Total weight, 14,023 pounds. Weight of skeleton: 983 pounds; of legs below knees: 967 pounds; of skin: 2119 pounds; of head skin: 496 pounds; of skull: 611 ½ pounds; of lungs: 299 pounds; of genitals: 75 ½ pounds; of kidneys: 35 pounds; of stomach and intestines: 2114 pounds; of heart: 51 pounds; of brain: 10 ¾ pounds; of left tusk: 33 pounds; of right tusk: 35 ½ pounds. Circumference of heart: 4 feet, 2 ½ inches; of front feet: 56 inches; of hind feet: 53 inches; of body behind shoulders: 14 feet, 11 inches. Thickness of skin: 1 ½ inches. Age: about 40 years.

There was other data on glands, eyes, muscles, tissues, and whatnot. Parts of internal organs were placed in glass jars, as were sections of blood vessels, tissues, and a half pint of blood.

Montano, pleased with results of his work with the elephant, skinned out the head for us, sewed the cut trunk, and made measurements for the taxidermist who'd mount the head for Carrie.

Two days later, where the river swung in close to camp, Ubusuku made a perfect shot with his spear on a three thousand pound hippo. The point of the thrown spear entered the beast's skull behind the eye, killing it instantly. The spear wedged itself solidly in the bone, and to withdraw it, Ubusuku had to bend his back and use every bit of his strength. As with the hatchet in the crocodile's back the weapon came out suddenly and the

Zulu turned a back somersault. He sprang to his feet, glared at the Wagenias. They didn't laugh.

Montano went through the same process with the hippo that he had with the elephant. His figures showed that the beast weighed 3224 pounds; the skin 440 pounds; stomach 831 pounds.

That night we had roast hippo for supper. Happily, Montano's thieving porters had left him some tinned butter, and spices. Hippo is excellent meat, reddish, of good texture, and tastes like pork. I cut out a beautiful sixteen-pound sirloin, spread it out, salted, peppered, and sugared it, sprinkled it with powdered thyme, dotted the meat with butter, rolled all tight and tied it securely, rubbed the outside with more butter, and put it in Montano's Dutch oven. I tied the lid down with wire and set the oven on a bed of wood coals, heaping burning brands over it until the metal heated through, then reduced heat by thinning the coals, and kept it at a moderate, even temperature for about 3½ hours.

Supper was late, but the savory steam that pervaded our camp grew more enchanting every minute. During the last half hour of the cooking all of us sat, gently drooling.

And the five of us ate every ounce of that roast.

Alexander Lake (1955) in Los Angeles studio while writing/consulting for Tarzan movies for RKO Pathe/Sol Lesser Productions.

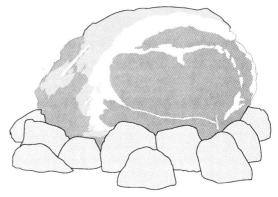

BUFFALO POT ROAST, ETC.

Among my most pleasant memories are nights beside African campfires when, having swallowed the last delicious portion of a roast of young zebra, or duikerbok, we'd move back from the fire, set mugs of tea on the ground beside us, and light our pipes. There was usually silence until the tea was finished, then someone would comment, and we'd all be off in a cloud of reminiscence.

That is what happened following the hippo feed. Carrie sat with his back against a tree, the smoke from his mellowed calabash pipe a thin cloud in the still air. Aylcough sat cross-legged, his big, black-bowled pipe steaming like a kettle. Davis sat on an empty paraffin tin, close enough to the fire so that every few minutes he could pick up a glowing stick to relight a char-rimmed brier that was continually going out. Montano was at a camp table, papers spread before him, his slender-stemmed pipe held to his mouth by a crooked forefinger. I sat on a short log cleaning my rifles and enjoying a battered corncob.

Fifty yards away the Wagenias, stuffed with cornmeal mush and half-raw hippo meat, were beginning to roll up in their blankets. Midway between them and us Ubusuku sat in regal solitude beside his own fire, fitting the tapering end of an antelope horn on the point of his spear. From time to time he'd take a piece of hippo meat from a pan on the coals, toss it from hand to hand to cool it, then pop it into his mouth. He seemed absorbed, but I knew he was alert to every night sound—a mouse scurrying before a ravenous snake, the swish of a nighthawk scooping insects from the air, the snorting of a lone hippo in the nearby river, a sudden, frantic rustling in the brush ...

Carrie said: "Brown Boy looks lonesome. Too bad he can't come and sit with us."

"He wouldn't come," I said. "He's a proud Zulu."

"Too proud to sit with white folks?"

"Yes. He works for us—is loyal, honest, and obedient, but he once said to me:

" 'The white man offers us salt with one hand while with the other, he steals our supper—' "

Carrie said: "I feel silly about my bet with Jones. The way Ubusuku handles the big animals has changed my ideas about hunting. I don't suppose even the lion would give Brown Boy a really bad time."

"I once saw Ubusuku kneel before a charging lion, rest his spear butt on the ground, and roll clear as the lion impaled himself. He digs pits for rhino—pits with sloping sides that squeeze the beast's feet together. As Jones told you, African natives were killing big game for thousands of years before guns were invented. You asked for that bet, Carrie."

"Well," Carrie said, "I'd like to call the thing off. I'll get a lot more fun out of being hunter for Montano. I'll pay off, of course."

"You'll have to pay off those others you bet with," I said, "but Jones won't accept your money unless Ubusuku fulfills the terms of the wager."

"Then I'll give the money to Ubusuku."

"You can't do that, either. Ubusuku's got three or four wives, but he'll be ruled by his father until the old man dies. Give the money to Umgugundhlova. Tell him you're rewarding him because he's the father of a mighty hunter. That'll please the old man, and Ubusuku will benefit in the long run."

"Good idea," Carrie said. "I'll do that. We'll talk details later."

Davis, who'd been in a huddle with Aylcough, walked over to Montano, talked earnestly a few minutes, then turned to me and said:

"Montano's moving over to Tanganyika as soon as he can get porters to replace the Wagenias. Instead of going back to Johannesburg, Aylcough and I are going to Tanganyika too. I'm going to take charge of the safari. Aylcough wants lion pictures."

"You'll have no trouble getting porters around Kasongo," I said. "And for lions, try the Serengeti Plains, where they're comparatively tame. Ubusuku and I'll pull out for home day after tomorrow."

The next day Carrie and Anatole went downriver to hire porters. Davis and Montano busied themselves sorting stores. Aylcough and two of the Wagenias went across country to photograph whatever they could. Ubusuku and I went hunting for meat.

Africa is the world's largest meat larder, and almost every pound of meat from young or old beasts and fowl can, with proper cooking, be served as a delicacy. There is no meat in Africa so insipid, strong, or tough that it can't be made enjoyable and healthful food. That goes for everything from elephant to water lizard.

Basic rules of good cooking are unknown to millions who daily "cook" food. For instance, housewives look at a piece of beef neck, or some other less choice cut, and say:

"This is tough and stringy. Best thing I can do with it is to boil it well." This they proceed to do, not realizing that the harder one boils meat, the tougher it gets. Boiling meat properly is one of the finest ways of preparing it, and one of the most difficult.

Take the tough-fleshed waterbuck, for example. When boiled as most cooks boil, the meat is practically unchewable. But simmer it gently and long, having first made sure that the chunks were cut *across* the grain, adding whole vegetables for the last hour of cooking, and salt and flavors during the final ten minutes, then thickening the juices with a little flour—and you'll have a "boiled" dinner that will live in your memory.

Many who appreciate good food consider elephant trunk the most choice part of the beast, and it is, when *simmered* until tender, and spiced appetizingly. Elephant feet, cooked by ordinary methods, are gooey and tasteless, but, baked until done, the edible insides then scooped out and mixed with plain gelatin and red-currant jelly, permitted to set until firm, then served with sour-sweet ostrich eggs and a patty of wild-game sausage, and you'll have a delightful meal that can be eaten as breakfast, lunch, or dinner.

SOUR-SWEET OSTRICH EGG

2 tablespoons vinegar (any vinegar), or 1 tablespoon lemon juice
1 tablespoon canned butter or hippo lard
1 teaspoon flour, or 2 teaspoons corn meal
1 teaspoon chopped onion, or 1/2 teaspoon onion salt

Melt butter (or lard) in frying pan, add onion, stir, add flour (or corn meal). Cook one minute.

Add six cloves, and a dash of ginger. Simmer, stirring occasionally, for at least 10 minutes.

Now add vinegar (or lemon juice), a dash of salt, and not more than 1 tablespoon of sugar. Bring barely to boiling, and slip in one whole ostrich egg (or 12 hen's eggs), cover, and poach.

WILD GAME SAUSAGE

This recipe was given me by a Basuto named Amalita, who cooked for Nicobar Jones for thirty years. On expeditions Jones and I did our own cooking, but Amalita lorded it in the kitchen of Jones's home. Amalita's wild-game cookery delighted such gourmet guests as L. Sam Marks, millionaire traveler who lived only to eat; Anders van der Wall, who burst and died after a prolonged Christmas dinner in Johannesburg; and the German, Gotthelf Kiessling, whose taste buds were so developed that he could detect and identify any one of thirty-six spices in foods even when only a few grains had been used.

This sausage recipe of Amalita's doesn't seem much different than that of the pork sausage of farm wives, but it differs significantly in proportion of fat to lean, and has been made less harsh by the use of savory instead of sage.

Cut 40 pounds hippo, rhino, wild pig, wart hog, or aardvark into small pieces. Add ten pounds fat, ¼ cup sugar, 1 tablespoon ginger, ¼ cup pepper, 1 pound salt, 1 tablespoon oregano, 3 tablespoons savory. Mix all together, and put through meat grinder three times. Pack into a sterilized stone jar and cover with a heavy layer of hippo lard or other fat. Keep cool.

To cook, fry in *boiling* grease until brown and crisp on both sides. Or place sausage patties in pan, cover with water, and keep just at boiling point until the water has evaporated. Then brown in the grease that remains in the pan. Or if you have canned butter, brown in that.

For stuffing fowls such as bustard, young ostrich, guinea hen, wild geese, flamingo, and other meaty birds, mix the sausage with an equal amount of cornmeal mush, or mashed potatoes, and pack tightly inside bird. Roast the fowl slowly.

On "rocking chair" safaris, where eating and drinking are sometimes more important than hunting, we often served curried dishes with the sausage-stuffed fowl.

Curry! Good curry! Honest curry! The delight of potentates, and the joy of men with good appetite! It puts soul into meat, and exalts the spirits of those who appreciate life's better gifts.

But be warned against the wishy-washy, uninspired concoction called curry in most homes and restaurants of Europe and America. Such curry is a byword and a hissing.

Genuine curry powder should be as much part of a hunting safari as guns and ammunition. It is easy to make. Keep proportions exact, and treasure the finished product.

CURRY POWDER

20 ounces caraway seed
2 pounds pale turmeric seed
½ pound Jamaica ginger
½ pound cumin seed
1 pound coriander seed
½ ounce cardamon seed
4 ounces cayenne pepper
½ pound black pepper

Powder ingredients well in a mortar. Dry the mixture beside fire, or in warm sunlight. Bottle tightly. *Vive le roi!*

Throughout the world the two favorite curries are Indian and Malay, but in Africa's interior, shrimps for the Malay curry are expensive, if one can obtain them at all. I've cooked Indian curry for hunters of all nations and never yet has one not demanded a second helping.

I made Indian curry with whatever meat was handy, preferring buffalo, sable, duikerbok, nyala, steinbok, zebra, and roan. Almost as good are wildebeest, wart hog, wild pig, aardvark, sitatunga, sassaby, gemsbok, springbok, lechwe, and giraffe.

Jones used to enjoy curried crocodile, but I've a mild crocodile phobia, so that meat doesn't go down easily. Snake meat is white and tasty, and, curried, is more palatable than chicken. Snake meat can also be prepared as one would ordinarily prepare fowl or fish, and is excellent.

Americans on safari, particularly those from the Middle West, throw their hands up at the thought of eating any meat but mutton, veal, beef, or pork. Italians, Portuguese, and Spanish will eat anything. Frenchmen will eat anything so long as it doesn't taste like what it is. Germans will eat anything if it's well cooked. Englishmen, dismayed at having to eat lion, for instance, do so, but make the experience a lark. Norwegians, Swedes, and Danes eat what they must without fuss, but also without fervor. Greeks and Russians eat anything with ecstasy, and are always hungry.

I once guided a man named William P. Perkins, a Texan, who cooked steaks into something resembling shoe soles. He shot a sable antelope, hacked out steaks, and fried them until they were about as chewable as the beast's hide would have been—then began a tirade about antelope steaks.

That night I cut a thick steak off the rump, lightly pricked both sides all over with a fork, rubbed salt and pepper in thoroughly, got the frying pan piping hot, poured in vegetable oil, let it sizzle a minute, dropped the steak in, turned it every minute for five minutes, dusted it with just a breath of garlic salt, let it cook another five minutes, turning it once, put it on a plate and handed Perkins a fork and a well-sharpened knife.

Perkins took a bite, chewed a couple of times, said:

"This ain't no Texas longhorn."

He ate the big steak without another word, then asked:

"What the hell did you do to that steak?"

"Sealed the juices in, seasoned it, and fried it in sizzling fat."

"But you pricked the steak with a fork. That lets juices out."

"Not if you rub the steak well with salt and pepper. They plug the fork holes and keep the juices inside."

"Could skinny Texas cattle be cooked like that?"

"Sure. Prick the steak well with a fork, rub in melted suet, salt and pepper, fry quickly in boiling fat—never cook a lean steak in a dry pan—turn the steak frequently, and serve rare, medium-rare, or medium—not well done. Remember that the slower a steak's fried the tougher it will be. Never let a steak get done on one side before turning.

"Broiling over clean, hot coals makes a tastier steak than does frying. Pricking, salting and peppering—and for too lean steaks, sueting—is the same for broiling as for frying. But pricking will ruin a steak unless the pan or coals are *hot.*"

"How about hanging meat?"

"Most meat is better for hanging, but duikerbok, sable, klipspringer, and nyala are excellent eating when fresh killed. Don't hang crocodile, snake, wild pig, wart hog, water or monitor lizard if you want them tasty. Hanging makes a big improvement in lion, leopard, most antelopes, elephant, rhino, hippo, and buffalo."

Prime carcasses, particularly those of deer and antelope, are often ruined for eating by carelessness. For instance:

Windpipes must be removed, and the animal bled *at once,* if meat is not to turn sour.

Skin should be taken off as soon as possible.

The underside of a carcass that is left on the ground quickly becomes tainted. Flies won't bother a carcass hung twenty feet up, or higher.

Make all cuts *across* the grain of the meat. Grain of the rump runs at an angle; grain of the round, straight across. Never *saw* the meat with the knife. Sawing the blade back and forth toughens ends of the fibers. And always before cooking wipe all game with a damp cloth. Pollen, dust, and dried blood ruin the flavor of meat.

Don't split the backbone of small animals.

Give your natives the shanks, brisket, flank, neck, and side ribs, leaving the choice pieces—round, rump, loin, shoulder, and prime rib roasts—for your party.

Boiling, frying, or broiling, when done with knowledge of the needs of various types of game, makes palatable dishes. But it is baking—slow, even, prolonged baking—that brings out wild meats' most gustatory qualities.

Meat may be baked in a Dutch oven set among hot coals, or hung over a flame. But for sheer savoriness and tenderness wrap a roast in dampened leaves or grass, then encase in a cocoon of clay. Put oven-hot rocks on the bottom of a hole in the ground and place the cocoon on the rocks. Cover it with other oven-hot stones. Fill in the hole and permit the meat to remain for twenty-four hours. Appropriate herbs may be wrapped with the grass or leaves.

Seat your guests beside the campfire. Dig up the roast. Go a little way upwind, crack the clay from the meat and peel off grasses and leaves. The appetizing odor will drift downwind and you'll be repaid for your trouble when you see the eager sniffings and the sparkle in the eyes of your guests.

Then there's barbecued game, which, like corn on the cob, is appreciated chiefly by Americans. Two desires are uppermost in the minds of most Americans when they first go hunting. One is to shoot a rifle merely to be shooting. The other is to eat barbecued antelope.

Here is a simple barbecue sauce that comes straight from a hunting client named Worthington, who'd been a member of the kitchen staff of a famous hotel in Tennessee. This sauce is good with all antelope meats, but is particularly effective with flavorless-fleshed reedbuck.

BARBECUE SAUCE TENNESSEE

1 cup vinegar
2 heaping tablespoons chopped sour pickle
¾ cup butter
2 tablespoons chopped onion, or 2 teaspoons onion salt
2 tablespoons Worcestershire sauce
2 teaspoons lemon juice
1 teaspoon brown (or burnt white) sugar

Mix all ingredients together and cook only until butter has melted. Keep warm, and serve with broiled, fried, or baked meat.

(Note: Europeans prefer that this sauce be made with browned butter.)

There isn't room in this book for the numerous safari-tested wild game recipes I've collected, but here are a few of the best:

BUFFALO POT ROAST *(Recipe by L. Sam Marks)*

Cut a 20-pound buffalo rump across the grain. Bone. Thread a strip of salt pork through the meat, or rub well with salted hippo lard. Marinate in vinegar water, lemon water, or any red wine for 24 hours. Dry with cloth, reserving marinade. Brown meat quickly and put in Dutch oven. Pour marinade over it. Add herbs to taste. Cover and cook slowly for about 6 hours. Lift out meat. Strain off fat. Slice meat and pour flour-thickened gravy over it. Serve with boiled vegetables and hot cakes.

BRAISED BUFFALO TONGUE

(Specialty of Anders van der Wall)

Trim cartilage from tongue. Put tongue in saucepan with water to cover. Add 1 grated onion, ½ teaspoon powdered cloves, salt, black pepper, and a dash of vinegar or lemon juice. Simmer for 3 hours. Skin and slice tongue. Serve with mashed potatoes, pickles, and sliced raw onions.

ELAND STEAKS

(Specialty of Amalita, Jones's Basuto cook, and equally delightful for sable, zebra, or wildebeest steaks)

Cut a thick rump steak. Slash one side in crisscross fashion with a sharp knife. Rub grated horseradish into slashes. Dunk steak in oil or melted butter. Fry (or broil) quickly, turning frequently until half done. Serve with fried onions and canned sour cherries.

A sauce that goes astonishingly well with potatoes baked in coals, and as gravy for fried cornmeal (mealie meal) mush, was concocted by Nicobar Jones when a wealthy client of his demanded something different. Here it is:

HIPPO HAM SAUCE

½ pound hippo ham
4 tablespoons grated onion, or 2 teaspoons onion salt
½ teaspoon black pepper
dash of powdered clove
dash of ginger
4 tablespoons vinegar, or 2 tablespoons lemon juice
4 tablespoons flour (white, graham, or pancake)
3 cups brewed tea

Cut hippo ham into small pieces. Fry. Add onions, cut fine, and fry for only 1 or 2 minutes with the ham. Add flour and tea. Stir in clove, ginger, vinegar (or lemon juice), and pepper. Cook 12 minutes.

Smoked hams from young hippo are one of the world's great delicacies, according to L. Sam Marks. Here is his recipe:

SMOKED HIPPO HAMS

To the fleshy side of a 120-pound hippo ham apply 4 tablespoons saltpeter and 1½ pounds brown sugar, rubbing well into the hock. Now lay ham on its side, fleshy side up, in a wooden tub or cask and cover with a 1-inch layer of good salt. Cover and set away for 6 weeks. Rub off salt, and rub in black pepper. Hang up and let drain for 8 days. Smoke with any green wood for 10 weeks. Cool. Return to tub and cover with salt mixed with 1 ounce saltpeter. After 6 days put ham in *strong* brine to which has been added 2 ounces each of saffron, ginger, rosemary, cumin, and 4 ounces of cloves. Soak in this brine for 7 weeks, hang up, drain well, rub with pepper, and smoke again with green wood.

(Note: Rhino, wild pig, and warthog hams cured according to the foregoing recipe are equally delicious.)

BAKED HIPPO HAM, MARKS

These famous Marks recipes are now used all over the world for ordinary pork hams.

Simmer a 120-pound ham for 24 hours. Remove skin. Punch ham full of pencil-size holes. Pour 1 gallon of champagne over ham, filling as many of the holes as possible. Place ham in suitable pan and rub well with mixture of ginger, flour, and powdered white sugar. Bake in moderate (375 degrees) baker's oven for 10 hours. *Do not baste.*

(Note: In cooking a 15-pound pork ham, simmer only 3 hours, use only 1 quart of champagne, and bake for 2 hours.)

GROUNDNUT HIPPO HAM, MARKS

Cut ½-inch-thick slices of ham. Grind groundnuts (peanuts) fine, and mix into a paste with melted, browned butter. Rub ham slices lightly with ginger, sprinkle with ginger ale, and spread with groundnut butter. Bake in moderate oven. Serve with honey toast, plain pineapple slices, and a glass of good sherry.

The following simple method of cooking python filets is also excellent for viper and cobra:

Put two 15-inch sections of python in baking pan. Brown 1 pound canned butter (or margarine) and pour over the filets. Dust with onion salt and sprinkle with lemon juice. Bake slowly until tender, basting frequently with the butter. Serve with boiled greens.

While the foregoing recipe for snake meats makes a tasty dish, gourmets prefer this more fanciful one:

PYTHON, YARBROUGH

Cut 4 pounds of filet from a young python, dip in flour mixed with salt, pepper, and ginger. Melt 1 pound butter in 2 quarts cream (or 6 cups evaporated milk and 2 cups water), and add 2 cups sherry wine. Add filets and simmer until meat is done. Make a sauce with cream and mushrooms. Serve with canned corn (tinned maize), and a green vegetable.

I have found that the legs of crocodile are best eating, but steaks from shoulders are popular. In preparing crocodile for cooking be careful to stay away from the neck, which has offensive musk glands on each side.

CROCODILE, F. ROBINSON

Cut thin slices of crocodile meat, preferably from a front leg. Add salt, ginger, and sweet red wine to some brown sauce. Broil or fry the slices of meat and pour the sauce over them. Sprinkle with grated cheese and dot with butter. Bake in a fast oven until browned. Serve with sauteed giant sliced mushrooms, fried rice, and chili sauce.

Many African game recipes call for mushrooms because they are available in season almost everywhere on the plains and in the forests. White mushrooms of eastern Angola and southwest Congo often grow to four pounds. In forests of Central Africa hundreds of pounds of "shell" mushrooms (almost identical with the American sulphur-shelf mushroom) can sometimes be gathered from one log. Pick the younger ones—they're tender, and taste like a dream when cooked in butter and canned milk. Then there's a golden-yellow woods mushroom, called the chanterelle—an apricot-flavored, delicate-textured delight. On the plains abound meadow mushrooms of many types.

Mushrooms have affinity with butter and cream, but can be overpowered by spices. They may be baked, boiled, fried, or pickled. Cut fine and added to pancake batter, mushrooms make a zestful treat. Creamed biltong (sun-dried meat) with mushrooms stewed in evaporated milk is a satisfying meal. With boiled noodles, stewed mushrooms add vitamins and *élan.* Incidentally, mushrooms are so nutritious that one can live on them exclusively for days and remain full of verve.

Four men eat breakfast at five o'clock. Two eat meat, and little else. The other two eat cereals, fruits, and starches. At lunchtime the meat eaters will still be going strong. The other two will have been yammering for a snack since ten o'clock. But, if one is to live on nothing but meat, the meat must contain at least 25 per cent fat. That's why in game cooking one should "lard" well. Most wild game is lean.

Lion meat does not take kindly to ordinary methods of cooking, but, properly stewed, is equal to hare, rabbit, muskrat, or cat.

JUGGED LION, OMOHUNDRO

Skin and clean a young lion, preferably one about 6 months old. Save 1 cup of blood and add 1 cup of vinegar to it. Cut meat into stew-size pieces and mix with uncooked onions and celery. Pour wine (any kind) over the mixture and let stand for at least 12 hours, stirring occasionally. Drain. Season with salt and pepper. Put all together again in more wine with favorite spices. A spot of garlic goes well too. Cook until fat rises. Skim. Bake until done, then add blood vinegar and take from heat without further cooking. Serve with stewed mushrooms and boiled onions.

There are times when small hunting parties find themselves without large game. Be not dismayed. Take your .22s and go out after small birds, mice, and squirrels. Use the following recipe and you'll be as well fed as if you'd eaten buffalo.

SMALL GAME KICKSHAW

Clean and split in half 36 small birds, squirrels, field mice, or an assortment of all of them. Boil in plenty of water and skim. Add salt, pepper, cloves, and onions. Simmer until tender in water to cover. Take from fire and bone. Put a 1/2-inch layer of mealie (corn meal) mush in a baking pan. Now a layer of meat. Another layer of mush, and so on, topping with mush. You won't, as a rule, need to add fat to this kickshaw, as mice are usually plump little rascals.

People's attitudes toward foods are curious. Persons who shudder at the thought of eating mice will dig a spoon into the backside of a lobster and eat with gusto. Field mice are clean, wholesome little beasts, and very tasty. Many persons who think snowbirds and songbirds a great treat when baked in a pie desert them entirely after they've tasted a well-cooked mouse pasty.

Everywhere in Africa are frogs—red frogs, yellow frogs, spotted frogs, giant frogs, and little hop-toads. All frogs are good eating, particularly their hind legs. They're meaty. African frogs have probably saved the lives of more lost and starving men than has any other food. Any chicken recipe is satisfactory for frog legs. Here is the easiest:

FROG LEGS, UGANDA

Fry fresh frog legs in butter. Add salt and pepper while cooking. Sprinkle with lemon juice or watered vinegar. Place on warm plate and drench with browned butter. Serve with mushrooms, tomatoes (if at hand), and any of Africa's many types of squash, baked or boiled. (Note: Many safari kitchens are stocked with vegetable purées. Best of all with frog legs is tomato hot sauce.)

Liver, be it lion, elephant, or antelope, is probably the most popular meat among old-time professional hunters. Liver is best eaten shortly after the kill. It should be cooked slowly—either broiled on a stick or fried in a not too hot pan. It mates well with hippo ham, pork bacon, or even hippo lard. Made into a paste, it once went everywhere with lonely old hunters and prospectors.

LIVER PASTE

Use any liver, preferably sable, buffalo, eland, duikerbok, springbok, lion, or zebra. Add an equal amount of fat meat (or lean meat and suet), and simmer long in a thin gravy of butter, flour, and milk. Drain and crush the mixture through a sieve. Add onion salt and the yolk of an ostrich egg (or yolks of 12 hen's eggs) for each 18 pounds of mixture. Add salt, pepper, powdered cloves. Beat and add the egg white. Add what's left of the original gravy, and bake from 2 to 3 hours in a moist oven, or in a pan set in another containing water. Do not skim off fat—the paste will take it all up again. Let cool until it sets—18 hours or more. Serve with anything and everything.

Liking for horse meat among Oregonians is said to amount to a passion. Mary Cullen, food editor of the *Oregon Journal*, is the cause of it all, for she's America's leading authority on the cooking of horse. One wonders what Miss Cullen could do with zebra, which is superior in almost every respect to Oregon horse. The following recipe is excellent for horse as well as for zebra.

ZEBRA STEAKS *SANS SOUCI*
(probably the world's tastiest steak)

Cut steaks off filet, or rump *across* grain. Pound well with meat pounder. Sprinkle with garlic salt, onion salt, salt, pepper. Pound seasonings into meat. Steaks will be thin and flat. Push them together so they become thick. Put a lump of suet on each one (or butter), and broil as for beef. Serve well buttered.

ZEBRA PATTIES
(Note: Wealthy Somalis consider this dish an aphrodisiac.)

Grind zebra filet or roast into hamburger. Put in large bowl and mix with evaporated milk. Use hands for mixing, and continue until the meat will absorb no more milk. Season and make into patties. Flour. Fry in hot grease (suet if possible), and watch out for scorching. Serve well buttered, with tomatoes, bread, and fried mashed potatoes.

Zebras—probably the world's tastiest steak—on the hoof.

African animals aren't noted for the size of their brains. The elephant's averages only eleven pounds. But there isn't an animal whose brains are not delicious when prepared as follows:

WILD-GAME BRAINS

Simmer brains for 6 or 7 minutes, drain, and remove skin and blood vessels. Slice into pieces for frying. Season with salt and pepper. Dip in slightly beaten egg (or in evaporated milk), and in cracker meal, fine bread crumbs, or corn meal. Fry golden in butter. Serve with fried eggs and lemon-butter sauce.

BRAIN HASH

(quantities don't matter in this recipe)

Cut brains into small pieces and mix with any chopped, cooked vegetables on hand. Add, if you like, any meat leftovers chopped small. Add a slightly beaten egg or two, and form into flat, round cakes, or roll into balls. Fry in deep fat at 375 degrees for 3 to 5 minutes. Or pan-fry in sizzling grease or oil. Serve with cheese, any green vegetable, and mashed, well-buttered squash (marrow).

Corel Professional Photos CD-ROM

The foregoing wild-game recipes are chiefly for safaris with well-equipped kitchen and pantry. For those who hunt and "live off the country," the recipes are good without the frills. If there's no milk, use water. If there's no butter, use rendered fat from any animal or fowl. If there are no spices, there'll at least be pepper and salt. Nutritious soups can be made anywhere at any time from whatever greens, wild vegetables, and game that happen to be at hand. A soup that really stays with you is made from groundnuts (peanuts), available almost everywhere in Africa. Use chopped groundnuts instead of meat, or use both.

Some people turn up their noses at wild-game dishes, failing to realize that, as Nicobar Jones used to say, "Proteins are proteins." The human body requires proteins, and does not differentiate between proteins of elephant, snake, frog, grasshopper, antelope, or corn-fed steer. All proteins go to repair tissue waste. On safari, meat eaters get hungry less frequently than vegetarians, and stand up better when the going is tough.

More and more African hunting parties are going in for popcorn. This is because an American named Ralph Luick developed a method of popping popcorn that puts it among the really interesting foods.

POPCORN, LUICK

(Note: It is important that the kernels be perfectly dry. The slightest moisture results in a mediocre product.)

*[**Editors note**: We tried this and found it so delicious that we now do it as a regular treat. Beats microwave popcorn all hollow and doesn't that very much more effort or time!]*

Melt ¼ pound butter (no substitute) in a 6- or 8-quart kettle. When the butter boils, it will foam. Stir the butter to keep from burning, until foam subsides. (The foam is water that is boiling out of the butter.) When the butter begins to brown, pour in one cup of popcorn kernels. Stir as more foam appears (water boiling out of the kernels this time). As this second foam subsides, the corn will begin to pop. Put lid on kettle and shake vigorously. Within seconds the corn will pop like mad, and in less than a minute the kettle will be filled with puffy, white, butter-soaked jewels. No additional salt required. Never was popcorn like this! It won't dry out, develops no "oil skin," and actually melts in the mouth.

Britishers and Germans have taken to eating Popcorn, Luick as a breakfast cereal. Eaten with cream and sugar, it makes ordinary patented breakfast foods seem mediocre indeed.

Some not too far-off day canned and potted African big and small game will be sold all over the world. For some time several Americans and Englishmen have been surveying the possibilities of such a venture, and are getting interested cooperation from Portuguese, Belgian, and French authorities.

Two cans of zebra filets, please.

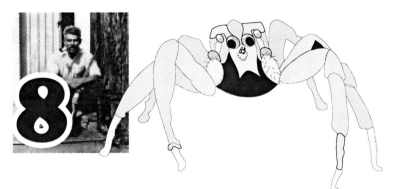

THE SPIDER AND THE QUICKSAND

Montano's camp required about three hundred pounds of meat a day. Sixty porters ate almost that much at a meal if they could get it. Ubusuku and I, skunked for hours, found hartebeest spoor just as we were about to give up. We'd had several chances at duikerbok, but shooting those little forty-pounders in knee-high grass is like shooting at rabbits. We'd need seven or eight of them, and the way they were diving into cover made that impossible.

The sun was in the last quarter of the sky when we came within sight of a 350-pound hartebeest bull. Keeping ant hills between us and him, we managed to get within a hundred yards, when he flipped his ears, raised his horselike head, whirled, and loped away. He hadn't seen us, so I knew something else had frightened him.

Grumbling at bad luck, I kept my eyes upwind, expecting to see a lion. Instead, a white man followed by two heavily laden natives pushed out from behind a brush screen. He saw us, held up one hand, switched a load he was carrying to the other shoulder, and came on. He was a short, wiry individual with a face so dusty and sweat-streaked that his teeth gleamed like those of a black-skinned Somali.

"Doctor Livingstone, I presume," he said with a grin.

Miki Carter, of California. I'd met him in Johannesburg shortly before starting out with Carrie, Davis, and Aylcough—an adventurous cameraman who made the world his beat. He set down his load of cameras and said:

"I went to Kindu. You didn't show up there."

"No. Going tomorrow."

"Don't tell me your tracker's already won that bet," Miki said in consternation. "I didn't hear about it until after you'd gone. I've had one hell of a time locating you. By God, if your native's lone handled all those animals already, he'll just have to do it all over again. I want pictures."

"How'd you find us? No one knows we're here."

"I'm with a white hunter—fellow named Manoli Fangoudis. Natives call him *Bwana* Manoli. We stopped at a village this side of Kindu and Manoli told the chief we wanted to find you. They got the drums going, or something, and next morning told us you were camped near the Ulindi toward Kama."

"I know Manoli. Where is he?"

"Hartebeest came hot-footing past us. He took after him."

"Manoli's from Kabale, Uganda. Good man. Likes to spear big game instead of shooting— The report of a 9.3 mm. Mauser crashed across the plain. "He's got our hartebeest," I said, then nodded to Ubusuku and added: "Take *Baas* Carter's Mangbetus to carry the meat."

"No," Miki said, "Manoli's got three Mangbetus with him. He'll be here pretty soon."

But Manoli hadn't got the hartebeest—he'd shot a buffalo cow. He came toward us, followed by his natives, the leading one carrying the buffalo's head atop his own.

Manoli's a big, well-proportioned African-born Greek who's been spearing lions and buffalo single-handed since he was eighteen. He began as an ivory poacher, but when he found he could barely make expenses, with ivory selling at $2.00 a pound, gave it up in favor of buffalo hunting. Buffalo sold to natives for about $7.00 a carcass. Even when hunting was good, Manoli often found himself so short of cash that he couldn't buy cartridges for his 9.3 mm. Mauser. Nor could he afford to hire native hunters. So he developed a technique for spearing buffalo.

I think every old-time hunter agrees that a wounded or angry buffalo is a tougher customer than a lion. First of all, the buffalo weighs fifteen hundred pounds—three times as much as a lion. A lion with a spear in him will often forget the hunter and fight the spear. Not so a buffalo. A lion knows when he's licked. A buffalo never.

Manoli usually used two spears on lone hunts—a wooden-shafted throwing spear, and a steel-shafted Masai spear. He'd sneak up on the buffalo and throw the wooden spear into its kidneys. Kidney wounds sometimes set up a temporary paralysis, making it possible to thrust a second spear into the heart without too much risk. But sometimes the jobs didn't turn out too neatly, and Manoli would find himself involved in fast action.

The Mangbetus brought less than two hundred pounds of meat from the kill, so I sent Ubusuku and Miki's two boys to lug another couple of hundred. While we waited, I told Miki and Manoli about Carrie's decision to concede the bet.

"I've already wired Hollywood I was getting pictures of your tracker at work," Miki said. "You can't let me down."

I grinned at Manoli. He grinned back. "Miki," I said, "Manoli will put on a better act for you than Ubusuku. A native killing big game with his bare hands, so to speak, is different, but a white man doing it is really something. If Carrie wants to drop the hunt, I don't feel I should prolong it. Jones has plenty of work ahead for me—said he'd write me at Kindu."

Miki took a letter from his hat and handed it to me. "He did write to Kindu," he said. "I picked it up for you."

Jones's note said briefly that as soon as the Carrie show was over I was to go to Libreville on the west coast of French Equatorial Africa and wait there for a Dutch entomologist named Kees Jonker, who'd ordered a guide.

After supper that night Davis and Aylcough, acting as referees in the matter of the Jones-Carrie bet, agreed to Carrie's request that he be permitted to concede victory to Ubusuku, and that the matter of payment of the wager be settled by Jones and Carrie.

Months later Jones accepted $5000 for himself, and another $5000 for Ubusuku's father.

Manoli agreed to spear a buffalo in front of Miki's camera. He'd make the kill by thrusting—not throwing. I'd act as gun support.

Early next morning five whites—Miki with his light movie camera, Aylcough with box camera, Manoli with spear, and Carrie and I with rifles—started out to locate buffalo. Shortly after noon we spotted a herd on a large, open, anthill-studded grass flat. We circled for an hour to get downwind, then began crawling on our bellies from ant heap to ant heap.

We finally made it to an ant hill about fifty yards from the edge of the herd. Here Miki kept us down while he changed lenses. When all set, Manoli whispered to me:

"I'll creep forward to about thirty yards of that near cow. When I'm ready for action, I'll raise my spearhead. You fire three or four fast shots to confuse the herd, and try to get the herd leader with your first shot. Maybe I'll get Miki some action before they stampede."

While Manoli, dragging the spear, wriggled forward through the grass, I picked out the herd bull, estimated his distance at eighty yards, and set my sights. Miki crouched behind his tripod.

Out of the grass about twenty yards ahead, Manoli's spear reared like a black mamba.

I fired. My first shot dropped the leader in his tracks. My second wounded a cow and she began running around crazily. The herd milled about, then began galloping in erratic, jumping circles. All was bellowing confusion for a few moments. Then a second leader took charge, and the frightened beasts wheeled after him at an angle in front of us.

My third shot clipped the new herd bull's horns. He plowed to a stop, bellowed, stood shaking and tossing his head as the rest of the herd thundered past him. Manoli ran to the bull, leaped in front of him, and thrust with his spear just as the bull did a half whirl. The spear missed; Manoli stumbled. The bull backed away snorting, dug in his feet, and with tail almost straight up drove head-first at Manoli. Manoli leveled his spear, held the butt away from his left side with both hands and let the beast's rush drive the razor-sharp blade into its shoulder. I expected Manoli to run. Instead, still holding onto the spear shaft, he was knocked to his knees, and dragged about sixty feet.

It seemed to me that Manoli's number was up.

I raised my rifle, and, to get an easier shot, stepped partially in front of the camera. Miki put his foot on my backside and pushed. The shot went wild.

I had no time to call Miki names, for Manoli got to his feet and jerked hard on the spear. It was stuck between the buffalo's foreleg and shoulder bone. The bull lifted his forefeet in a wrenching, twisting jump and again Manoli went to his knees. He pulled himself erect by the spear handle, and, hopping on one foot, wrestled to loosen the spear.

Action was so fast—the man and the animal changed places so rapidly—that I didn't dare shoot. As I ran toward the struggle, I could hear Miki shouting to me to get out of the picture.

Suddenly one of the bull's lunges drove the blade into its lungs. He stood like a statue for a second, then with a coughing snort sprayed Manoli with blood. The struggle began again—the spear point working around in the chest cavity, but impossible for Manoli to pull out of the animal. Manoli tugged, pulled, and thrust. He was up and down, sometimes swung off his feet by the beast's plunging, sometimes flat on his belly, but he hung onto that spear all the while.

The bull seemed to weaken abruptly and I had a chance to shoot, but saw that Manoli would be the victor in another minute, so stepped back out of camera range. The bull lowered his horns for a sweep, but his strength was gone and the lowered head sank slowly until the nose rested on the ground.

On one foot like a stork, Manoli thrust again. The bull moaned and crumpled, then lay quiet. Manoli fell beside him, gasping air in great, painful gulps. His whole body shook with the pounding of his heart, but little by little the sobbing breaths quieted. Finally he lay still, eyes shut as if asleep. His hands still grasped the spear handle.

When able to talk, Manoli said:

"I think my ankle's broken."

He was right—it was.

Miki, smiling smugly as he sealed film in a tin, saw me scowling at him. With a grin he said:

"I know exactly what you're thinking—and—the same to you."

That night we really ate. I curried buffalo meat, and Miki donated two cans of green Kenya plums. Manoli came through with a tin of IXL berry jam from New Zealand. Davis had found some ripe wild melons, and we had a pudding made of corn meal, liver, and birds' eggs.

It was one of those nights when firelight has a touch of red in it, and flames curl and twist as if trying to get back into the wood from which they came; a night when coals glow and wane, making shifting patterns of ruby and gold; a night for seeing pictures in the embers.

The fire burned low and one of the carriers piled on fresh wood. Flames leaped high and sparks exploded in little bursts. Anatole brought a four-quart kettle of tea, and, as often happened beside campfires, I was asked to spin a yarn.

"For months on end I go—trading, hunting, foot-slogging," I said. "Usually nothing much out of the ordinary happens, then comes a job that makes up in excitement and danger for all of the listless months.

"I took this fellow, Jonker, that Jones wants me to meet in Libreville, up the Ogooue two years ago. That was quite a trip."

Entomologist Kees Jonker, drinking morning coffee at a folding camp table beneath an *okoume* tree in the Gaboon district of French Equatorial Africa, stared glassy-eyed at a green and yellow spider dangling eighteen inches in front of his face. His clean-shaven upper lip and the tip of his big nose were pasty white. The guy was scared stiff.

"The spider's harmless, Jonker," I said.

Jonker stood up, coffee slopping from his tin mug. "It doesn't matter whether they're poisonous or not—they fill me with intolerable fear," he said. "That's one reason I'm in West Africa—to whip this fear. Sometimes I think I've overcome it, then I see a spiderlike creature unexpectedly, and—"

"I know," I said. "I've guided men with several kinds of phobias; fear of horses, fear of things falling, fear of dead bodies, and several who feared blood."

The spider hanging over the table suddenly squirted silk from its spinnerets and plummeted to the table top. Jonker crushed it with the end of a stick—and shuddered. I said:

"Your fear seems so great, Jonker, that I think this trip's a mistake. Rains have been heavy. The lowlands where we plan to go are teeming with fearsome small things. Let's call it off."

"No," he said. "If this phobia stops me now, I'll never cure it."

Jonker was a two hundred-pounder with all the courage in the world—until it came to spiders. He'd become an entomologist partly in defiance to his fear.

"Okay," I said. "We'll start upriver tomorrow."

I shouldered my rifle and set out, hoping to find a young antelope or maybe a red buffalo calf for supper. There was plenty of game in the clearings, but I couldn't get near it. I prowled for miles and finally settled for a yearling hippo. When I got back to camp, dusk was falling. I sent my head boy, Lagone, and his nine Bakele (Bakalai) porters, to bring in the meat, then sat by the fire and watched Jonker finish putting up a white canvas insect trap. The canvas was a 6 x 9 sheet that Jonker erected like a sail. When firelight played upon it the thing became sort of luminescent, and insects came from all directions to cling to it.

Jonker and I ate hippo liver for supper, drank a lot of tea, lit our pipes, and watched insects and beetles bang into the canvas "sail." From time to time he sprayed the insects with a Flit-like solution and they'd fall to the ground at the bottom of the trap. Jonker sorted them out with his fingers, bottling those he wanted.

The night grew black and the firelight threw shuffling shadows around us. At one bottom corner of the trap my eye caught a quicker, more solid shadow. It darted at the little pile of dead insects, then vanished. I stared for several minutes without seeing the dark movement again and had decided the light was playing tricks on me, when it appeared once more for a brief instant.

I stepped around the canvas trap, and stopped suddenly. Squatting within a yard was one of the most devilish-looking animals in Africa—a whip scorpion. I have no phobias, but large whip scorpions (*amblypygi*) give me the creeps. The little beasts look like something out of hell—and stink. A man who fears spiderlike creatures usually goes into dithering panic when he sees a whip scorpion.

The unholy things have segmented, flat bodies about the size of a poker chip. They have eight true legs, four to a side. The back three pairs bend forward and upward at the joints so that the vicious little animal seems always about to spring. These three pairs of legs are about twelve times longer than the body is wide—spreading ten to eleven inches. The front pair of true legs aren't legs at all, but stringlike "whips," twenty-five to thirty inches in length. The whips writhe and twist in all directions until they touch an insect, whereupon the scorpion pounces so fast that the eye can barely follow it. The victim is clasped in a pair of "jaw-legs," twice as long as the true legs and armed with cruel fangs along their inner edges. The whip scorpion's prey never escapes, but is held in the "toothed" embrace until the scorpion sucks the body dry.

Jonker, fumbling for an insect, reached around the edge of the canvas. The scorpion leaped. The spiked jaw-legs wrapped around Jonker's fingers: Jonker jerked his hand away. The scorpion clung. Jonker, squawking like a stricken parrot, shook the beast off, then fell to his hands and knees.

I tried to help him to his feet, but his legs buckled and he knelt, head down, every muscle twitching. He began to shake. I said:

"You're suffering from shock, Jonker. Lie down and I'll cover you with blankets."

He didn't seem to hear me, so I pushed him over on his back, put two blankets over him, and sat watching while the shaking slowly lessened. An hour later he said:

"What was it?"

"A whip scorpion."

"It bit me."

"They're not poisonous."

He sighed and sat up, threw the blankets aside, said: "I'm warm again," then, bitterly: "This is no place for me—I'm not even half a man."

"Look, Jonker," I said. "Beat that fear. Next time you see a whip scorpion, pick it up."

"I'll do it," he said, sighed, and added: "God!"

I'd planned to take Jonker to a little sandy valley up one of the tributaries of the Ogooué. At this time of year the place would be swarming with frogs, toads, shrews, land crabs, scorpions, centipedes, wasps, spiders, and all manner of worms. Next morning I said:

"You're a pretty sick man, Jonker, when your phobia acts up. I'd like to see you whip it, but—"

"*Please,*" he protested. "My mind's made up. I'm scared to death, but I'm in the mood to see the thing through. Don't say anything to make me weaken."

"Right," I said, and told Lagone that Jonker and I would go up the left bank of the river. "Break camp," I said, "and follow us."

We stuck around until the porters started making up the loads, then Jonker and I set out up the red-watered Ogooué. We were heading into a situation where death would dust our feathers—but, of course, we didn't foresee that.

The undergrowth was dense close to the riverbank, so we cut north through the trees about a half mile where going was easier. This was great country for a zoologist; a country of giant squirrels, snakes, small antelope, okapis, red buffalo, femurs, occasional leopards. But Jonker concentrated on butterflies, mosquitoes, wasps, bees, ants, and all manner of small creatures. On his back hung a square wooden box packed with small, wide-mouthed bottles. In his pockets were tweezers, long needles, tiny scoops and shovels. With Jonker's size and brawn the pink butterfly net held in one hairy hand seemed grotesquely out of character.

It was slow going, for Jonker continually stopped to turn over logs and rocks in his search for insects. Occasionally he'd pop one into a bottle. He studied spiders, too—particularly those that drape sheets of web over bushes.

"You know," he said, "I've lain every day for months on psychoanalysts' couches, trying to find some childhood association that might account for my fear of spiders. No use—there seems no reasonable explanation of it. When a spider touches me, my heart pounds, and I sweat. If I hold one in my hand for more than a couple of seconds, I vomit."

We hit the tributary on the third day and followed it northeast. Small streams danced down gentle slopes on both sides of the branch. Springs bubbled from soggy ground. Tall trees were oddly interspersed with short ones, and most trunks were entangled with rubber vines. Mosquitoes dive-bombed us. Gnats flew into our ears, up our nostrils, and into our mouths. They caused so much misery that we'd have turned back except that they suddenly vanished as if blown away by a strong wind.

Shortly before sunset, from the top of a low, treeless hill, we looked down into our little valley. Where once had been a firm, sandy floor, was now a lake that shone like molten copper in the dying light. Coarse grasses grew to the edge of the water, but trees and bushes seemed to have drawn back as if fearful of seeing their reflections.

We chose a camp site at the edge of the trees, then I walked around the lake, looking for streams that fed it. There were none, so I knew the lake for what it was—a sheet of water overlying quicksand.

I'd had unpleasant experiences with quicksand. I knew that most such deathtraps are created by runoff water that's gone underground, then forced its way upward through normally firm sand, making the sand loose and treacherous.

I went back to where Jonker and the natives were making camp, and said:

"That water's only about two inches deep, and it covers the most deadly form of quicksand. Everyone's to stay away from it—don't put even one foot in it."

The Kaffirs drew aside, talked together for several minutes, then Lagone said:

"Pay us, master, and we will go."

"It's only quicksand, Lagone," I said. "It can't hurt you if you stay away from it."

"We must go, master." Why?

"If we do not go away, a devil voice will call and call until we plunge into the evil waters."

I laughed, reassured Lagone, refused to pay them off, and told them to talk no more about their devil. They built a fire and sat around it in silence. Jonker and I curled up beside our own fire and slept.

In the morning Lagone and his porters were gone.

"I'll stick around a couple of days, Jonker," I said, "and if they don't come back, I'll go downriver and pick up a gang of Bakotos. Bakotos aren't so superstitious."

I went hunting, leaving Jonker in camp to set up his insect trap and to fiddle with his specimens. I walked all day and never once got within shooting distance of a supper. Back at camp I switched my .303 for a .22 and returned to the woods looking for squirrels. I got two big fellows, skinned and cleaned them where they fell, then pushed back to camp again. I broiled the squirrels on a stick, put them on tin plates, and looked up to see Jonker studying something on the ground.

"Some sort of spoor," he said.

I examined the tracks. "Brush-tailed porcupine," I said. "I've an order for two of them." I followed the spoor with my eyes, saw that it entered a large, cavelike hollow beneath a nearby silk-cotton tree, and made a mental note to try to capture the beast alive next day.

As the night grew darker I piled brush on the fire. The insect trap glowed warmly in the firelight. Beetles crashed into it and fell stunned at its base. And, exactly as had happened four nights before, a whip scorpion shuffled close, grabbed a beetle, and darted toward the cave where the brush-tail had holed up.

"Jonker," I asked, "what do you plan to do when you see another whip scorpion?"

He looked up from the kit of bottles and said:

"Pick it up—I guess."

"Don't you know for sure?"

"Yes. I'll pick it up."

"Okay," I said, "the time has come. There's a whip scorpion in the hollow under that tree. Go in and get it."

Jonker looked at his hands. He wove his fingers together, said, "Sure. Tomorrow."

"No, now," I said.

"Now?"

"Yes, now."

"Give me a little time," he said, and walked away. He was back in a few minutes, carrying a pair of goggles. "I'm not going to crawl in that hole without goggles," he said. "The bloody thing might—"

"Goggles are okay," I said.

Jonker's goggles were ordinary pilots' goggles, but were held snugly around the head with a wide elastic band. He put them on and held his hands before him, looking at them, shaking his head, then he picked up a flashlight, turned the beam on the mouth of the big hollow, and strode toward it stiff-legged. He lay on his belly and crawled into the opening. Only his feet were outside when his light went out. A moment of silence, then a scream that prickled my skin. Jonker backed out, rushed blindly into the sail-like insect trap, fell, got up, and stumbled, still screeching, toward the fire.

I grabbed him, then almost screamed myself. A great, hairy, ten-inch West African giant spider was clinging to Jonker's face. Jonker pawed at it madly. It clung. He jerked loose from me, then grabbed the spider with both hands and pulled. The beast came away in his hands—all but one leg that was caught under the headband of the goggles. I reached for the spider leg, but Jonker ducked and ran blindly—toward the quicksand.

I grabbed up my flashlight and followed, yelling.

Almost instantly, it seemed, Jonker was thirty feet from shore, and sinking.

At the edge of the quicksand I held the light beam on him, saw him standing erect, his back to me, still fighting the spider leg. The water was almost to his knees.

"Lie flat on your back, Jonker," I yelled. "Lie down! Damn it— lie down!"

He half turned toward me. I saw him hurl the spider leg away from him.

"Lie down, Jonker!" I shouted. "Lie on your back and spread your arms wide!" He answered:

"I held that leg in my hands. Did you see?"

"To hell with the leg," I said. "Are you sane now?"

"I'm all right, just shaking."

"Stop shaking," I said, "or you'll shake yourself down to the bottom of the sand trap. Lie down on your back. Spread your arms. Lie perfectly still."

Jonker threw himself backward so hard that water splashed around him in sheets. Angrily I said:

"Don't make another move. Don't talk. Just listen to me. Don't try to pull your legs out of the sand. Don't—"

He yelled something.

"Shut up," I said. "I can get you out if you'll do exactly as you're told. When I ask you a question, just answer yes or no. Are you over your fright?"

"Something's happened to me—I'm not even nervous."

"Have you had experience with quicksand? Yes or no."

"No."

"Are you apt to get panicky if you start sinking deeper?"

"Nothing will ever frighten me again."

"Are you sinking now?"

"A little, maybe—not much."

"If you're sinking, it's because you're talking. Stick to yes or no. There's no reason to get panicky. Keep in mind that *if you can float in water, you can float in quicksand.* Keep your arms spread wide. Don't move at all. Keep your chest up, and filled with air. Forget your legs. I'll tell you when to try to pull them out. I'm going back to camp now, to get a rope. You all right?"

"Yes."

But there was no rope in camp—the porters had taken the only two we'd had. I severed a rubber vine with a hatchet, tried to pull it from the tree, and got nowhere. I thought of trying to knock a platform together, but a man in Jonker's near-hysterical condition was apt to begin struggling. His abrupt return to sanity might be merely a phase of shock. There was no time to waste. I'd have to try to rescue him the hard way.

I cut two saplings, trimmed them hastily, ran back to Jonker. I held my flashlight where I thought he was; saw nothing but smooth water. I felt a wave of weakness, but almost at once the beam found him. He lay quiet as death.

"Okay, fellow," I said. "I'm coming in after you. But first I'm going to throw a pole out to you. Don't try to grab it, just—"Hey, do you hear me, Jonker?"

No answer.

"Jonker!" I shouted.

No answer. The guy'd passed out.

I played the beam of the flashlight over him. He seemed limp, and was sinking at the hips. I threw one of the poles as close to him as I dared. I laid my own sapling on the water, one end near the shore, the other end reaching toward Jonker. I figured he was at least thirty feet out, and my sapling was only about twelve feet long. That meant I'd have to move it twice. I felt a compulsion to hurry, but forced myself to act deliberately. I placed my flashlight carefully on the grass and lay down on the firm bank so that the sapling in the water was at right angles to my hips. Then I rolled into the quicksand—rolled over and on top of the sapling, two complete rolls, then lay on my back, arms outstretched, and rested. My feet sank an inch or two and I eased them from the sand ever so gently. I rolled over again, the sapling supporting my hips. Again I rested.

As I lay staring upward, the sky began to lighten. I turned my head cautiously, saw a yellow, gibbous moon peeping above the ragged tree line on a hill. I rolled again, off the end of my sapling that time, and lay floating entirely unsupported.

Trying to not move an unnecessary muscle, I worked the sapling across my chest, then pushed it toward the top of my head. With arms up, I began to sink. My impulse was to hurry, but I stayed with slow motion. I lifted my head, drew the sapling under it until it was stopped by the back of my neck.

By this time I was panting from exertion. I lay still until my breathing quieted, but couldn't stop the pounding of my heart. I hooked one arm over the sapling and pulled it under a shoulder blade. Again I rested. Then with my other hand I worked the sapling under my other shoulder.

By this time my feet were down at least a foot. It took a long time to ease them to the surface. I rested again, then with outstretched arms worked the pole under me down to my hips. Again I rolled and rested—rolled and rested.

I was within ten feet of Jonker when he moved. I said:

"Lie still, Jonker. Still!"

He tried to sit up, and I shouted: "Lie still, you son of a bitch!"

Jonker said: "I know where I am. The water's over my belly."

"Now listen," I said. "There's no need for me to come closer. There's a pole here for you. I'm going to try to push it under you. Don't make any move to help until I tell you."

I had to roll over once more to reach Jonker's sapling, but I got it, pushed one end toward him, and thanked the Lord for the moonlight.

When the end of the pole touched him, I said: "Now, Jonker, move one hand very slowly, and steer the end of this pole under the small of your back. Got it? Okay. Now gently lift your belly."

"It won't lift," he said. "My hips just sink deeper."

I was sinking myself, but took a chance and pushed. The pole went under him easily. I felt an impulse to cry, cursed instead, said:

"Reach out and grasp the pole on each side of you, Jonker. Work it slowly under your hips. Then rest. Rest a long time. Don't use your hands after you get the pole in place. Keep your arms stretched out. Don't worry about your feet. I'm going back to camp now to tear that insect trap into strips and make a rope and pull you out. You all right?"

"I'm all right—I think."

I said: "You can't sink with that pole under you if you *lie still.*"

The trip back to firm ground was tough. Each time I rolled along my pole I had to rest longer. No one who hasn't worked himself out of quicksand can ever know how strength ebbs. I made it—felt solid ground and crawled out to safety. I got to my feet, wobbling with weakness, and rested awhile by the campfire. I saw the squirrels, wolfed one, felt stronger.

I cut the canvas sheet into strips, knotted them into a rope, tied a twelve-inch chunk of wood to one end, went to the edge of the lake, tied the other end of the improvised rope around my waist; with something close to prayer I heaved the wood chunk at Jonker. It fell across him. I said:

"Okay, old-timer, now do what I tell you, and work fast. Get hold of that rope and untie the wood. Tie the rope tightly around one wrist. Be sure it's on for good, for if it slips off you're a goner. Okay?"

"Okay," Jonker said.

I sat waiting for several minutes. Jonker didn't seem to move much, but finally he said:

"You can pull my arm off, and the rope won't come untied. But my legs are in pretty deep."

"Start working your legs to the surface. Move first one, then the other, just a fraction of an inch at a time. It may take an hour to get them reasonably clear. Is the pole still under your hips?"

"Yes, and my arms are stretched wide."

While Jonker labored to free his feet, I talked to him. I knew that if he got excited and worked too fast he'd sink deeper. I said:

"Easy does it, Jonker. Take all night if you want. Quicksand's strange stuff. Gentle water pressure from underneath floats sand so that each grain is suspended free. Such sand has no traction because the water pressure exactly balances the weight of the sand. Take the pressure away and the water comes to the surface, the sand settles and becomes firm. A month from now, when the underground water's dried up, you'll be able to walk across this lake. Did you know that if you pull a cow or an antelope out of quicksand, he'll charge you the minute his feet hit firm ground? Horses won't do that."

I talked about this and that—most of it silly stuff, I remember. Once when I stopped, to rest my voice, I heard Jonker panting. I said:

"Rest now, Jonker."

"I'm all in," he said. "I can't keep on. I've got my legs straight out and my feet are only down about six inches now, but I've pains in my chest— can't breathe." There was panic in his voice. I said:

"All right, fellow. The time has come. I'm going to start pulling. If you ever struggled, struggle now!"

I dug my feet in, leaned forward, pulled. I pulled until I thought the rope would cut my waist. I pulled until my ears ached, and blood ran from my nose. I heard Jonker yelling in pain, but he seemed far away. He threshed so violently at times that he almost pulled me toward him.

Suddenly there was no strain on the rope and I stumbled forward and fell. I thought the rope had broken, and lay there too pooped and sick at heart to do anything about it.

The rope nagged at me and I sat up. Jonker was on his feet within a yard of the bank. I jerked the rope frantically and poor Jonker fell forward on his face. I went hand over hand along the rope, keeping the strain steady. I got hold of his free hand and pulled him onto the grass. Then I sat down and fought to keep from blubbering.

Back at the campfire I examined Jonker's wrist. The rope had torn his flesh to the bone. I got the first-aid kit, poured antiseptic on the torn flesh, then sewed it together as best I could. When I'd bandaged and taped it, I said:

"That'll have to do until we get to Libreville, Jonker."

Jonker didn't answer—he was sound asleep.

African elephant — challenge.

WYNKEN, BLYNKEN, AND NOD

Many men don't recognize adventure when they meet it. One type calls adventure a "mess." "I got into a mess," these say. Another type looks on adventures as vexations. These say: "The elephants became nuisances, so we shot a couple of them." A third type sees strange and unusual happenings only as perversities.

On the other hand, there are men like George Vossos, who see adventure in every struggle no matter how minute—the attempts of a beetle to solve the problem of crawling over a stick in its path, the struggles of a turtle that's fallen on its back, the efforts of a longtailed bird to fly against wind, sunshine contending with an encroaching cloud.

Such men strip away nonessentials so that the problem stands out starkly. The beetle must climb over the stick—he has food in his mouth for his hungry brood. The stick is a formidable obstacle, and while overcoming it the beetle is spotted by a ravenous bird. Will the beetle's brood be fed? Has the beetle sufficient strength or ingenuity to escape peril and achieve his goal?

To those who see things as drama the struggles of the beetle may well be more exciting than the charge of a lion, for the lion, except for some queer twist of fate, is foredoomed to failure. All of the lion's strength, determination, speed, and anger will be futile against the devastation of a well-placed bullet.

Usually wild game—even big game—is not dangerous to humans. To one who knows its behavior pattern the killing of an elephant with a heavy-calibered rifle is about as dramatic as shooting a pig in a pasture. The drama is there, however, for those who *think* it is. A man filled with fantastic myths about big beasts quakes and quivers as he faces them. He sees rage in eyes that protrude with fright, sees killing lust in a trunk sinuously feeling out the air for danger smells. He jerks the trigger; his shot wounds instead of killing; the beast screams in pain and the "hunter" frantically empties the rifle magazine. The elephant dies slowly, sometimes noisily.

The hunter "knows" he heard the wings of death. His mouth is dry from fear, lungs tight with suspense. He's experienced drama—the drama of a story that exists chiefly in his mind.

"Lions," said Carl Akeley, America's famed museum hunter, "are gentlemen; if they are allowed to go their own way unmolested they will keep to their own paths without encroaching on yours." Akeley felt almost the same about elephants, yet he was horribly mangled by one. It was his own fault, however— he forgot to keep an eye out for an elephant he'd bypassed in the brush while stalking another. Akeley knew those elephants had long been pestered by hunters, knew they'd developed an abnormal hatred of white man's smell.

Time was when white camera hunters would no more think of facing big game without gun support than they'd think of bathing with clothes on. Today a camera hunter who hires gun support does so in order to protect camera and film rather than himself.

Walter J. Wilwerding, of Minneapolis, is probably the world's top wild-animal artist. His paintings of big game are major art exhibits in many countries. In 1929, on his first African safari with easel and camera, he was ably "supported" by professional hunters. After taking hundreds of close-ups of everything from crocodile to lion he decided that gun support was pretty much window-dressing, so on a 1933 African sketching and camera hunt he had gun support only occasionally. Wilwerding's longest, most successful safari was in 1953. He painted and photographed leopards, elephants, rhinos, hippos, buffalo, crocodiles, baboons, gorillas—everything. Much work was done at close quarters, yet there was not one gun in his outfit!

True, he encountered drama now and then. On a river he killed the engine of the boat so he could drift close to a drinking elephant. He got close all right, and the elephant showed resentment by attempting to tip the boat over. With no rifle there was only one thing Wilwerding could do—get the engine started. He did it, after some minutes of intense drama. That drama will be reproduced on canvas—quite a contrast to the usual photograph of a fatuously grinning rifleman beside a carcass.

Hollywood's Miki and Peg Carter have captured many unforgettable moments on moving-picture film. Peg, known everywhere in Africa as "that beautiful camera hunter," becomes angry when support guns kill even threatening beasts.

Wanda Vik-Persen specialized in stills of charging big game. Like Peg Carter, Wanda preferred dodging to shooting, and waxed sarcastic when a beast was killed.

I once came across an Englishwoman, whose name I've forgotten, who'd set up her camera in the open beside a water hole. Day after day she photographed the game that came to drink. Rhinos paused to peer at her. Elephants watched, eyes bugged. Giraffes would look down on the woman with puzzled eyes, then spread their legs and drink. Not only did this woman have no gun, but she worked alone except for one native who cooked and did camp chores.

A melancholy Norwegian named Reidar Aas used to sit on a camp stool at a water hole north of Lisala on the Congo, and *talk* to the animals. He believed that animals' fear of man was but the reflection of man's fear of animals; that animals sensed fear emanations and responded in kind. He maintained that anger stems from fear, and that beasts who were not afraid were never angry. Anyway, he proved his theory to his own satisfaction. He feared nothing that breathed; prowled among snakes, held consultations with beasts. And he was never attacked, although he said that at times he had to talk fast to keep larger game from devouring him.

Don Rolph, of Los Gatos, California, Miki Carter's twenty-eight-year-old sound man, works even closer to wild animals than Carter. While Miki shoots the pictures, Rolph edges so near to the beast with his directional parabolic mike that he records the sounds of their breathing. One day on the Serengeti Plain, in 1953, while working with feeding lions, cubs chewed through Rolph's mike cable six times. Another day, when he set the shiny mike down for a moment, a cub ran off with it.

Photographer Ace Williams, producer of television shows using wild African game, employs support gunners only as color in the stories he films.

Truth is that if one uses a little common sense, and does not annoy animals, he can walk the length and breadth of Africa unharmed except by flies, ticks, ants, bugs, and mosquitoes. I've known traders who for years invaded Africa's wildest areas without carrying a firearm. They lived on wild fruits, vegetables, and what meat they could trap or could buy from natives.

The thrills experienced by "hunters" whose delight is in turning living animals into bloody carcasses are real enough. First, there's the thrill of standing at a safe distance, pressing a trigger, and hurling sudden death. The sense of power gives a boost to maladjusted egos. Second, there's the thrill of seeing blood—not their own—but the animal's. In some men blood lust is so dominant that they drool at sight of a bleeding beast. Mixed with blood lust is often the desire to give pain. I've guided men who danced and screamed in apparent ecstasy while watching agonized struggles of a dying animal.

That type of hunter is more numerous than one likes to believe; and they've one trait in common—they take no chances of being hurt themselves. The sporting idea that an animal should be given a fighting chance for life seems fantastic to them. They see no ignominy in shooting beasts from jeeps, trucks, or tree platforms. They look with disgust on the guide who suggests that when a wounded animal runs away the sporting thing is to go after it and kill it.

Fake camera hunters are invading Africa like hordes of locusts these days. They wander among natives and through farmers' fields taking pictures for background. Then they go to Nairobi or some other large city and buy yards of film of charging beasts and combine it with their own. Result is a motion-picture record of a very brave man facing violent death.

Sometimes these pseudo heroes are hoist on their own petards. More and more they're being sold film that includes charges by the single-horned rhino of India; and close-ups of enraged Bengal tigers. There are no single-horned rhinos or Bengal tigers in Africa.

True sportsmen are of all nationalities, of course, but I think when the tale is told you'll find that Englishmen lead the rest. Americans are too keen for victory—the kill is the thing. They do it sporting, giving the animal the breaks when possible, but if the beast gets away, a Yank's apt to act as if his favorite football team had suffered a defeat.

With the better-type Englishmen "the game's the thing." If, after they've made a good try, the beast outwits them, they're likely to yell after it: "Well played, old thing."

Most Germans I've guided take their hunting seriously. They become good hunters quickly because they pay attention to details. Germans learn spooring, for instance, by patient study. They like to plan an attack on an animal as if about to besiege a city. With the exception of certain Prussian officers I've worked for, most Germans are happy to give beasts the edge.

Frenchmen are emotional hunters, inclined to let an animal escape if it arouses their sympathies. It's almost impossible for a French sportsman to shoot a beast that displays likable traits—an impala buck that stands defiant so his doe can escape, a lion that's been rolling and tumbling with half-grown cubs. But if an animal's mean, the Frenchman will pump bullets at it with weird cries and shoutings.

Then there are hunters like Harry Krebs, but not many, thank the Lord. Krebs, in his thirties, big and powerfully muscled, was willing to pay well for the opportunity of accompanying Miki and Peg Carter, Arthur Aylcough (the same Aylcough who'd acted as referee in the Jones-Carrie wager), and myself on a picture-taking safari into the northern Congo. Krebs said all he wanted out of the trip were some antelope heads. We took him along because we'd have to shoot antelope for meat anyway.

Krebs seemed normal enough until we got into the Mangbetu country, when he began demanding first shot at each beast. Aylcough, who was collecting heads himself, usually let Krebs have his way, but developed a slow burn. When there was a choice between two beasts, Krebs insisted on having the one with the longer horns.

Aylcough was a quiet fellow, and Krebs should have known that quiet men pack the most dynamite. He either didn't know, or didn't care, for he kept right on making a pest of himself, and grabbing the advantage whenever possible.

One morning two impala bucks stood, hindquarters screened by brush, forequarters in plain sight. Both bucks had fine horns. I said: "One hundred sixty yards. Krebs take the near buck, Aylcough the far one. Shoot together."

Both knelt, aimed, and let their shots off. Both bucks fell. Krebs's horns measured 24 ½ inches, Aylcough's 27 ¾ inches.

"World's record horns!" Aylcough said. "My giddy aunt!"

Krebs stepped deliberately over to Aylcough's buck and banged one horn with his clubbed rifle. The horn broke off near the head.

Aylcough cold-caulked him with a right hook. Peg Carter said:

"... eight, nine, ten, and is *he* sunk!"

I offered Krebs his money back, and the loan of a tracker to guide him to Kilo. He refused. I couldn't very well ditch the guy, so he stayed with us.

A week later we camped in a beautiful, brush-ringed glade through which ran a clear, shallow stream. Elephant spoor was plentiful, and Miki, Peg, and Aylcough seemed about to get their longed-for elephant sequences at last. Elephant feeding noises were continuous that night. One big fellow actually walked between two pup tents. By dawn the beasts had quieted and we saw three of them at the brush fringe flapping their ears, squeaking with contentment.

Peg and Aylcough got out still cameras; Miki, his "hand organ." Our five Mangbetu boys set about preparing breakfast. The three elephants, instead of lumbering back into the bush, lined up a company front, spread their ears wide, and waved sinuous trunks in our direction. They showed no fear. The big beasts were about a hundred yards away, too far for stills. Miki changed lenses and ground out a few feet of film.

A large bull pushed through a thicket. The three, squealing in anger, rushed him. He lumbered across one end of the clearing and disappeared among heavy foliage. The three pals moved around in the open, heads bobbing, then wheeled toward us, stopping less than seventy feet away. Again they spread their ears and peered at us with nearsighted eyes. Peg said:

"Wynken, Blynken, and Nod."

They were of a size, between ten and eleven feet high at the shoulders. Wynken's tusks were broken at the tips. Nod's were beautifully curved but not large—probably thirty pounds each.

Blynken's tusks were so small that at first we thought him a female. All were about twenty years old, we judged.

Grass in the clearing was coarse and long, but had been well trampled. A few low bushes, smashed down by heavy feet, made gray-green splotches here and there. Seemingly bored with watching us, the beasts ambled to the edge of the clearing, where Blynken tore a leafy branch from a tree and began swishing flies off Nod's back with it. Wynken, not to be outdone, got a branch of his own and went after flies on Blynken.

We were standing there chuckling at them when a shot blasted behind us. Blynken lifted his trunk high, screamed in agony, sat down as if weary, fell over on his side, struggled to his feet, and stood swaying as if about to fall again. Wynken and Nod, trumpeting, were almost hidden by the trees when with one accord, they turned, lined up at Blynken's sides, leaned their shoulders against him, and tried to help him away.

Two more quick shots! Wynken shrieked as a bullet plowed into him, dropped his ears, hunched up his back, and stood still. Blynken, unsupported, staggered a few steps and again fell on his side. Also hit, Nod ran for the trees.

The shooter was Krebs. I turned, saw him, rifle across arm, but was too stunned by the sudden tragedy to do anything but stare. Behind me I heard Peg crying and Miki cursing. Suddenly Aylcough tossed me his rifle, and with strangely stiff shoulders, walked toward Krebs.

Krebs, rifle across his belly, said: "Stay away from me, goddam you!"

Aylcough, face expressionless, jerked the rifle from Krebs's hands and tossed it aside, slapped Krebs's right cheek with an open hand —and the fight was on.

It was a honey while it lasted. Krebs lunged and swung, lunged and flailed, the speed and power of his rushes forcing Aylcough back. Aylcough's heel caught on a trampled bush and he sat down hard. Krebs kicked him in the chest, then jumped on him.

Miki and I raced to pull Krebs off, but before we got to them Aylcough had got a wristlock and was holding Krebs helpless. Aylcough loosed his hold abruptly, and chopped Krebs hard on the side of the jaw, pushed him away, and got to his feet. Krebs rose bellowing. Aylcough jabbed him with three fast, straight lefts, feinted with his right, then drove a hard left to Krebs's solar plexus. Krebs began to double up, but Aylcough straightened him with another left, pushed his head back, and socked him in the floating ribs with a right hook that didn't travel more than four inches, yet lifted Krebs off his feet.

Krebs fell on his side, rolled over on his back, and lay gasping for breath. Aylcough got hold of Krebs's ankles and pushed his knees up against his chest. Krebs's breath came back.

Alycough reached for his rifle and walked to Blynken. He saw that Blynken was dying, and put a bullet in the beast's brain. Wynken still stood hunched up, making coughing noises. When approached, he walked draggingly away. Blood indicated the wound was low in the stomach. Chances were he'd recover, so we let him go. Nod was nowhere in sight.

We were a sad lot as we gathered beside the pup tents. No one knew exactly what to do, so we just stood, saying nothing. Krebs crawled from his tent, looked around, and went back in. I called one of the Mangbetus and said:

"Joe, you go with *Bwana* Krebs as far as Kilo. See he arrives safely, then go to Ngoroloo's village and wait there for *Bwana* Miki." Then I called Krebs out and told him to be on his way. Half an hour later he was gone.

We shifted camp, worked with buffalo, antelope, and rhino for three weeks, then, en route to Lake Albert, stopped again at the Camp of the Three Elephants. Nod was there and so was Wynken, still standing with hanging ears, back humped. He stood broadside to the trees at the clearing's edge— a very sick elephant.

Nod, one ear drooping because of Krebs's bullet, eyed us for several minutes, then moved toward us. Peg knelt low in the grass, her camera in front of her. Miki set up his movie camera behind Peg. Aylcough stood, still camera ready, behind Miki. A little to one side of Aylcough I stood, rifle bolt back, finger on trigger.

Nod kept coming.

His good ear drew back suddenly in a quarter cock—sign of a coming charge. He lifted his trunk, then curled it back between his tusks. I said:

"Get out of his way, Peg—he's mean."

Too late. With a quick shuffle forward, Nod was within reaching distance of Peg. No chance, if he reached his trunk for her. But Nod hadn't seen Peg, for he stopped within five feet of her, and, coughing with anger, eyed Miki.

Aylcough said: "Shoot him, damn it!"

I didn't dare. If I killed him instantly, he'd fall on Peg. If I wounded him, he'd trample her to death. Miki moved quickly to one side, hoping to lure Nod away. Instead, Nod moved forward, one great foot missing Peg by inches. Again Nod stopped, eyed Aylcough, hung his tusks straight down, shoved out his trunk with tip curled under. He trumpeted, lifted his tusks, curled his trunk back under his throat, and charged like a battering ram. Miki ran left, Aylcough right. Peg rose from the grass behind the elephant, took a picture of him from the rear, then scuttled after Miki.

Shrilling and trumpeting, Nod took after Miki and Peg. I swung my rifle for a shot, but the beast stopped to tear up a bush, giving Miki, Peg, and Aylcough time to clamber onto the flat-bed truck, where the four Mangbetus were already huddled. Aylcough got back of the wheel, stepped on the starter, and started bumping across the clearing.

Nod, screeching without letup, lumbered after, saw the pup tents, hurled them in all directions. I cut across the clearing, turned at the trees, and saw Wynken standing miserably. I dropped to one knee and put four slugs in the animal's side, a little below and behind his ear. I heard the slugs hit solidly. He didn't even twitch his ears, but a moment later collapsed, the big heart riddled.

Aylcough wheeled the truck among the trees and over the rough, stump-studded roads the boys had cut. He moved in low gear despite the raging elephant behind him—a broken axle could mean death.

I pushed at an angle through the shrub, met the truck on a curve, climbed aboard, and sat on the floor boards beside Peg. Miki ground away at his camera like a butcher making hamburger. Five times Nod was within trunk distance of Miki, and five times the beast stopped to tear up bushes. Five times I raised my rifle to shoot, and five times Miki said:

"No—not yet! Not yet!"

Abruptly we left the trees, bounced over a log, and rolled onto the plain. Aylcough shifted into second gear and stepped on the gas. The car jerked, then quit.

Nod came thundering.

The Mangbetus jumped and ran. Aylcough lifted the hood to tinker with the engine. Peg grabbed Miki. He shook her off and kept turning the camera crank. I aimed an inch above Nod's eye, and squeezed the trigger.

Nod's legs folded. His great, seven-ton body crumpled and hit the back of the stalled truck in a sliding crash. Miki, tripod, and Peg were all in the air together. I can still see seven legs—Miki's, Peg's, and the tripod's—flailing frantically.

It isn't enough to say, "All's well that ends well." Truth is, as any professional white hunter would tell you, I was a fool. I'd taken chances with clients' lives. That my clients insisted on taking those chances is not a valid excuse. The lives of the party were my responsibility—pictures or no pictures.

The soft spot above an elephant's eye is only about two inches in diameter, and it isn't in the same place on all elephants. It just happened that Nod's was where I'd aimed. Luck.

But the risk paid off for Miki and Peg. Film exhibitors are unanimous in declaring that Miki's sequence of the wildly charging Nod is the most thrilling ever screened.

I said good-by to Miki, Peg, and Aylcough at Kilo, went to Albertville to pick up another hunting party, found them on a binge, tried to sober them up, failed, so telegraphed Nicobar Jones for orders.

Four days after Jones's reply I'd ridden 120 weary miles northwest from Albertville on the Congo shore of Lake Tanganyika, to help Ives Jenssen, dean of old-time ivory hunters, celebrate his ninetieth birthday. I'd brought along two bottles of Cape brandy to urge his tongue to tales of adventure.

I pulled up my horse as the forest trail broke abruptly into the open and sat looking at Jenssen's deep-thatched, two-room hut squatting contentedly in bright sunlight in the center of a ten-acre clearing. His vegetable garden throve; yellow roses climbed over the walls of the hut.

The barking of a dog from behind the house grew hysterical, and my horse pranced nervously. I kicked him in the flanks and rounded the house at a canter.

Jenssen, bloody, and dead, lay on his back on newly plowed ground. Five filthy-feathered vultures fluffed and shuffled angrily as Lascar, Jenssen's big white boarhound, kept them from the body with vicious rushes. I hit the ground and killed three with the butt of my rifle. The other two, with broken wings, flopped obscenely across the field. I dropped them with two fast shots, then, sick at heart, knelt by the body of the old white hunter. Lascar lay near, panting.

One side of Jenssen's chest was crushed. Flies swarmed on dried blood. Elephant tracks in the soft ground seemed to indicate the killer. I got a blanket from the hut and covered my old friend.

Nicobar Jones, my first hunting boss, had taught me most of what I knew about big game and antelope, but it was Jenssen who'd introduced me to the Africa of the treetops—the fascinating green continent of semigloom that few men know—the continent of tree snakes, pottos, flying and booming squirrels, monkeys, lemurs, dormice, bats, angwantiboes, and a multitude of other tree-dwelling animals and insects.

Jenssen had taught me well. But that had been long ago, before he'd retired to live peacefully in his lonely forest clearing. And now, on his ninetieth birthday, he was dead.

With a tightness in my throat I examined the elephant tracks more closely, and got another shock. The elephant had only two legs. All the tracks were oval—hind-feet tracks. There was no sign of even one round front-foot track.

I examined the body more carefully. Jenssen's chest had not been crushed by the weight of an elephant's foot; it had been stove in with a blow from the side—a kick from a heavy boot, I guessed. Yet, there was no shoe print anywhere among the maze of elephant tracks.

I followed the spoor to where it disappeared into leaf mold at the edge of the trees. I walked back to Jenssen's body, remembered his Pygmy servant, Tock-Tockie, and yelled for him, although I felt sure he'd not answer—felt I'd find him dead too if I hunted long enough.

I wrapped the blanket snugly around Jenssen's body and started to carry it to the hut. My horse whinnied softly and I paused to listen. Hoofbeats. At the side of the hut a mounted man appeared— an assistant territorial administrator, Henrik Poullet, who'd once been pointed out to me in Albertville. I put Jenssen's body back on the ground and stood facing Poullet. He stared at the blanket wrapped body, pulled his revolver, and said:

"Take off the blanket."

I did. Poullet scowled at the crushed chest, pondered the elephant tracks, said: "Killed by an elephant, I see. But who fired two shots? On my way to Yambi I heard them and came here."

I pointed to the vultures. Poullet holstered his revolver.

Three sweating natives wearing white shirts and khaki shorts trotted from beyond the hut and halted behind Poullet. He tossed his reins to one and dismounted.

I said: "A man wearing elephant feet over his boots killed Jenssen, Poullet."

"Don't be ridiculous," he said.

I pointed to the tracks. "All oval," I said. "Hind feet. Not an inch deep. The ground's soft. An elephant would have sunk three or four inches. An angry elephant would have stomped the body, then likely have covered it with branches. Some man did this—a white man. No native would be dumb enough to try to fool police with phony elephant feet clues."

Poullet looked scornful. "You talk like an ass," he said, and told two natives to carry Jenssen's body to the hut.

"Ask your trackers," I said.

"I know every white man in this area," Poullet said. "None of them would kill a man. Nor do I think you would. But you must stay here until I have time to get the police. As for this idea of a man wearing elephant's feet ..." He laughed nastily.

"Ask your trackers."

Poullet turned to the native who was holding his horse. "Well, Wabo?"

Wabo said: *"Ndovu* was a man. *Ndovu* does not kill thus. Nor is he without front feet."

Poullet turned to the second native and said:

"Tell Wabo he is a fool, Wanyutu."

Wanyutu said: "It is not Wabo who is a fool, *Bwana.* "

Poullet slashed him across the chest with his rhino-hide whip. I said:

"What's the matter with you, Poullet? The boy only answered your question."

I watched Wanyutu open his shirt and finger the purplish welt.

"Poullet," I said, "I'm going after Jenssen's killer. A man so stupid as he was shouldn't be too hard to track down. When the police get here—"

Poullet whirled angrily. "Shut up," he said, and drew his revolver again. I tucked my rifle under my arm and went to the hut. Poullet followed, stood glaring at Jenssen's body on the floor, wrote a chit, and told one of the natives to take it to the magistrate at Albertville. Then he said to me:

"I can't hold a gun on you for six or seven days, but if you leave here, Wabo will follow you. You can't get away."

I grinned. "Let's bury Jenssen," I said. I wrapped the body in an extra blanket, took a shovel from a kitchen corner and handed it to Wanyutu, and then went into the garden. We buried Jenssen beside a bank of red geraniums. I watched Wanyutu fill the grave, then I said:

"You're a Kikuyu, Wanyutu."

"It is so."

"But you work in the Congo."

"I was unhappy in Kenya."

"The dead man was my friend," I said.

"When one buries a friend, he buries part of his own heart."

"Wanyutu," I said, "I want to find my friend's killer."

"I too have read the spoor, *Bwana.* Even my son, who is in his first year as a herder of goats, would not be deceived by the spoor. The killer's brain is filled with maggots. Not many men are so mad. He would be easy to find. You will leave this place and search until you find him who kills aged men. I will go with you."

"But, *Bwana* Poullet ..."

Wanyutu shrugged. "We will go, O Hunter, and Wabo will follow us, but he will not tell *Bwana* Poullet where we are. Wabo, too, is Kikuyu."

That night when Poullet's snores had become regular I slipped from the hut into bright moonlight. Wanyutu and Wabo waited for me at the edge of the trees. Wabo said:

"Wanyutu knows a clearing not far within the forest. Go with him, O American, and go safely." Then he disappeared into the night.

Half an hour later Wanyutu and I entered a small, moonlit glade in which someone had built a crude shelter of woven branches. We made a small fire and squatted facing each other across it. I said:

"Wanyutu, I want you to visit the homes of all white men in this area. There can't be more than ten or twelve. Talk to servants. Find out in which houses elephants' feet are used for walkingstick stands. Find a foot with a stone-gouge at the base of the second toe."

"It comes to me that I will find that foot, *Bwana,*" Wanyutu said. He left at dawn.

I was hungry, didn't dare shoot, so made a snare from a vine and some withes. During the next twenty-four hours I caught a squirrel, a large green bird, and a plump gray monkey. I broiled them on a stick and ate them with raw shaggymane mushrooms. Midmorning of the second day, Wabo came. He said:

"Mpelembe, the messenger *Bwana* Poullet sent to Albertville, met a white police sergeant and eight black constables on the very night he left. Yesterday they came to the hut of the dead one. Six of the constables are trackers and they have been told to find you. *Bwana* Poullet is very angry."

"Who remains at the hut?"

"None remain, *Bwana.* The white men follow the trackers."

"My horse?"

"*Bwana* Poullet rides his own horse and leads yours."

"And Lascar, the big white dog?"

"*Bwana* Poullet has shot the dog, *Bwana.*"

"Fine—just fine," I said. "I'll have a talk with *Bwana* Poullet one of these days. Can you find Wanyutu?"

"I will find him."

"Good boy," I said. "Tell him to come to me at Jenssen's hut when he finds the elephant feet."

Wabo hesitated, then blurted: "If you wish it I wild put a spear through the back of *Bwana* Poullet."

"Thanks, Wabo," I said, "but I've other plans for him. Go now, and find Wanyutu."

I spent the rest of that day in Jenssen's hut going through his things. There were faded letters written in Norwegian, dated more than fifty years before. From the handwriting I could tell they were from a girl. There were two faded photographs of an elderly woman—Jenssen's mother, I guessed. I found many notes about birds, animals, and insects—some quite recent. There were knives, and a box of odd-calibered bullets. In a battered cigar box were thirty-one British gold sovereigns. Nowhere did I find a clue to the killer.

Scouting outside the hut, I came across a narrow trail leading into the woods and to a small circular opening in which was a short bench and a crude table. Jenssen had built himself a hideaway. I slept there in my blankets that night. When I wakened in the morning I noticed a tree that showed evidence of having been climbed. On a hunch I scrambled into the lower branches— and my hunch paid off. Wedged in a crotch was an old-fashioned dispatch box wrapped in a piece of waterproof tarpaulin. I dropped it to the ground, slid down, opened the box, and found a single, folded parchment. It revealed something about Jenssen I'd never known:

In 1926 and 1927 he'd been an investigator for the League of Nations Advisory Committee on the Traffic in Opium!

Things began to clear in my mind. The guy who'd killed Jenssen had probably been hopped up. That would explain his insane rage, and his bizarre attempt to hang the killing on an elephant. Jenssen had likely discovered a dope-smuggling setup. This meant that I might run into something big—and bad.

Back in the hut I ate raw carrots for breakfast and had scarcely washed them down with cold coffee when Wanyutu arrived with news that he'd found the telltale elephant foot.

"It is in the house of a hide buyer. His name is Faure. His first name is Remi. He is a small man and very timid. He has no wife."

I got my rifle, shoved some carrots in my pockets, and followed Wanyutu. Three hours later I entered Faure's house without knocking, Wanyutu following. Faure stood beside a rough wood table, a needle poised for a shot in the arm. I grabbed the syringe, pushed him into a chair, and said:

"You killed Jenssen, you son of a bitch."

No answer. He just sat, twitching. Pupils of his eyes were rimmed with silver. Wanyntu handed me the stone-gouged elephant's foot.

I held it up and said:

"I'm going to kick your ribs in just as you kicked in Jenssen's—"

"Martinelli—he did it—Martinelli," Faure said hoarsely, then doubled over, fell to the floor, and began to shriek. He turned on his back, face paper-white, sweat like raindrops beading his forehead and lip. He said:

"Please—the medicine—for the love of God!"

I pulled him into sitting position, handed him the syringe, and he began to cry. He steadied his shaking left arm between his knees and shoved the needle into a vein. The plunger went home slowly. His face grew red. He sighed deeply, lay back smiling. I waited a few minutes, then said:

"All right, begin talking."

Faure got to his feet and said:

"Martinelli hid my supply. All I had was in this syringe. I'll burn again in a couple of hours, but ..."

He talked a mixture of Belgian-French and English. The gist of his story was that he'd been delivering dope to a Lake Tanganyika boatman—dope supplied by an Italian communist named Carmelo Martinelli. An addict, he'd had to obey Martinelli's orders, or "burn." Jenssen had somehow got on to the racket and had sent a letter by Tock-Tockie, to be delivered to Kenya Police. Martinelli had learned of the letter, followed Tock-Tockie in a car, and had run him down.

Tock-Tockie died. Martinelli had then taken Faure with him to Jenssen's hut, and after kicking the old man to death, had gotten himself crazily high on heroin. He'd then sent Faure for the elephant feet. Eight hours later, when Faure got back to Jenssen's, Martinelli put on the elephant feet like boots and stamped around the body.

I said: "Faure, you and I are going to call on Mr. Martinelli. Where does he live?"

Faure pointed through a window at the ridge of a thatched roof showing above a mound about a half mile away.

Martinelli opened the door to my knock. He was blond and chunky. When he saw Faure he grunted as if surprised, then turned slightly crossed brown eyes on me. I banged him under the chin with the heel of my hand. He staggered backward, tried to recover and fell forward on his face. After I dragged him into a front room, I sat in a chair and watched him until he got to his feet. In excellent English he said:

"If it's stuff you're after, I have none."

I said: "You killed Jenssen."

"I don't know any Jenssen," he said.

I turned to speak to Faure, and Faure was gone. Wanyutu stood by the closed door. I said: "Where's Faure?" Wanyntu pointed to a door at the opposite side of the room. I opened the door to a kitchen—empty. I gave Wanyntu my skinning knife, said: "Watch Martinelli," and ran through the kitchen, opened the back door, and saw Faure high-tailing across the veld with what looked like a cigar box under his arm.

I went back to Martinelli and said: "Faure's taken off with a box of your morphine."

Martinelli gasped as if he'd been punched in the belly, and jumped at me with fingers like claws. I clipped him with a short hook to the side of the chin. He went to his knees. I jerked him erect, pushed him down in a chair, and said to Wanyutu:

"Go find Poullet and the police sergeant. Bring them here—fast." Then I sat on a chair opposite Martinelli—sat for more than twelve hours. Martinelli spoke twice, each time for permission to sniff heroin. I let him sniff.

When the sergeant and Poullet arrived I charged Martinelli with Jenssen's murder. I repeated Faure's story, and the sergeant believed it. He placed a native constable at each door of the house, and motioned me outside. In French he said:

"My name is Lenotre—Andre Lenotre. I cannot arrest Martinelli on mere say-so. Where is the witness, Faure?"

"He's run off with Martinelli's drugs. If you'll permit it, Sergeant, I'll follow Faure and bring him back."

"*Bon.* Why not?"

"Poullet—"

"*Quel salaud!*" Lenotre said, and spat.

I called Wanyutu, told him to follow Faure, then turned and shook hands with Lenotre. He said:

"I'll hold Martinelli here for six days. That's the best I can do without the witness."

"You'll have your witness, Sergeant," I said.

I untied my horse from Poullet's saddle, put my rifle in its saddle boot, and galloped after Wanyutu. At Faure's house a native servant was telling Wanyutu that Faure had ridden away on a horse, taking with him a bundle of food, a revolver, and a little box.

By questioning natives, Wanyutu and I managed to stay pretty close behind Faure for three days—Wanyntu running beside my horse. We finally trailed him to a small, homemade dock on Lake Tanganyika. Nosing about among the blacks, Wanyutu learned that Faure had traded his horse for a boat and was headed for a fisherman's shack on the opposite shore.

Leaving my horse as security for a flat-bottomed rowboat, we followed. We found Faure's boat tied to a fallen tree, but the shack was empty.

We followed a faint trail across a quarter mile of marsh, hit hard terrain and dry, high grass. A deep, rocky, waterless wash cut a gash diagonally across the plain. Finding anyone in this arid wilderness seemed hopeless—Faure had all of East Africa to hide in. Sergeant Lenotre could hold Martinelli only three more days. I was certain that when the guards were withdrawn, Martinelli would disappear. I'd have to find Faure within a few hours. I did. Rather, he found us.

Night fell, and I was almost too pooped to build a fire of twigs and grass to cook some big frogs Wanyutu had captured. We ate, and I dozed sitting up, too weary to lie down. A grunt from Wanyutu brought me awake—and there was Faure, standing just within the circle of firelight.

He was hopped to the eyebrows. He stared vaguely, waving one arm as if swimming. He said:

"There's animals out there and I can't find my revolver." Then on a flat stone beside the fire he spotted two cleaned and skinned frogs that we hadn't cooked. He grabbed and wolfed them raw. "Someone stole my food," he said.

The guy was high, all right, but he still hugged that little box under one arm. He'd remained standing all this time, but now he sat down, nodded sleepily, struggled to remain upright, gave up, and fell back sound asleep.

I hid the box in the gully, then came back and lay down near him. We had no blankets, but neither the chill nor coughing and snorting of hippos in the lake disturbed us.

Wanyutu and I were up at the crack of dawn, but Faure slept until well after sunup. He wakened clearheaded but sick, and begged for "just one sniff." I refused. Wanyutu speared a four-foot lizard, and we ate. Faure wanted no food, but pleaded again for his drug. I said:

"After you've answered some questions, Faure. To whom does the boatman deliver the dope?"

"Most of it goes to Kikuyu secret cults."

"Do they have money to pay for it?"

"It's free to them."

"Why?"

"All I know is that communists are behind the deal. Martinelli told me it's Arabian opium."

"Go on."

"Give me my medicine, first—please."

I got the box from the gully and gave him a big pinch of gray powder. He held it on the back of his hand, sniffed it, rubbed his nose with the heel of his hand and began talking so fast I could hardly understand him. He said he'd delivered one package to the boatman in December, and three weeks later assassins of the *Dini ya Jesu Kristo* (Cult of Jesus Christ) had murdered Assistant Police Inspector Dominic Mortimer and two of his native constables. Six weeks later Faure had delivered another shipment, and within a few days members of the *Dini ya Msambwa* (Cult of Good Guardian Spirits) had attacked a Catholic mission at Malakisi in North Kavirondo Province. Eleven of the attackers had been killed.

"Assistant Superintendent Walker of the Kenya Police had his head bashed during that affray," Faure said, and wept. I said:

"Okay, Faure. You're going back to testify against Martinelli."

"Yes," he agreed, then, taking me by surprise, grabbed the box and ran up the gully. I said: "Go get him, Wanyutu." The Kikuyu took off, spear in hand. He stopped suddenly, sniffing the air, and yelled back to me:

"We must run, *Bwana. I* smell the dogs."

Sure enough, the air held the taint of wild hunting dogs. A second later a sudden gust brought the full force of nauseating stench.

I picked up my rifle and called: "Hurry, Wanyutu. They'll kill Faure."

We stumbled up the rocky wash, mounting to a protruding ledge so we could see the surrounding plain. We heard the dogs' bell-like *oooing.* Then there they were—about thirty beautiful white-yellow-and-black brutes racing after a terror-driven antelope. Before them swept the most revolting odor in all of Africa—a stink far more sickening than that of mating crocodiles. We could see up and down the gully and across the plain on either side, but Faure was not in sight.

Every animal in Africa fears the hunting dog. For the sheer hell of it he kills game both big and little, day and night. He kills wildebeest, buffalo, zebra, hyena— everything except the elephant, hippo, and rhino. He sometimes kills men. He is deadlier than the leopard, has tremendous endurance, and fears nothing—not even the lion.

The dogs hunt in packs of from three to a hundred, and chase their prey in relays. They seldom attack an animal's head, but take turns running alongside, slashing the beast's flanks with their long white fangs— slashing away until the animal's bowels protrude, then pulling the guts out little by little until the victim crashes in death. They tear the carcass to pieces in silent ferocity, then trot away in quest of another jolly chase.

Hunting dogs roam almost everywhere in Africa, and night or day makes no difference—they kill whenever they come across an animal. With the smell of fresh blood in their nostrils they ignore the sound of a rifle. Their stench grows stronger under excitement, and few men get a whiff without gagging.

The antelope stumbled. The pack fell back, leaving the leader beside the faltering beast. The dog grabbed the trailing entrails in his teeth and braced his feet in a skidding stop. The antelope crumpled. Instantly the dogs were at him. Their *oooing* ceased and they shredded the carcass with no sound except a sort of lecherous panting.

I shot the leader and his pack tore him to pieces exactly as they'd torn the antelope. I was about to fire again, but realized I had only ten cartridges—nine in the magazine and one in the breech.

The dogs separated into three packs and began running in a wide circle, five-inch ears stiffly erect; sweet-toned *oooing* singing through the air. And then from the grass in the center of the circle Faure rose to his feet. Instantly two of the dog packs stopped and faced him. The third pack, belling excitedly, raced toward him. The pack leader shot ahead, fang-slashing Faure as it passed. Faure screamed, holding his box above his head with both hands.

I shot fast and three dogs dropped. The packs joined to rend the carcasses. Faure ran. The pack separated into two, and followed Faure at a slow, easy lope. When they drew up on him they paused to let him get ahead, then took up the tantalizing chase again. I said:

"I've only seven cartridges left, Wanyutu. I'll drop as many dogs as I can. While the others are rending them, you cut in with your spear. Let's go."

"No, Bwana," Wanyutu said.

Then I remembered that Kikuyus would rather die than touch a hunting dog.

I raced across the plain. I knelt, aimed carefully, pressed the trigger. A dog jumped high and was torn to bits almost before it hit the ground. I gained about thirty yards before the brutes took off after Faure again. Panting too hard, I missed the next shot, but the bullet ricocheted and wounded a dog. He went the way of the others. Five shots left—and at least twenty-five dogs.

Faure kept running, but was stumbling. The biggest dog raced alongside him, looking up at his face. Faure doubled back. The big dog stopped and watched while another dog loped beside Faure, snapping at his side.

Faure finally dropped, and as the dogs bunched, I let loose with my five remaining cartridges—almost without aiming. Six dogs dropped. One bullet had got two. The pack ignored Faure while they ripped into their fallen comrades. I went up, swinging my rifle by the barrel.

Upwind, beyond the dog stink, a Tommy gazelle came out from behind a low bush to dance stiff-legged in the sunlight. Without one backward glance at me or at Faure the dogs raced after the Tommy.

Faure, poor fellow, was dead, the little box beside him. His left side was torn and bloody, but his wounds hadn't killed him—he'd been run to death. We covered him with rocks from the gully, safe from hyenas and vultures.

Sergeant Lenotre met me as I pulled my horse to a stop before Martinelli's house and threw the reins to Wanyutu. I handed Lenotre the box of dope and said:

"Faure is dead, Sergeant."

"So is Martinelli," Lenotre said. "He shot himself the day after you left."

I told the sergeant the story Faure had told me about the dope and the Kikuyu societies. He said:

"That story you must tell to the authorities at Leopoldville."

Poullet came out of the house, scowling. I drove my left into his belly, and when he tipped forward I clipped him on the chin with my right. He fell like a wet sack. I said to Lenotre:

"When Poullet wakes up, tell him that punch was for a dog named Lascar."

Motioning Wanyutu to follow, I mounted again and rode off to report to Leopoldville.

STUFFED HEROES

If you read African hunting articles you've probably seen pictures of Bos, a bull buffalo; Archie, a greater kudu; and Percy, a big male rhino. Magnificent animals with near-record horns—the three of them have been dead for more than thirty years. Today their carcasses are papier-mâché, covered with their own hides, but they're still magnificent animals—papier-mâché or not.

The animals have made a fortune for their owner, an East Indian, of Nairobi (formerly of Dar es Salaam), who, at the rate of $25 per photograph, permits "hunters" to pose beside the "trophies."

Bos, Archie, and Percy have near-perfect heads. The animals have not changed their poses since they were stuffed. Archie rests his nose on the ground, his beautiful, fifty-six-inch horns pointing up. Bos lies with neck stretched out, his horns spread a full fifty-five inches. Percy lies in practically the same position as Bos, his twenty-nine-inch front horn sweeping aloft like a curved dagger.

Bos, Archie, and Percy have been killed a hundred different ways in a hundred different magazine articles by a hundred different writers. Bos seems to have always been "red-eyed with hate." Poor Percy, whose original death was from a single .257 bullet through a temple, shows up in stories as an "insane monstrosity intent on murder." Archie usually "slashed at me with horns that could tear the bowels from an elephant."

Actually all three animals were killed in 1920 by Nicobar Jones, who shot Bos while the buffalo was peacefully chewing his cud beneath a thorn tree; Archie as he stood motionless on a hillside, staring upwind; and Percy as he voided dung in a tiny clearing in the brush.

I've a fondness for barroom hunter-writers. They're harmless fellows, smart enough to know they can pick up better hunting yarns in pubs than they can on the veld. Many professional hunters are thirsty souls, and for a free drink will lay the thrills on thick. Stories by pub hunters are almost always overwritten. Like this:

"The antelope was a beauty. He stood broadside to me, his marvelous horns piercing the blue sky. I raised my rifle, looked along the barrel, but couldn't keep the front sight still because of the wild thumping of my heart. Was I to toil for days through Africa's heat and dust to locate this magnificent beast, only to lose it because of overpowering excitement? God forbid! Exerting every bit of my will power, I steadied the rifle and squeezed the trigger ...!"

And he drops a 130-pound bushbuck with fourteen-inch horns.

If he writes about fishing on the Thika, he says:

"I could tell he was a whopper by the way he rocketed the fly. No ripping the lure, but one wild, foaming rush, instant capture, and the lightning-like spurt for what the fish thought was the safety of the brush-lined riverbank. Cautiously I felt the line, realized the hook was well set, and began reeling in. I might just as well have set off a charge of dynamite under the rainbowed beauty, for he charged across the current like a speedboat gone mad, the tightly angling line cutting a foaming fin on the water. Back and forth, back and forth, every moment fraught with threats of disaster to rod, line and leader ..."

And on and on until at last, exhausted but triumphant, the angler lands an eight-inch trout.

Hen O'Toole was one of these pub hunter-writers. The day he arrived in Nairobi he went on a bender and spent two weeks staggering up and down Delamere Avenue, being thrown out of night clubs because he didn't wear a white tie. He'd almost worn out his welcome at the bars when he reached the conclusion that the best way to get off the liquor was to go on safari. He hired a white hunter friend of mine, Pelman O'Connor, and spent three months teetotaling it down the Congo. However, at Port Francqui on the Kasai River, his thirst got behind him and pushed him face first into a case of Johnny Dewar.

By the time O'Toole had killed the twelfth bottle, he was no longer welcome in Port Francqui, so O'Connor took him upriver a few miles and made camp. Three days later I came along with a two-man hunting party and camped a hundred yards downstream from them.

As always when I expected to remain in one place for more than a day or two, I had the natives knock up a john. This one was made from bits of packing cases, some canvas, and three or four flattened-out paraffin tins. The door was a sheet of galvanized corrugated iron. It was a good solid john, even though it looked like the patched-up hut of a karoo Hottentot. What's more, it was a two-holer.

My clients were Ben Solomon, a wealthy, bighearted, laughing, uneducated Londoner, who'd made his money, as he said: "in 'errings," and a chinless Englishman named Stephen Buccleugh— a real man, even though he acted and talked like something out of Wodehouse. Both were after heads, and were getting them.

On the evening of the day we made camp Solomon and Buccleugh were having a sundowner at a folding table between their pup tents when O'Toole came over, saw the bottle, picked it up, read the label, and said:

"Haig and Haig! A poem in *Usquebaugh!*"

Buccleugh said: *"Usquebaugh.* Water of Life, what? Have one."

O'Toole handed the bottle to Solomon, who poured a jolt into a tin mug and handed it to O'Toole. That was a mistake, for O'Toole's thirst overwhelmed him again and he stayed to kill the bottle.

Early next morning he was back, bringing his thirst with him. An hour later, when he staggered back to his own camp, Buccleugh said:

"This cawn't go on, y'know. The chap's a bit of a cadge, what?"

"Not a bad bloke," Solomon said, "but 'e does soak hit hup like a blinkin' sponge."

"Chap's kidneys not too good," Buccleugh said. "Pumps ship after each drink. Must tell him to use the W.C. Cawn't have people pumping ship all over the lot."

So when O'Toole came back that afternoon for more drinks, he was shown the john and requested to use it, which he did, frequently. In fact, by the time he was high again, he'd worn a path to the corrugated-iron door.

That evening one of the porters remarked that the boys were tired of antelope meat and asked me to shoot a hippo. Late that night I bagged a young five-hundred-pounder that came fussing to the river's edge. I had the boys lug the carcass to camp and lay it behind the john, planning on cutting it up in the morning.

O'Toole showed up at breakfast, and without permission reached into Buccleugh's liquor box, took out a bottle, pulled the cork, and gargled a long, slow drink.

Buccleugh was angry, but said nothing. However, Solomon was less polite. He said:

" 'Ere, 'ere, that won't do abaht 'ere. W'y don't you tyke the bloody bottle and go 'ome?"

O'Toole did. I said:

"One time Hollywood's Larry Crosby, public-relations man for his brothers Bing and Bob, decided to go fishing and forget Crosby legends for a while, so he and I went up the St. Joe River in Idaho's panhandle after Dolly Vardens, rainbows, and cutthroats.

"At our camp we had a daily visitor who came to cadge drinks just as O'Toole does. He was an old, bearded trapper named Rourke, and his thirst was something to see. Anyway, we got tired of it, shot a black bear, seated him on the john, and when Rourke pushed open the door, he squealed like a woman, high-tailed it out of camp, and never came back."

Buccleugh said: "Hah! Bear on the W.C. Might frighten a chap, what? Suppose the fellow— Oh, by Jove, that was the thought behind the rag, what? Jolly good. Frightened the chap away. Wish we had a bear."

"We've a hippo," I said.

Solomon laughed. Buccleugh looked puzzled. I said:

"I could shore up the seat of the john, have the boys set the hippo on it, close the door, and ..."

I thought Buccleugh would choke. "Just like the bear," he cackled. "Why not?"

The hippo's legs were stiff and we had a hard time getting the beast into the john, and seated. No matter how we tried, we couldn't keep the back legs from sticking out straight. We finally got him into a more or less natural pose, closed the door, and waited for O'Toole to show up. He arrived after lunch, in pretty bad shape, and parched for a drink. After he'd taken a couple of quick ones, we put a half-filled bottle on the table, told him to make himself at home, got our rifles, and went off into the brush. Hidden from O'Toole, we circled and lay behind a bush close to one side and a little in front of the john.

We'd been there only a few minutes when O'Toole, carrying the bottle in one hand, fumbling at his fly with the other, staggered to the john door and pushed it hard with a foot. The door opened part way, banged against the hippo's outstretched foot and slammed shut.

O'Toole said: "Excuse me," backed away a few feet, said: "Hurry it up, will you?" uncorked the bottle, wiped the top with his palm, tipped it, drank, corked the bottle, placed it upright on the ground, and said:

"Jazz it up in there. I can't wait all day."

Buccleugh was so red with repressed laughter that even h his ears glowed. Solomon stared, entranced. O'Toole waited a few minutes, cursed, walked up, and kicked the door. "For cripe's sake!" he said angrily.

He took another drink, placed the bottle at his feet, put his hand on the door, pushed cautiously, peeked through the slight opening, staggered backward, tripped over the bottle, and sat down. He sat for a few minutes mumbling something we couldn't hear, picked up the bottle and stared at it, then started to throw it, but hesitated and set the bottle down, got to his feet, and approached the john again. With a hand on the door he paused, said: "Come out, goddamit!" and jumped back hurriedly.

Nothing happened.

He pushed the door open as far as it would go and put his head in the opening, leaped backward, picked up the bottle, hurled it at the hippo, staggered to within a few feet of where we lay, moaned: "Oh, my God!" and began to run. He started in a half circle, seemed to get his direction suddenly, and headed straight for his own camp.

By this time Buccleugh was almost hysterical. In all my life I've never seen a man laugh so hard. Solomon said: "Poor devil," then abruptly he too began to laugh.

I had the boys wrestle the hippo to a spot under a tree and directed its cutting up. An hour or so later O'Connor came over to say good-by. He said:

"I think O'Toole's coming down with fever. He's got the boys breaking camp. Says he's off to the States the quickest way."

So we told O'Connor what had happened.

Yes, liquor on safari has created funny situations, but usually too much liquor results in trouble, accident, and tragedy. White hunter Ira Wisdom had a client with jitters after a five-week drunk, who shot himself through the head when a red spider fell into a cup of coffee he was drinking.

Most shooting accidents on safari are caused by liquor, as are many safari breakups. It was liquor—good, old, Portuguese *aguardente*—that was responsible for one of the most highly dramatic safari mix-ups I ever experienced.

Death lurks beside every African jungle trail, and he frequently delights in making a fool of a man before killing him. Every professional hunter knows this. When things begin to go haywire on safari, the hunter knows that nine times out of ten blood will flow and skulls will crack before the fleshless prankster is put to rout.

So I knew something of what to expect when on June 18, while fording the Chiumbo River in northeastern Angola, I led Hans Seimens, a young German archaeologist, and our nineteen porters, into the midst of hundreds of swarming, poisonous water snakes.

The porters, their bellies filled with grated manioc (tapioca), and happy with my promise of hippo meat for supper, had laughed and sung, with loads balanced on heads, as they followed me thigh-deep along the ford.

About halfway across we began wading around the end of a small island that shouldered the stream. As I cleared the island's tip, I was suddenly surrounded by a writhing, wriggling mass of light green, blunt-nosed, stub-tailed serpents that had been feeding on the monstrously bloated body of a dead hippo. The carcass, covered with scum, was held to the island's bank by an overhanging bush. The snakes, panicked by my abrupt appearance, twisted and shuttled in all directions. Some squirmed toward us, heads high, eyes glaring coldly, tongues darting. I tried to sidestep them, slipped into a hole, and went in over my head.

Close behind me Bembe, my head porter, yelling in terror, slapped at the serpents. One sank its teeth in his finger. Bembe whipped his arm frantically, but the snake clung like a dog.

The rest of the carriers, panic-stricken, dumped their loads and high-tailed it back to shore. I struggled back to the ridge of the ford just in time for the dead hippo, swinging clear of the bush, to bump into me. I jabbed at the distended belly with the muzzle of my rifle. The barrel sank deep into rotting flesh. I jerked the gun clear and was promptly sprayed with a stream of liquid putrefaction. Gasping and retching, I ducked under the surface again. When I came up for air the carcass, gas hissing from the hole in its guts, was ten yards downstream, slowly deflating. I waded ashore.

Seimens was kneeling beside Bembe. The other carriers had vanished into the trees. Seimens had slit Bembe's finger and was sucking the wound. He spat out a mouthful of venomous blood. I took his place, cut the wound deeper, and packed it with permanganate-of-potash crystals from the small first-aid kit I always carried in my haversack.

Seimens, who'd been about to step into the river when the porters had stampeded, had been knocked down in the rush, tramped on, and generally roughed up. He'd controlled himself while aiding Bembe, but now he really let go. He cursed the porters, damned the snakes, and almost wept over the dunking of his precious baggage. He said:

"It is finished. I have lost everything. I—"

"Come on, Seimens," I said, "let's get the loads out of the water."

We worked for an hour lugging stuff ashore. Seimens seemed whipped. I felt sorry for him. A college professor in Germany, he'd scrimped for ten years so he could finance a one-man archaeological expedition to a mound of skulls near Taba, in Angola's Canza district. He'd wangled a leave of absence without pay, bought tools, instruments, and camping equipment, and had landed in Mossamedes broke—still almost 1300 miles by trail from his journey's end. When, over a bottle of gin, he'd told me his story, I'd impulsively offered to guide him without charge.

At dawn, March 4, with nine Huambas and ten Mundombes as carriers, we'd gone east to the Cuanza River, north to Kwanza, then east along what is now the right of way of the Benguela Railroad, to the Chiumbo River. We'd followed the river north, and at sundown on June 17, had camped seventy-five miles below Canza, having made roughly 1200 wandering miles in 105 days. We'd had no more than usual troubles—swamps, mosquitoes, a little fever, rains, hot sun, and some mountain climbing. And we'd had some mighty pleasant stretches.

Seimens had been a happy man as we'd broken camp beside the Chiumbo on the morning of June 18. His lifelong dream was about to come true. Then—the snakes.

Now, as I threw down the last rescued bundle, I looked at Bembe. He was dead.

We opened the load containing shovels; dug a grave and buried Bembe. I said:

"The porters won't be back, Seimens. Swarming water snakes are one of their most dread superstitions. One of these days we'll send their wages to their chiefs. In the meantime, I've got to locate a native village and a *chefe do posto.* The Government will force natives to act as carriers in a case like ours."

Seimens didn't answer. He prodded loads until he found the one containing *aguardente.* He opened it, exposing twenty-four quarts. He uncorked one, tipped it, and let the liquor gurgle down his throat. Someone grunted. A squat, dark brown native with white eyelashes stood at the edge of the brush staring at the bottles on the open tarp. I said:

"You're a Ka-Konga."

He looked at me sideways with eyes like a lizard's. He said:

"It is true, *ilustrissimo senhor.* I am Chicreta. I am a *pombeiro* [trader]. I want *aguardente.*" He pointed to the bottles.

"Get me twenty *carregadores* [porters] and I'll give you a whole bottle of *aguardente.*"

"Will you pay eight *angolares* [about 25¢] a day?"

"Six *angolares.*"

He turned toward the brush and shouted. Twenty-three husky Ka-Kongas strode into the clearing. "*Carregadores,*" Chicreta said, and reached for a bottle. I let him take one and thereby opened a door to hell.

Chicreta's men were under such stern control that I guessed he'd been in the army. He had a constant thirst and kept begging for *aguardente.* Refusals invariably turned his weird eyes dead-black.

The next five days were through gameless country and the porters grew sullen from meat hunger. The sixth day I told them to rest in camp while I went hunting. Seimens stayed to guard the baggage. I made a three-mile sweep into a small valley without raising so much as a hare. I hit the river again about five miles from camp and worked along the reeds until I spotted a small antelope drinking. Climbing a high rock near the river's edge to get a better shot, I slipped, threw out my arms to prevent a fall, and dropped my rifle into the water.

I stripped, waded out a few feet, and went in over my head. I dived, scraped the mud bottom with my hands, came up, dived again and again. The only result was to stir up slime; my rifle was gone. That .303 had been my pet, and I felt pretty low as I pulled into camp.

Seimens, sitting beside the dead fire, looked up when he heard my footsteps. His eyes were swollen almost shut, the bridge of his nose broken, his face smeared with dry blood. Porters and baggage were gone. He said dully:

"They've stolen the loads. Chicreta beat me with his fighting stick."

I helped him to the river and washed his face. The cold water snapped him out of it. I said:

"Where's your rifle?"

"One of the porters took it."

"Okay," I said. "Lie down and rest a while. I'll be back."

I walked into the trees to think. No rifles. No ammunition. No baggage. A gang of really bad natives controlled by a drunken leader. The nearest Portuguese authorities 150 miles away at Henrique de Carvalho, the renegades heading, I figured, for the Congo border.

Disgusted by my incompetence, I think I'd have quit had it not been for that blighted look in Seimens's eyes. I hurried back to camp.

"Okay, Seimens," I said, "let's get going. I think Chicreta's heading for the Congo. I'd like to catch him before he crosses the border. Belgian police wouldn't like what I'm going to do to that guy."

"Chicreta's a killer," he said.

"Chicreta's crazy," I answered.

Feeling naked without my gun, I took up the porters' spoor. As I'd guessed, they'd turned due east. The Congo border was less than 125 miles.

Within an hour we found the body of one of the porters, Chacahanga, lying beside the trail, head bashed in by a bottle. His load, chiefly scientific instruments, lay unopened near his feet. In a small leather bag that hung from his neck I found an outdated army labor-company pass. It had been signed by "Sergeant Chicreta Kahinga."

That solved the puzzle of Chicreta and his twenty-three carriers. He'd deserted the army with his whole squad.

We hid the pack, buried the body, slept, and in the morning picked up the porters' spoor again. It was easy to follow and every six hours or so we'd come to an empty *aguardente* bottle. Evidently Chicreta wasn't sharing the liquor.

During the next four days Seimens and I ate only what we could get with our hands—a cobra, fish scooped from shallow overflows of creeks we passed, frogs, a hare I knocked over with a stone, mushrooms, odds and ends of berries, wild manioc, the hind ends of hundreds of black ants.

Shortly after noon on the fifth day, when less than thirty-five miles from the Congo border, the spoor turned abruptly north. We followed it, puzzled by Chicreta's evident change in plans. Within a mile I became more puzzled, for an elephant's spoor showed up and there'd been no elephants in that area for years.

Even more bewildering, the elephant tracks overlay those of the porters', and the spoor of a woman overlay that of the elephant. I concluded that an elephant and a woman were following Chicreta's gang. It was fantastic— impossible. I wondered if I'd gone balmy.

The tracks led across a sandy flat, through an almost brushless glade and to the edge of a grove. Here the porters' tracks became a jumble of milling prints. An empty bottle stood against a low bush. Then the porters had fallen into line and marched again, skirting the trees. The woman and the elephant had turned off into brush. I said:

"Seimens, these tracks tell a story that only a Pygmy could read."

"I am weary and sick. How far ahead is Chicreta?"

"About ten miles."

"We come upon them. What then?"

"God knows," I said. "Something. I've been hoping he'd get too drunk to—"

The trunk of an elephant appeared above a bank of brush. The brush parted and the big beast pushed into the open—a yellow-skinned native on its head. Following came a black-skinned woman, bent and wrinkled.

The elephant was very old. His skin was warty and loose. As the beast shuffled to a stop before us, the man slid to the ground. The old woman threw herself on her knees, wrapped her arms around my ankles, and began to kiss my feet. I helped her up, pushed her aside, and said to the man:

"Speak."

"*Ilustrissimo senhor,*" he said, "you have come. I will now get back Opudo, my wife. She is beautiful, O Father, and I would not have her to also be the wife of the snake-eyed Ka-Konga who has stolen her. Furthermore—"

"Wait. Who are you?" I said.

"I am Senza. I am the husband of Opudo. The *pombeiro* and his *carregadores* came. The snake-eyed one saw Opudo as we stood aside to let them pass. He took her in his arms and would have raped her, but instead, drank from a bottle. Then he tied her hands. All of the *carregadores* are in my house and one stands outside the door with a gun."

"The one you call Snake-eyes is not a *pombeiro*. He is a thief and a murderer. How can your hut hold so many?"

"My house is not a hut, *Senhor.* It has much room, for I have many palm trees and gather much oil. I am the husband of Opudo. She—" His voice broke. He held out his hands and said:

"She is beautiful, *Senhor.* Do not let her become the wife of —"

"Tell me about this elephant, Senza," I said.

"I was my elephant's keeper in the forests of Congo, O Father. We pulled trees that had been cut down. My elephant is ancient. When I was discharged from the work corps, they would have shot him as too old to work. We loved each other, the elephant and I. I begged the major to give him to me. The major laughed and gave me the elephant and together we came into my own country and married Opudo."

The old woman wailed. I said: "Be quiet," and she stopped.

"Where is your house, Senza?" I asked. "How long have the *carregadores* been in your house?"

"My house is in the forest, O Father. It is not far. They took Opudo at sunrise while we were gathering wild fruits. They have been in my house since the tree shadows were the length of three men."

"About seven hours. Have you a gun, Senza?"

"My gun is within the house, O Father."

"We'll help you, Senza, but first, I must think."

I walked off by myself and sat in the shade of a bush. After a while I had Senza take me to his clearing and I peered out from behind a shrub. Our baggage was piled at one side of the house. A porter sat on his haunches before the door, Seimens's rifle across his knees. The house—about twenty by thirty feet—had window openings at the sides. I moved so I could see the back wall. No windows there.

The house was made of saplings plastered with dung and mud. The roof was reed thatch. From inside came drunken laughter and loud curses.

When Senza and I got back to Seimens and the old woman, the elephant was snorting and coughing, holding his trunk high and backing around in a circle. Senza said:

"*Quissondes.*"

Sure enough, army ants were streaming in a narrow band across a patch of bare earth.

"Will your elephant obey orders, Senza?" I asked.

"He is an obedient child, *Senhor.*"

"Could we sneak him up behind your house and have him push through it?"

"He would put his forehead against my house, but he would not push, O Father. He has been taught that a hut must not be hurt."

"If he'd smash through your house, Senza, he'd rout the *carre gadores.* They'd rush in all directions. I'd fell the man with the rifle, and with it in my hands, I could handle a hundred Ka-Kongas."

"My elephant will not push my house, O Father. Furthermore, he might crush Opudo, my wife."

"Would you rather Opudo were dead, or the wife of that... ?"

"Dead, *Senhor,*" he said hoarsely.

The old woman squawked like a chicken and poured dust on her head. I said:

"Seimens, you'll stand in front of the house, hidden among the trees. You'll do something to attract the attention of the man with the rifle. Shake bushes. Grunt. Anything.

"Old woman, you will stay here.

"Senza, you, the elephant, and I will sneak up behind the house. You will tell the elephant to put his head against the house and push."

"He will not push, *Senhor*, as I have told you."

"The elephant will push, Senza," I said.

"Get going now. Take up your positions. I'll be along. When I'm ready to start things, Seimens, I'll give a bird call. Like this," I said, and whistled.

Seimens nodded and followed Senza and the elephant.

I got the empty liquor bottle from beside the bush, picked up a small stick, walked to the army ants, and began pushing them into the bottle. A few of them scrambled up my arm, sticking what seemed like red-hot needles into me. The pain was intense. Sweat burst out on my forehead.

I managed to get forty or fifty ants into the bottle's neck.

When I reached Senza and the elephant in the bush directly behind the house, I gave my bird call, waited a few seconds, then stepped to where I could see the front of the house. The native with the gun stood staring toward the brush.

I hurried back to Senza, said "Come on," and tiptoed across the clearing. Senza followed silently. Even the elephant's big feet made no noise.

We stood within five feet of the back wall of the house. It seemed that Chicreta was now sharing the *aguardente* with his followers, for many talked at once, some voices drunkenly shrill. I nodded to Senza.

Senza pulled his elephant by an ear and whispered an order. The elephant put his head against the wall and curled his trunk back between his front legs. That was all.

I pulled the cork and held the ant bottle upside-down over the elephant's upturned trunk tip. Nothing happened. I banged the bottom of the bottle as if it were catsup.

The elephant suddenly sat, lifted his trunk, and screamed. Then he lunged to his feet and banged his trunk repeatedly against the house. Mud flew; saplings splintered. The big beast dropped his backside, turned completely around and backed through the wall. With the thatch falling about him he sat down, lifted both front feet, trumpeted, got up, and whirled round and round.

Shrieking Ka-Kongas scrambled from the debris. The elephant's trunk grabbed one, lifted and banged him hard against the wreckage. Natives scattered every which way, some stumbling as they ran.

The guard ran too, dropping the gun. I got it, checked the chamber, then ducked as the elephant tossed part of the roof within a foot of me. I heard Senza yell, and whirled to see Opudo racing for the trees with Chicreta hard after her. Praying that the gun was zeroed correctly, I led Chicreta's ankles about a yard and squeezed the trigger.

He went down with a bullet through a foot.

It was a nice melee. Seimens chased natives with part of a tree branch. Senza rolled on the ground with two of the porters. The elephant's screams were continuous as he smashed his bleeding trunk against an old wood stove.

To save him further agony, I shot him through the heart. He stood still for a second, then collapsed head-first, burying his tusks deep in the earth.

A stone bounced off my back. I turned in time to duck another stone hurled by a porter named Chacaiombe. He rushed me. I jabbed him in the stomach with the muzzle of the rifle. He bent double, his chin near his knees. I tapped the side of his chin with the rifle butt. He stretched out on his stomach, muscles of his calves quivering. He was out cold.

That was the end. Seimens came into the clearing without his club. Senza stalked back ahead of Opudo. We dragged in three injured porters and two who'd been killed by the elephant. All others got away.

Senza took a letter to the *chefe do posto* at Henrique de Carvalho and returned with twenty carriers and a note asking me to report to the police at my convenience. We were less than sixty miles from Seimens's graveyard of skulls at Taba. Considerably older-looking than when I'd met him, Seimens went off with the new carriers to do his digging.

I turned Chicreta and Chacaiombe over to Senza and Opudo to hold for Portuguese authorities, and then I took off for Henrique de Carvalho to buy a new rifle.

Alexander Lake at his typewriter about 1940.

WITCH DOCTOR

Near the Cuchibi River in Eastern Angola, I sat on a stool beside the low "door" of a Mucassquere hut. Batu, a graying, snaggle-toothed "witch doctor," squatted at my feet. A naked two-year-old girl, face shiny from recent washing, played nearby with pebbles. Suddenly she threw some pebbles in the air, and laughed gleefully as one struck Batu on the forehead. Batu growled like an annoyed baboon and the little girl ran for protection to her mother, who was boiling water in a black cast-iron kettle at an open fire.

The baby, arms about one of her mother's bare legs, peeked at Batu, pretended more fright, skipped close to the fire, slipped, grasped the edge of the steaming kettle, and pulled it over on herself.

I picked up the shrieking youngster, saw terrible scalds on her face, chest, and one arm, and stood helpless. Batu said: "Ow!", picked up a glass bottle that held my drinking water, broke it on a stone, selected a razor-sharp, shell-shaped fragment, cut a deep gash in his forearm, and let the hot blood pour over the scalded skin of the baby.

Almost at once the little girl's screams subsided, her agonized writhing stopped, and she lay quiet except for tremulous catches of breath. With gory fingers Batu spread blood to other small burned areas.

The mother whimpered and wrung her hands. Batu said:

"Bring a newly-washed white cloth, woman."

The mother returned with a clean flour sack. Batu carefully bandaged the scalded areas, then said:

"The baby will sleep much. Give her milk when she is hungry. Do not let her scratch. The cloth is to keep off flies. Do not remove it. I will return when the cure is complete."

Batu did return—three weeks later, removed the cloths, revealing pink new skin where the scalds had been. I said wonderingly:

"No scars!"

Batu gave me an odd look. He said:

"I have told white doctors how blood, warm and fresh from the veins, puts out fire in flesh. They say, 'Yes, yes, Batu,' but they do not believe. Yet, that blood does this has been known to Mucassqueres since the moon gave birth to the first man."

Once in Kitchini country I sprained an ankle so severely that I was ill with pain. A witch doctor, Capogoni, rubbed my leg, ankle, and foot with dirty-looking gray salve, then bound the sprain snugly with strips of soft antelope hide. During the night pain diminished and swelling receded so that the bandage had to be retightened. That sprain got well much faster than any I'd had before. Capogoni refused to tell how the salve was made, but gave me a snuffbox full. When I got back to Johannesburg, I asked Old Doc Brennan, a former British Army physician, to analyze the salve. A few days later he said:

"*Extractum solani liquidum.*"

"Whatever that is," I said.

"Potato salve," Doc said. "Raw Irish potatoes mixed with oil. You can buy it in chemist shops. It's as good as anything ever devised for relieving swellings in sprains, gout, and lumbago."

"Potatoes?"

"Potatoes contain potash salts—the healing ingredient."

"Doc," I said, "a Masai *laibon* (witch doctor) once cured a client of mine of tapeworm. White doctors had failed."

"Patient probably wouldn't follow orders," Doc said. "I'll bet the *laibon* gave your client crushed pumpkin seed to eat, and restricted other foods."

"Yes—for three days," I said.

"Sure cure," Doc said, "for most intestinal worms. Pumpkin seeds contain olein, palmitin, stearin, glyceride of linoleic acid—"

I broke in. "If I collect native medicines, Doc, will you analyze them for me? I've a hunch—"

"That native medicine is pretty much like white medicine? Sure, I'll do what I can—maybe learn something myself."

That's how I began cultivating witch doctors—good ones and evil ones. I met and questioned scores of them, from chiefs of the Masai Engidongi Clan, which supplies all witch doctors for the Masai tribes, to the human-flesh-eating witch doctors of the Fan tribe, of French Equatorial Africa.

I think my associations with African witch doctors were the most interesting of my African experiences. As my understanding of native methods of healing grew, so did my knowledge of white healers. I came to realize that in basic principles the "Medicine" of blacks and whites are about on a par.

Both white and black physicians achieve their cures more through "faith" than through drugs. Ninety per cent of "drugs" prescribed by healers of both races have no virtue in themselves, but are a means of inspiring faith. As one witch doctor said:

"I give sick man white water—no get well. I give him red water —get a little well. I give black water with big stink—man get well slow. Give man black water with big stink, make dance in lion skin, beat devils with two sticks, and make screams and screams—man get well *quick.*"

A white physician told me: "I have patients with varying diseases for whom I prescribe colored water. It benefits most of them because they *believe* it will, but some patients find no help in pleasant-tasting water. They must have it bitter, so I add something to pucker their tongues and they too get well."

An Ovampo witch doctor once told me that he cured many diseases by the simple expedient of cutting off little fingers and "letting the devils run out."

Some white faith healers of religious groups exorcise demons by use of a holy name.

An American surgeon recently said that he'd removed normal organs from eighty women because no amount of argument could convince the women that the organs weren't diseased in some way.

Ovampo patients, after having fingers removed, get well. They have faith in the cure.

The "demon-freed" often get well. They have faith.

The eighty organless American women got well. They too had faith.

These facts puzzled me for years until I was told by one of the world's leading physicians that practically every disease from which humans suffer is "mentally originated." "The list," he said, "includes stomach ulcers, colitis, hemorrhoids, heart disease, diabetes, arthritis, asthma, hay fever, allergies, most forms of indigestion, headaches, and general miseries. This doesn't mean," he went on, "that because a disease is mentally inspired it is less real. But it does mean that the cure must come through the mind."

African natives of some tribes eat hearts of leopards and lions to acquire bravery and strength. Americans and Europeans eat fish as a brain food. Lion's heart does not stimulate courage, nor does fish have any particular affinity for the brain. Yet lion-heart-eating Zulus under Shaka were Africa's most courageous soldiers, and thousands of white students swear that even small amounts of fish in the diet wipe vapors from their brains.

African witch doctors effect cures. They average as many cures (of most diseases) as do their white contemporaries.

A partial list of modern faith-healing methods, as noted by America's renowned Dr. Howard W. Haggard, follows:

Osteopathy, chiropractic, Christian Science, prayer, spiritualism, astrology, application of appliances such as radio belts, drinking of mixtures like radioactive water, and psychoanalysis.

Reverend Norman Vincent Peale, one of America's most publicized preachers, an advocate of prayer, employs psychiatrists, psychologists, and religious counselors to build up patients' faith. He gets results. So do other faith cults. So do African medicine men and witch doctors.

But, so far as I can learn, faith cures fail when it comes to virus and deficiency diseases. These require antibiotics and vitamins. When a man requires Vitamin A, he gets more of it from a single carrot than he'd get from all faith cures put together, according to Old Doc Brennan. "And," he added, "all the vitamins in the world won't cure arthritis resulting from mental disturbance."

Well, I'm no authority on these things, but I've learned that, except in one phase, medicine men and white physicians begin with the same basic concepts—faith healing and drugs. The exception is that modern doctors also use sanitation. I believe that if African medicine men employed effective sanitation measures, their percentage of cures would be as high as those of graduates of the finest medical colleges.

Modern faith healers adjust their vocabularies, procedures, and gadgets to the minds of their patients. So do African witch doctors.

Unhappily, all African witch doctors have been built up in the public mind as wild, vicious, devil-possessed breeders of hatred and death. That, of course, is not true. The sincere and kindly far outnumber the evildoers, as sincere, kindly white physicians outnumber diplomaed rascals.

I've known witch doctors who believed they were controlled by evil spirits. I've known a few who advocated cannibalism, and practiced it.

And I've known evil white doctors. I've known some who were wholesale abortionists with "hospitals" on a level with abattoirs. I've known white doctors who were drug peddlers, and worse.

Native African witch doctors have long lists of drugs and medicines that have for centuries proved beneficial. Most of these "drugs" are compounded from vegetables or fruits or flowers. For example:

For erysipelas, some witch-doctor healers rub the affected parts with an ointment made from bean flowers and pods. A tea made from green bark of the bean plant is often given to reduce fever.

For gravel, four cupfuls of boiled beet juice each day.

For influenza and some fevers, an hourly dose of salted liquid from boiled red peppers. Some add palm wine to it.

For rheumatism, the brew from boiled celery—not less than a quart a day.

Flaxseed is used widely as poultices in pneumonia, pleurisy, boils, and abscesses.

Boiled juice of garlic as a preventative of scurvy.

Syrup from dried grapes for dysentery.

Olive oil for gallstones.

Syrup of onion juice and sugar for sore throat, and for easing pains of burns and scalds. Onion juice in hot milk for sleeplessness.

Pumpkin seeds beaten to a pulp and mixed with milk is the witch doctor's favorite cure for intestinal worms. In small quantities it is a gentle laxative.

Scores of other native remedies are equally simple. According to chemists, healing ingredients in the foregoing medicines are linoleic acid, oleic acid, enzymes, B-amylase, urease, uricase, d-limonene, linseed oil, diallyl disulfide, allyl-propyl disulfide, malic and tartaric acids, oleuropein, olein, palmitin allyl sulfide, stearin, glyceride of linoleic acid, vitamins A, B, C, E, and niacin.

Like most humans, I'm most deeply impressed by things I don't understand, so I'd probably have great faith in the curative powers of a bottle of medicine on which the label bore the words: "diallyl disulfide and allyl-propyl disulfide." On the other hand, if the label read merely "oil of garlic," I'd likely need my faith built up with psychoanalysis, or perhaps even with drumbeats and cavortings by a witch doctor.

Evil witch doctors spend little time attempting to cure diseases. Their activities are almost entirely political or religious. They claim supernatural powers and the ability to bring death to whom they will. They rule their followers by fear so great that many actually die when placed under a "spell."

An example of evil witch doctors is the Engidongi Clan of the Masai tribe. So powerful is the influence of the Engidongi that the British have quarantined them on the Loita Plateau. The Engidongi supply all *laibons* for other Masai clans in Kenya and Tanganyika. A *laibon* is primarily a witch doctor, but he is also a chief. He takes orders from the quarantined Engidongi leaders, and is supposed to be immortal, except when a curse is put on him by another *laibon.*

Masai tribesmen fear their *laibons* so much that they dread even to look at one. Yet they gladly pay high prices for charms assuring prosperity and fertility. Engidongi leaders direct all cattle raids, and are given a percentage of all cattle stolen. Through the *laibons* the Engidongi leaders tell tribesmen whether they should, or should not, obey British rules and regulations.

A tribesman under the curse of a *laibon* almost always dies—of fear.

Then there's the Kikuyu tribe of Kenya. I know some of its leaders, and I've met Mau Mau organizers. Witch doctors are blamed for much of the unrest among Kikuyus, but wrongly. The troublemakers are the native religious leaders who have organized cults with such names as the Men of God; Cult of the Holy Ghost; Cult of Jesus Christ; Cult of Msambwa. Teachings are a weird mixture gathered from Catholics, Seventh Day Adventists, Salvation Army, Methodists, and Jehovah's Witnesses.

The *Watu wa Mungu* (Men of God) consists of two branches, one of which observes Saturday as the Sabbath; the other, Sunday. Their leaders are known as *arathi* (prophets), who resist everything modern, including sanitation and disease prevention. Like the *Dini ya Jesu Kristo* (Cult of Jesus Christ), the *Dini ya Msambwa* (Cult of Msambwa), and the *Dini ya Roho* (Cult of the Holy Ghost), the Men of God want white men pushed out of the country. In a general way their slogan is: "The time has come. Let us wash in the blood of white men, and of black men who oppose us. Why do we wait?"

Many of Kenya's African leaders secretly belong to one of these cults. Thus politics combines with religion to create Africa's greatest threat against white supremacy. In a general way this unholy combination is the Mau Mau.

Witch doctors are used by cult and political leaders to further their programs, but witch doctors, as such, are involved very little in the rebellion.

In Basutoland, a mountainous British protectorate in South Africa, witch doctors are the pawns of 1300 chieftains who call themselves the Sons of Moshesh. Moshesh founded the Basuto tribe about 1830.

The Sons of Moshesh now fight bitterly among themselves for power. To gain this power, they murder innocent relatives and either eat some of the victim's flesh or mix it with blood and seasonings and use it as a salve. To the Sons of Moshesh power doesn't necessarily mean political power. Many of the murders—and I know of more than a hundred—are committed to assure success in unimportant undertakings. The most gruesome part of these killings is that the flesh must be cut from the victim while he still lives.

Witch doctors do not commit these murders—they are done by "friends" of the chiefs involved. The witch doctors do, however, boil up the good-luck pastes—with appropriate incantations.

British authorities have hanged many of these murderers, yet in 1952 there were at least fourteen known "medicine" killings.

I once lived within eighty miles of Maseru, Basutoland's capital. I met and talked to many witch doctors. All lived in fear of the Sons of Moshesh, and did the Sons' bidding. But the witch doctors I knew were not bad men. I'm sure that if authorities could get rid of Head Chieftainess Mantsebo, and slap down the Sons of Moshesh, most witch doctors of Basutoland would become what they'd prefer to be—simple medicine men.

Most African medicine men and witch doctors have detailed knowledge of many poisons, and witch doctors of political-religious status are adepts at poisoning enemies. The same kinds of poisons used for murder by witch doctors are also used by medicine men as curative drugs.

Formulas for mixing poisons are handed down from father to son, and from cult teacher to pupil. The formulas are supposed to be secret, but almost every native knows them. To make poison for arrows and spears, boil in water the smaller branches of the trees *akocanthera friesiorun* or *ancanthera venenata.* When the liquid has become blackish and gooey, wipe a band of it around your arrow a couple of inches *behind* the head. When fresh, this poison will kill an elephant within an hour, a smaller beast within minutes. However, the poison soon becomes dry and brittle unless covered with a wrapping of thin hide. The older the poison, the slower its action. If you want to do a really quick job of killing, add a little sap from the shrub *sapium madagascarensis.* But be careful—one drop in an open scratch will start your blood foaming in your veins. When the foaming blood reaches your heart—you've had it.

Another equally deadly poison is made by mixing entrails of the deadly *ngwa* caterpillar with juice of the euphorbia tree. This poison is a favorite with Bushmen.

Other poisons much used in Africa are: brews made from wild foxglove; *strychnos; strophanthus;* and from poison glands of snakes, and scorpions. Because it supposedly brings painless death, a poison made by soaking the yellow flowers of the *ngotuane* tree in water is often used to put human enemies out of the way. The victim just tightens up until there's no movement left in him. The desert rose, whose pretty white and pink flowers cheer the wastelands of East African deserts, is the source of poison almost as virulent as that made from the akocanthera trees.

But you don't need poisons, to kill. You can medicate a man to death as did the fourteen physicians who attended King Charles II. One of the fourteen was a Dr. Scarburgh. Here is his account of the treatment the king was subjected to when, on February 2, 1685, he was taken with a convulsion and became unconscious.

First, a pint of blood was taken from veins of one of his arms. Then he was bled again, from a shoulder. He was given an emetic, then a purgative, then another purgative. This was followed by an enema containing cinnamon, cardamon seed, linseed, saffron, camomile flowers, fennel seed, aloes, cochineal, beet roots, mallow leaves, violets, rock salt, sacred bitters, and antimony. Came another enema, and another purgative. The king's head was shaved, a blister raised on his pate, and a sneezing powder given. Several purges followed, then drinks of barley water, licorice, sweet almond, wine, absinthe, anise, and brews of thistle leaves, mint, and rue. More wine. Plasters of pitch and pigeon dung were bound on his feet. More bleeding. More purges. Then came medicines that included dissolved pearls, melon seeds, gentian root, nutmeg, quinine, manna, slippery elm, cloves, flowers of lime, cherry water, lily of the valley, peony, and lavender. These were topped with about a teaspoonful of *extract of a human skull.*

Charles's condition didn't improve, so he was given Raleigh's antidote—a concoction made from more than fifty ingredients. Then, the king was given a besoar stone (gallstone of a goat) to swallow. Lastly the physicians administered their most powerful combination—Raleigh's antidote, pearl julep, and ammonia.

The king died.

An Ovampo chieftain named Andahe, taken with convulsions, was treated by a witch doctor named Angero. Andahe died, and Angero was taken into custody by German Southwest Africa officials Charged with murder, he gave the judges a list of ingredients he'd used in his medicine. Here it is:

Owls' eyes, crocodile dung, viper's flesh, toad skin, a monkey hand, and a hawk's head—all boiled together. Angero strained the concoction and administered the liquid. He was acquitted because the judges found he'd created nothing but a nourishing soup.

When I gave the recipe for Angero's "soup" to a noted dietician in one of America's veterans' hospitals, he said:

"So far as nutrients are concerned, that soup is equal to most soups we serve our patients. Even the crocodile's dung would have some food value. Boiling would kill any unhealthy germs."

Where witch doctors fall down is in the treatment of diseases such as sleeping sickness, syphilis, polio, and other virus diseases. Because they make no cures in such cases, they often go on homicidal onslaughts similar to the one to which poor King Charles was subjected.

If one thinks only of nutrition, cannibalism supplies satisfactory salts and proteins. However, most African cannibalism—and cannibalism still exists among a few tribes—is only occasionally the result of a need for food. Some tribes eat their dead as a form of burial that quiets the ghost. Others eat human flesh because it's supposed to have magical properties. But most cannibalism is indulged in as a part of tribal ceremonial rites. Responsibility for the practice in such cases must rest on the shoulders of witch doctors. Among the Fan tribe of French Equatorial Africa certain ceremonial routines require the eating of human flesh that has been buried for some time. Fresh flesh won't do.

To me the most fascinating phase of witchcraft is what I call the "hyperphysical." The manifestations I've seen and experienced are beyond belief—as are the things I've been told.

Dr. Clifford Nance, who was in Africa studying witchcraft, told me the following experience. He said:

"Sukumbana was a Zulu witch doctor. He was about fifty—tall, lean, and cadaverous. He talked little, groaned much, and liked to be called 'Tony.' He had 'cast the bones' for me several times, and had foretold incidents of a minor nature. One night as we sat beside his fire he said:

" 'I look at the bones, but I do not see them. My spirit goes through the Hole and talks to your spirit. That is how I know.'

" 'Could my spirit go through the Hole, O Magician?' I asked.

" '*Yebo,* You-Who-Are-Young. But you must tell your *ehlose* (spirit) the things you wish to know when it goes beyond the Hole.'

"Tony was serious, but I was having a joke. I said:

" 'I will tell my *ehlose* that I would talk to a spider, or something.'

"Tony groaned, said: '*Ai! Ai! Ai!* spat on his palm, threw the bones on the ground before him, groaned again, got to his feet, and said:

" 'Come.'

"I followed him into the darkness until we were beyond the sounds of the kraal. We stopped a few yards from a large *moepel* tree that seemed a monster shadow. Tony told me I must now breathe deeply. 'Deep—deep,' he said. Still thinking of it as more or less a joke, I took deep breaths until I felt dizzy. Tony said:

" 'Sit and rest. Think only of a giant spider.'

"Almost immediately, I got a strong mental picture of a great spider with twelve-inch legs. Tony said:

" 'Stand and breathe deep once more, *umganaam* (friend).'

"I began taking more deep breaths. As I puffed like a grampus, Tony told me I must think of the air as strong wine; that I must feel the wine flowing in my veins; must *picture* the wine pumping to every part of me; must feel the wine in the tips of my ears, toes, fingers. Sure enough, I began to tingle throughout my body. I felt a bit drunk, and I was no longer joking. Tony said:

" 'You are weary, *umlungu* (white man). You will sleep. Come.'

"He led me to my hut, watched me roll up in my blankets, and said:

" 'When you shut your eyes, you will pass through the Hole. The spider awaits you. My spirit has talked to her spirit.'

" '*Her* spirit?'

" '*Yebo,* O Venturesome One. She is the mother of all spiders.' Tony snuffed the candle with his fingers, but didn't put it out. I saw him lift a foot to step through the door....

"Howling winds awakened me. I was in a galvanized-iron shack somewhere in the Kalahari Desert. Sand hissed and whispered against the sheet-iron walls, and the hut echoed with the noise of something banging on the door. I loosed the latch, and the wind sucked the door open with a clang. As I struggled to close it, something brushed past me—something shaped like a man. He was followed by two shadows that scurried beside his feet like mobile dinner plates. I got the door shut, and lighted a candle.

"My visitor was a man—shriveled and wrinkled, with sunken eyes, cheeks, and lips. He wore dirty clothes so much too large that he seemed hung with cloths. I said:

" 'It's a wonder you didn't blow away.'

"He didn't answer, but looked anxiously into the corners of the room, making coaxing noises, as if to a dog. I remembered the 'shadows' that had come in with him. 'They're probably under the cot,' I said.

"He knelt, looked under the cot, and whined: 'Come here, you.' He wasn't obeyed. He shrilled: 'Damn your blood! Come here!'

"From under the cot came a giant black spider. It was twice the size of any I'd ever seen. It was hairy, and its eight, high-elbowed legs spread at least twenty-four inches. Belly to floor, the beast moved draggingly, as if against its will. I stepped hurriedly up on a chair.

"The candle flame flickered as if blown by a breath. Outside, the wind carried voices. Sand hissed continuously against the metal walls. The old man grasped the spider with eager, clawlike fingers and sank his yellowed teeth into the beast's abdomen. He sucked the creature dry and threw the deflated carcass to the floor, where it lay with legs curled tight against the body.

"I leaped for the door, and had the latch in my hand when I was jerked back by a powerful arm. The old man was no longer old, but hale and vigorous. His body had filled out its clothes. The face was sanguine and haughty. I backed against the wall. He said:

" 'You came through, you fool. Why did you come through?'

" 'I don't understand.'

" 'The Hole. Why did you come through?'

" 'A joke,' I said. 'I thought it was a joke.'

" 'So did I—long ago. Now I am what I am.'

" 'Are you dead?'

" 'Neither dead nor alive—a cacodemon—an incubus—a slave to Gita. Compelled to forestall complete death by drinking blood of spiders. So you will be.'

" 'No,' I said. 'It was a joke. This is a dream—I just now fell asleep.'

" 'Come,' he said, and opened the door.

"The wind had died. Clouds scudded blackly across a lopsided moon.

"I stepped ahead of him into the night. He pushed past me, and led the way. At his heels scuttled the other giant spider. As I followed over sand ridges, I tried to wake myself. I shook my head, slapped my face. It hurt. I didn't waken. *I wasn't asleep.*

"We walked in silence beneath a moon that seemed to race across the sky. A lone hill like a monstrous ant heap loomed before us. My guide pulled aside bushes and uncovered the opening of a cave. Then he took my hand and led me in to absolute darkness.

"After a while, light gleamed ahead—a phosphorescent glow. The air was warm—humid. It smelled of rotting leaves and stagnant water. Abruptly, we moved into a room seemingly without limits. I knew we were in tropical country because I watched snakes and lizards scurry out of our way—species that lived only in the marshes below the Bambuto Mountains of Nigeria.

"Everywhere were giant spiders. They flashed like wind-driven leaves across the cave floor. They crouched and stalked mice and toads—and worms like grubby serpents. My guide began to shrink. His trousers folded about his ankles. I watched the skin wrinkle on the back of his neck, and grow old and dead. He scooped up the big spider at his feet, sucked it empty—and was a 'man' again.

"There were others like him around us, but I saw them as in a fog. Occasionally one reached down, grabbed up a spider and gorged. We stopped at the edge of a circular sandy stretch. What I thought was a blackish-brown hummock rose on hairy legs and looked at me with glassy eyes set close to a horny beak. My guide said:

" 'Gita,' and moved away from me.

"I stared at Gita, and once again tried to waken. I beat my nose with a fist. I scratched my cheeks. I stamped my feet. Blood trickled from a nostril. I watched it drip on my shirt. I looked again at Gita.

"She was a monster. Her legs spread at least four feet. She breathed through holes in her sides, and over the holes between her last two pairs of legs were covers that fluttered as she breathed. Men—demon men—came between us carrying a naked, chocolate-brown, dead body, its face covered by a green cloth mask. The men laid the body on the sand before Gita. Then they moved out of my vision.

"The dead native lay on his back. Gita lowered her body, moved a bit forward, crouched, beak poised as if about to rend the dead flesh. I yelled:

" 'The face! Let me see his face!'

"Gita leaped backward, sideways, turned, ran, then stopped like a checked hunting dog. She seemed to be listening.

"Then I heard it—a terrifying clanking of armored land crabs. They moved toward us—thousands of them—purple, and so damp that they seemed to be sweating. They moved jerkily, eyes protruding on little sticks from their heads, claws wide open, waving aloft, the stringlike 'palps' waving and twitching at the sides of their mouths.

"They surrounded the corpse, pinched bits of flesh from the body, and sat back, stuffing it into their mouths.

"Gita scurried off in terror.

"Suddenly the place was deserted except for the crabs—the corpse—and me.

" 'The face!' I screamed. 'I want to see the face! I think I know who...'

"I opened my eyes. The candle still burned in my hut. Tony was gone.

"Three months later," Dr. Nance continued, "I received a letter from my partner, in the French Cameroons. One of our favorite safari boys—a Hottentot named Jim—while ill with fever, had been bitten by a giant spider, had become delirious and had rushed out into a swamp. They'd found Jim's body almost entirely eaten by land crabs.

"No, my 'dream' hadn't been a telepathic demonstration—Jim hadn't died until twenty-eight days *after* I'd 'gone through the Hole.'"

Another weird witch-doctor-inspired experience was that of Charlie Weems, who, back in the nineties, freighted goods by ox wagon from Portuguese East African ports to miners and prospectors on the Rhodesian side of the mountains.

Weems had lost two outfits during bad storms on the Hump, and was almost broke. A Chibisa-speaking ox driver suggested that Weems buy a protective charm from a certain Nyasaland witch doctor. Weems did.

From that day forward until he retired rich, Weems's wagons were conducted over the Hump by a small, shadowy figure that met them wherever danger threatened. The figure invariably rode astride a lead ox, and disappeared when danger was past.

Weems, telling the story, said that the "figure" never spoke, and vanished if a human moved within thirty feet of him. Weems "knew" that the little protector was a ghost.

Giraffes.

CYRIL AND THE BUSTARD

Each year increasing numbers of scatter-gun addicts flock into Kenya, Tanganyika, Congo, Uganda, Angola, French Equatorial Africa, and parts of Rhodesia, to indulge in bird shooting that for variety and excitement cannot be equaled anywhere else on earth.

Game hunters are not noted for reticence in matters of the chase, but are given to vocal marathons in which the game grows faster, larger, and more dangerous with every telling. Wing shooters, who, world over, outnumber all other types of hunters, are a different breed. They're usually secretive as to when, where, and how they get their bags. This is one reason why the general public knows little about the joys of African bird shooting.

It could be that bird hunters can find no adequate words with which to express their emotions as they watch hour-long flights of yellowthroat, pintail, and black-face sand grouse rocketing toward them low under a dawn sky. The water in the big shallow-banked pan lies brownish-gray and still in the morning light. Scattered trees and shrubs that line the water hole's edges have crept out of the night to assume the weird shapes and dusty robes they'll wear during the hours of sunshine. Out of nowhere a flock of hundreds of sand grouse—the size of small pigeons— comes scooting, dodging, and ducking. They fly straight at the gun, fearing neither hunter nor the roar of his piece. Over the pan the birds circle, then, as one, whistle into a plummeting dive. No sooner is the first flight settled than another sweeps in. Then, a third flight, a fourth, a fifth ... On and on they come from all directions, and they keep coming—sometimes for an hour and a half.

The first time a man watches a *quarter-million* sand grouse flashing over his head like feathered bullets he's sometimes so overpowered by the multitude that he doesn't fire a shot. Even if he remains unhypnotized, he gets no birds the first day because he's reluctant to slaughter them at point-blank range. He soon learns, however, to concentrate on trailing and scattered birds. This makes for real shooting, for the little aerial speeders can jink out of the line of fire quicker than a man can press a trigger.

No bag limits are imposed on African birds, and only two or three colonies require a license fee—usually a nominal one. However, scatter-gun enthusiasts are sportsmen, and I've seldom been on a shotgun safari where hunters killed more birds than could be eaten. This permits a big bag, however, for hungry native porters and camp boys can consume a lot of grouse.

Then, there's the kori (greater) bustard—the world's largest game bird. He stands four feet high and weighs from thirty to fifty pounds. He is long-beaked, long-legged, long-bodied, and as difficult to stalk as an impala. Even at close range the average shotgun load does little more than tickle the big fellow. He flies strongly, and few men have got one on the wing with a shotgun. When a man does bring a kori plummeting to earth in a thudding crash, that man will sometimes be so overcome by his feat that he'll live in a daze for hours.

On open veld the kori bustard can see for miles, and stalking him requires that a man take advantage of every bit of cover, and snake through grass on his belly like an overfed monitor lizard. Even expert stalkers may spend days vainly attempting to get within .22 range of the wary devils. I've known hunters to become so exasperated by continued failure that they finally bagged the quarry with a .375—even a .450. Not sporting, but understandable, for no true bird hunter wants to leave Africa without having his picture taken with a greater bustard that he himself has shot. It's quite a picture—usually the hunter and a native, holding up the bird with wings outspread—eight to nine feet.

I don't know how many species of bustards there are in Africa, but I've seen seven. Tastiest are the lesser bustard, the Arabian bustard, and the European bustard. These run heavy to white meat, and when properly cooked are superior to chicken. The kori bustard is excellent eating too, but not when fresh-killed. Hang him for forty-eight hours, however, or let him soak in cold water for twenty-four hours, and you have a tenderized version of American turkey that will leave delightful gustatory memories. When kori hunting, be sure to have along a couple of the largest covered pans that you can get. Cut the kori into pieces, brown in hot fat, season and bake covered until done.

Around his neck the kori bustard wears what looks like a stocking that's been pulled over his head. The "stocking" hangs loose and empty at the base of the throat. In mating season, the kori bends his head back to his tail feathers, inflates the stocking into a ball and thus presents a picture that is certain seduction for any member of the opposite sex who sees it.

One September I took a shotgun party of three to a bush-scattered savannah northwest of Stanleyville. Near six large, yellow-flowered acacia trees we found ruins of what long ago had been a European's home. Whoever the housewife had been, she'd planted a garden, for over the ruins were growing pink and red roses, orange San Carlos vines, and lavender bougainvillaea. Nearby great clumps of pink and red geraniums sprawled beside stands of pink and red flowered bamboo. Off a little way yellow canna lilies ran wild.

Our natives cleared out briers for a campsite, and we pitched our pup tents among the rioting flowers.

My clients were a Scotsman named Robert Thompson, an Englishman named Howard Fowler, and a twenty-one-year-old English boy named Cyril Taylor. Thompson and Fowler were in their thirties, solidly-built 180-pounders. Both had served several years in the ranks, and on leaving the army, had gone into business and done well.

Cyril Taylor was an oddity. He weighed about 145 pounds, was slender, gray-eyed, blond-haired, and painfully diffident. He'd been reared by a mother who'd kept him in dresses for too many years, and had done everything else she could to make a sissy of him. On his twenty-first birthday he'd written Nicobar Jones, saying he'd reached his majority and wished to go on a "strenuous and difficult" hunting trip to "try to overcome an unfortunate behavior pattern imposed upon me by a too-doting mother." The lad had enclosed a check for $6000 as "earnest money."

I was due to meet Thompson and Fowler within five weeks, so we cabled Taylor that if he cared to join a hunting party, he should meet us at Stanleyville on September 1.

The kid was a ridiculous figure when he arrived. He'd evidently been reading books authored by "Colonel Blimps," for he wore a belted tweed shooting jacket, khaki shorts, rolled heather stockings, low, hobnailed shoes, a Lincoln-green sport shirt, and a white solar topee. Thompson and Fowler, dressed as African hunters should be —in tough khaki shirts, long trousers, heavy army boots, and comfortably battered felt hats—didn't spare Taylor's feelings. As they shook hands, Thompson said:

"Could it be you'r-re a bloody duke?"

Fowler said, "Why, Clarence!"

Taylor flushed, swallowed, and mumbled something about "feeling a bit of an ass ever since I put these silly rags on."

I liked the young fellow—I'd guided too many men to be fooled by appearance. The boy had a straight eye, stood up well, and had a chin that promised guts in a tough spot. At first meeting an unobservant person would undoubtedly take him for a pansy, but I knew at once that he was really only a mother-cursed lad who'd never developed male confidence.

Thompson and Fowler almost had fits when Taylor opened his baggage and displayed a Lang over-and-under, single-trigger, beautifully en-graved, 12-bore shotgun, and a Grant .256 side-lock double rifle. The two pieces must have set him back at least $2500. They were marvelous firearms—I got a tremendous boot out of just holding them. Both had been fitted to the kid.

Fowler handled the pieces with obvious envy, and handed them back without comment. But the guns aroused a mean streak in Thompson. He behaved abominably toward Taylor, sneering at the boy, insulting him at every opportunity. I could have stopped it, of course, but it was Taylor's problem—he'd work out his own answer.

The day before we left Stanleyville I took Taylor shopping and got him outfitted with sensible hunting clothes. At the hotel we stopped at the bar for a quick one. Thompson and Fowler were already there. Fowler looked the kid over, grinned, and said:

"Much better."

Thompson recited in singsong:

> "You may br-reak- you may shatter-r the vase if
> you will, But the smell of the pansies will cling
> to it still."

Taylor flushed, licked his lips, said nothing. I had half a mind to bawl him out for taking it so meekly, but held my tongue when I noticed his eyes—cold and calculating. The kid wasn't humiliated —he was icily angry.

Two weeks later we'd made camp beside the ruined house.

Next day Thompson and Fowler, with four natives as retrievers, went after quail. Taylor watched them out of sight, went to his chest, and, to my astonish-ment, took out two pairs of six-ounce boxing gloves.

"Mother doesn't know it," he said, "but two years ago I started boxing lessons with an old army sergeant who'd been a good man in his day. I became pretty good myself."

I massaged a glove with my fingers. "How good?" I asked.

"Well, I outboxed some of England's best amateurs—in the gym, that is. They all told me I've a rather nasty right. I think I have too, but there's something in me that prevents my letting it go. I've never really wanted to lay it on a man, but now I do."

"Thompson?"

Taylor nodded. "I intend to have a go at him."

"Well," I said, "you'd better be good. The guy outweighs you, and you can tell from his walk that he can handle himself." The kid was just too light to go up against Thompson. I thought it over a minute, then said:

"Before you tackle Thompson, let's see how you stack up against me." I reached for a pair of gloves. They'd never been used, so I broke their backs and pushed my hands into them. Taylor tied them, and while he put his pair on, I smelled mine. New leather. A good smell. We had a bit of a job tying his gloves, but managed it, mostly with our teeth. I said:

"Odd that you should have brought gloves along."

"Didn't quite know what to do with them. Didn't want to leave them around the house. Mother —"

"You're a funny guy," I said, and snapped his head back with a playful left. His left struck like an adder, getting my nose three times before I could slide away—and the third left was so hard that I tasted blood on my soft palate. He stood up well, beautifully balanced, his left out, but a bit low, his right cocked in front of his shoulder. I said:

"You're fast, all right, kid."

Taylor smiled, feinted, snapped another left. I moved my head enough to let it slide over my shoulder, and he stiff-armed the side of my neck, throwing me off balance. Then he drove his right into my floating ribs so hard that I grunted. I dropped my left, shifted, and drove it hard into his solar plexus, shifted again, slipped a left, moved in close, and hooked the side of his jaw with a short, hard right. He went to his knees. I stepped back. He looked up at me and again, I saw that coldly calculating stare. I thought: *This guy's no sissy.*

As we sparred around looking for openings, he said:

"You've got a right good right yourself."

"I'm twenty pounds heavier than you," I said. "It makes a difference."

"I think I'm feeling my oats. I've an inclination to hang a right on you. Curious about it," he said.

"Hang it on me if you can, but remember, you're asking for it."

His left flickered. I drew in my chin. His right shoulder tightened. I figured his right was coming, and let my own right go, thinking to beat him to the punch ...

My face was in the grass—my hands under me. I pushed hard against the ground, trying to raise myself. Nothing happened. I pushed again. My rear went up, but my face stayed where it was. I made a tremendous effort and rolled over on my back. The kid knelt beside me, whimpering—his gloved hands pulling at me.

Fresh air suddenly filled my whole body. Strength came back with a rush. I sat up, pushed the kid back, and got to my feet. I fell my jaw, found it wasn't broken, and said:

"It was your right, wasn't it?"

"I let it go."

"I've fought them all," I said, "and that's one of the few times I've ever been out."

"I wore long golden curls until I was six," he said.

"Well," I said, untying my gloves with my teeth, "you're a big boy now—it's time you learned some of the facts of life."

"Such as?"

"Such as you're about as good a man as I've met."

Taylor's face started working and I thought he was going to cry. I said, "Oh hell," threw my gloves on the grass, and walked away.

Four of our boys had gone with Thompson and Fowler. Just before putting the gloves on with Taylor I'd set the remaining eleven boys to gathering wood and dried antelope chips for the fires. Now, as I fooled around camp, paying no attention to the boys as they came and went, I heard Taylor say:

"What's the matter with the silly asses?"

I looked up to see two wood-loaded natives edging around Taylor like dogs that feared they might be kicked. They dumped their loads on the pile and walked past Taylor again, eying him sideways, eyes showing lots of white.

Three other natives came to add wood to the pile. They too eyed Taylor as if he were dangerous, and when the kid said: "What the devil!" the three jumped as if stung. When still a third group sidled past, giving Taylor the frightened eye, I called Jumbo, the head boy.

As Jumbo drew near, he wriggled, held both hands above his head, bowed timidly to Taylor, and said:

"We have seen, *Bwana.* Now we know."

I laughed and said: "It is well that you saw, Jumbo. For *Bwana* Taylor's hands are filled with thunder." Then to Taylor, I said:

"The natives saw you lay me out. From now on, if you play it right, you'll be the big guy around here."

"Certainly a novel role for me," Taylor said. Then he waved a lordly hand at Jumbo and said gravely, "Carry on, my man."

Jumbo beamed like a Burmese idol.

At sundown Thompson and Fowler returned, sweaty, hungry, and fagged. The four retrievers, loaded down with plump European quail and spurred yellow-necks, gave them to the other boys for plucking. Disliking the job, the boys went at it apathetically.

Thompson stood his shotgun against a tree, dropped his haversack to the ground beside it, and called:

"Have the Kaffirs get those feather-rs off faster-r, Jumbo. I'm bloody well famished."

"Yes, *Bwana,*" Jumbo said.

The boys continued plucking in their slow, deliberate way. Thompson watched a few moments, then said in exasperation:

"The blighter-rs ar-re going to take their-r own sweet time. Might as well give or-rder-rs to a bloody stump."

To the boys Taylor said quietly, "Make it fast, men."

You'd have thought every boy had been jabbed with an electric needle. Feathers flew. In minutes seventy fat little carcasses lay naked on their backs.

Thompson stared from the natives to Taylor and back again, lips moving silently as if talking to himself—his neck growing redder and redder.

Taylor winked at me, snapped his fingers at the natives, and said:

"I would eat, friends. On with the cleaning."

Never were birds gutted so quickly.

Thompson still didn't speak. I said:

"Better get washed, Thompson, or you'll be late for supper."

He moved to where a basin of water stood on a small packing case beside his pup tent. As he washed, he splashed, snorted, and mumbled. At supper, as he gnawed hungrily at bird after bird, he eyed Taylor speculatively, but said nothing. Once or twice, when the boys serving us spoke to Taylor with unusual servility, Thompson nearly choked. When he'd tossed the last bare bone into the fire, he wiped his mouth with a handful of grass, swallowed a tin cupful of tea, and said:

"Taylor-r, I obser-rve that you've br-ribed the Kaffir-rs. I have nothing to say about it except that if you've put the boys up to making a fool of me, it will be you I'll give the hiding, not the blacks."

Fowler said, "Let's have no talk of hidings."

"I'll no be made a lout of," Thompson said sullenly. "And a hiding is what our-r little fair-ry would have had fr-rom me long ago if he wer-re somewhat mor-re of a man."

Taylor took a deep breath and got to his feet, looking at me questioningly. I shook my head. The kid sighed and sat down again. I said:

"Taylor didn't bribe the natives, Thompson. It's just that they have wholehearted respect for him."

Thompson turned to Fowler and said angrily:

"So help me God, if this goes on I'm going to tur-rn in my bloody str-ripes."

Later, when making the rounds to see that camp was shipshape for the night, I noticed a light in Taylor's pup tent and peeked in. He was propped on one elbow, reading. Five or six books were stacked as a stand for his candle. I said:

"Slip something on and come out. I want to talk to you."

He came out on hands and knees, dragging a robe behind him. He put it on and we walked out of earshot of the other tents.

"About Thompson," I began.

"What about him?"

"He intends to beat you up, comes the opportunity."

"So I assume."

"Look, Taylor," I said, "it's all right to go he-man, but Thompson outweighs you at least thirty-five pounds. That guy's no setup. He was bayonet champ of his army outfit. I admit you're good with the gloves, but with Thompson it'd be bare hands."

"Of course."

"There is such a thing as good sense," I said testily.

"I fancy I'm not too smart," he said, "but thanks, anyway."

There was no use arguing—his mind was made up. "Well," I said, "if you must—you must. But pick your own time, at least."

"I will. Thanks," he said, and went back to his books.

The next day Thompson, Fowler, Taylor, the fifteen boys, and I chased guinea fowl—ordinary black-and-white, bluish-headed, wattle-dangling guinea fowl. Chased is the word. The taunting-voiced birds were everywhere, scuttling about on the open veld and huddling in bunches in the brush.

Ten of the boys moved forward in a line, pushing guinea fowl ahead of them. Thompson was at one end of the line, Fowler at the other, Taylor and I in the center. Behind us came four rifle bearers, for, when bird hunting in Africa, anything may pop up—from lion to nasty-tempered rhino. Jumbo, whose dignity wouldn't permit him to hunt birds, brought up the rear.

The line advanced slowly at first, then faster, until the guineas took fright and streaked for cover—hundreds of them. But guinea fowl don't take wing until really hard pressed, so we ran them. The sun was hot and the breeze had died. As we panted after the scurrying birds, dust settled on our sweat-wet faces, got up our nostrils and into our mouths. At the edge of the brush the guineas lifted into the air with noise like a cyclone. Guns boomed. Feathers flew. Birds collapsed in mid-flight and bounced as they hit ground. Boys laughed and shouted. We fired, loaded, fired, loaded, and fired again.

Twelve birds bagged out of all those hundreds. A hungry man needs at least one whole bird. Fifteen boys, four whites. Nine more birds required.

We walked more than two miles before we came on a flock that hadn't been frightened off by the guns. Again the long line, the walk-up, the chase, exploding shells, and falling birds.

Five miles back to camp, with a quick bathe in a small stream en route. A pot of tea while the boys warmed up quail left from last night's supper. Gun cleaning. An hour of relaxing under the trees, and back out on the veld again—this time to track down and go through an almost identical campaign with blue-breasted vulturine guinea fowl—the size of small turkeys.

These birds stuck more closely to the brush, and when they rose, it was with thundering wings that carried them every which way.

We bagged fifteen—enough for a second day's eating, so called it off and spent a couple of hours alternately dunking in the little stream, and sitting naked in the sun.

As I sat on warm sand, puffing my pipe, shooing flies off my bare shanks and watching the others disport in the water, it occurred to me that although Taylor had carried his Lang over-and-under all day, he hadn't fired a shot. I wondered why. At the first opportunity I asked him.

"Well," he said, "I've never shot a gun—not even at the Grant & Lang factory. I just haven't been able to bring myself to the point of taking my very first shot in front of Thompson."

"For Pete's sake, why?"

"I can't explain. I cringe at the thought of him laughing at me. Silly, I know, but there it is."

"And you're the guy who wants to go round-and-round with him!"

"That's different. Nobody's going to be laughing then. But to shoot at a bird and miss ..."

"You give me a pain in the fanny," I said. "Act your age.

"But ..."

I walked away.

"Right-o," he called after me. "Next time out."

While we ate breakfast next morning, Jumbo signaled to be quiet, and motioned us to follow him into the acacia trees. He walked as if stalking, and we imitated him. Beside the last tree he knelt and pointed to a lone kori bustard standing motionless about 150 feet away.

The great bird stood broadside to us, his skimpy, dark topknot hanging down behind his "ears," long, bare legs sticking out below his heavily feathered body. He gave the same impression as a man wearing a topcoat, but no pants.

I waited while Thompson, Fowler, and Taylor went back for their guns. They returned as quietly as Indians, guns loaded. The bustard, except for an occasional slight fluffing of feathers, hadn't moved. I whispered:

"Fifty yards. Use choke. One shot each, after he takes wing. Thompson first, then Fowler, then Taylor."

They spread out—Thompson to the left, Fowler in the center, Taylor to the right. The bustard seemed to sense danger, for he fluttered his wings a little and turned his head nervously. I threw a stone at him.

He lumbered into the air, headed toward us. The heel of Thompson's gun caught on his right shirt pocket, throwing him off. He made a clean miss. The kori changed direction, increased his wing beat, and really scudded across our front. Fowler fired and got two tail feathers. Taylor pointed his Lang, shut both eyes, and pulled the trigger. The bustard, headless, hit the ground in a crumpled heap.

The kid trembled as he turned the dead bird on its belly and spread the enormous wings. I held my steel tape to them. Nine feet, two inches!

"Well bowled, Taylor," Fowler said.

Thompson grunted.

Taylor was embarrassed, and mumbled something about "feeling like an ass." I intended saying nothing to him about the shot being a fluke, but that evening, as he lay reading in front of his tent, I noticed his book was *Pickwick Papers.* Reminded of Tracy Tupman, I couldn't resist the opportunity to rib the kid. I said:

"Lend me your book a minute, Taylor."

I flipped the pages, found Dickens' account of the shooting party at Wardle's, and read aloud:

> *"Tupman," said the old gentleman, "you singled out that particular bird?"*
>
> *"No..." said Mr. Tupman— "no."*
>
> *"You did," said Wardle. "I saw you do it—I observed you pick him out—I noticed you as you raised your piece to take aim; and I will say this, that the best shot in existence could not have done it more beautifully. You are an older hand at this, than I thought you, Tupman; you have been out before."*

Taylor grinned sheepishly and said: "I thought of Tupman when I opened my eyes and saw that bustard thud to the grass. How am I to go shooting with these chaps again, now that they think I'm such a whiz?"

"Maybe if you keep your eyes shut you'll do all right," I said impatiently. "What do you care what they think?"

He flushed.

"Truth is," I said, "nobody gives a damn if you can shoot or not. I'm beginning to figure you out, Taylor. I think you've been acting like a sissy all these years only to attract attention to yourself. Snap out of it, kid. You're important as hell to your mother, but you don't mean much to anyone else—not yet, anyway. Tomorrow we're going after button quail with .22's. First thing in the morning you and I are going out to do a little practice plinking. In half an hour you'll be good enough to pot those little buttons at fifty yards. And then, you're going out on your own with Thompson and Fowler—I'm not going along."

"Decent of you," Taylor said huffily.

"Go ahead and stamp your foot, now," I said.

Taylor laughed aloud and pushed his left playfully against my still-sore nose. I shifted left, jolted his stomach with a right, stuck the palm of my hand on his face and pushed him on his fanny. He looked up, grinning. He was learning.

After breakfast next morning I handed Taylor my .22, took an empty jam tin, and we walked out behind the canna lilies. I tossed the can about fifty feet, showed the kid how to hold the gun, line the sights, and *squeeze* the trigger. He hit the tin his first try. He was a natural. I moved the tin about thirty feet further out. He hit it five shots out of seven. I said:

"Button quail rise and flutter low for about 150 feet. They're about the size of the jam tin, and look like big fat bumblebees. Idea is to hit them on the fly. Unless you're a whiz with a .22, you don't drive birds, you 'walk them up.' That is, you walk toward a covey until it takes flight. Usually the birds fly straight away from you. This gives you easy 'going away' shots. Pick a bird in level flight and let him have it in the behind. You're letting your shots off fine now, while plinking at the tin, but chances are you'll start jerking the trigger when your target's on the wing. Don't do it. *Squeeze.* Remember, birds coming straight in, or birds going straight away. You'll be surprised at the way your .22 will bring 'em down."

"Supposing the others want to *drive* the buttons?"

"They won't—not with .22's. In driving, the guns stand behind low cover. Beaters scare the birds toward you. When the birds are close on the other side of your cover—low shrubs, hedge, or even a solid fence—the beaters chase them up. The birds whir over the cover, spot you, and instantly scatter in all directions—up, down, right, left. Pick a bird, lead it, dust it with six-shot; pick a second bird, and a third. If you get three out of a flurry, you've done about all that can be expected.

"In a few days we're going to drive spur fowl. In my opinion, they're the sportiest bird in Africa, and there're at least twenty-seven varieties of them. In Kenya, they're known as 'yellow-necks'; in this part of the Congo, as 'red-necks'; most everywhere else, as 'bare-necks.' I've shot them in Rhodesia, Angola, Kenya, and Tanganyika. I've shot them high in mountains, and in low dust country. The books call them 'francolins,' but don't let that worry you—they're just quail."

"You know," Taylor said, "Jones's cable, saying I could join a hunting party, didn't mention birds. I thought we'd be going after lions, and whatnot."

"Bird hunting's more fun."

"The devil!"

"Well, it is in Africa, anyway. There are so many birds and so many ways of getting them that no matter how many times you go after them, something new and exciting happens."

"Like what?"

"Like seeing a hundred thousand flamingos in a single flock. They're red and white, but, from a distance, look pink. In flight—a great pink cloud. Standing in water—a mile-square pink carpet. Or, the spectacle of a thousand sacred ibis on an Ethiopian river— white, black-headed with black-tipped wing feathers. When taking off and landing, the sacred ibis' wings make marvelous, curving patterns. Or, the sight of flocks of snow-white, beautiful, dumb, pestiferous egrets of West Africa—once eagerly sought for their plumes, but now only pains in the neck. Egrets can soil more hats in an hour than San Francisco pigeons can soil in a day. If they stayed in water where they belong, they'd be enchanting, but they've got a yen to be land birds, and make a mess of it. They can't judge distance, and when they try to land on a fence, for instance, they miss the top rail with their funny feet and crash squawking to the ground. I've seen them try to land on the ridge of a roof, miss, and burn their bottoms sliding down the slope. Then, there's—"

"Hold up a minute. Can you eat flamingos, ibis, and egrets?"

"Properly cooked, you'll never eat better fowl than ibis. Flamingos taste a bit fishy if eaten as is, but a young one, packed with stuffing made of *fried* onions, *baked* chestnuts, chopped parsley, rosemary leaves, *fresh* bread, lemon juice, and grated lemon rind; then, while roasting, basted frequently with orange juice! It's a dish superior to any goose ever cooked."

"I'm hungry," Taylor said.

"Keep an edge on your appetite until I serve breasts of those spur fowl I mentioned," I said. "Rubbed well with canned butter, baked for twenty minutes, basted four times with rich antelope stock, and served with sugared sweet potatoes—you'll think you're eating poetry."

"But sporting birds ..."

"All birds are sporting birds if you make shooting them a sporting affair. Myriads of ducks that nest in the north fly to Africa between seasons—teal, widgeons, mallards, spoonbills, sheldrakes, Egyptians, African geese—gray, knob-billed, pink-foot, spur-winged, to mention a few—are fast fliers and provide extraordinary shooting. To be appetizing, geese should be cooked like flamingos.

"Small waders are usually wary rascals. Among plovers, I've had the best sport with the gray, golden, and spurred. The spurred plover's the one that picks crocodiles' teeth. There are black-and-white crows, ravens—"

"Crows!"

Kafue Lechwe—confrontation.

"Crows are very sporting birds with a small-calibered rifle—and excellent eating, too, if hung, or soaked a day or two in cold water. I've made many a hearty meal of crow. Then, there are doves, pigeons of all colors from white to green, ardetas, plotuses, starlings, linongolos, and scores of others—all in prodigious numbers—on plains and uplands, along marshes, rivers, lakes, pans, and pools. They offer scatter-gun addicts the kind of sport they look forward to when they get to heaven."

Taylor sighed. "You know," he said, "if I'd known we were going to hunt birds, I'd have brought my dog."

"Can't hunt with dogs in Africa. Snakes bite them. Leopards and baboons kill them. Buffaloes crush them. Antelope gore them. Tsetse flies destroy them. Ticks poison them. Crocodiles swallow them."

"I've been half expecting to see lions or something out on this trip. I've read—"

"You'll see them, but not right here. Biggest game in this particular area are duikerbok and hares. But ten miles out, you'll see larger antelope, buffalo, and, occasionally, elephant. When we go after spur fowl, you may see all three."

It was after sundown when Thompson, Fowler, and Taylor dragged into camp with seventy-two button quail. Taylor had bagged fourteen, which was good for a man first time out. From the strained manners of Thompson and Taylor I judged things hadn't been too pleasant, but nothing was said about it, so I asked no questions.

Next morning, however, the trouble came into the open when Thompson, always crabby early in the day, called Taylor a bloody nymph.

Taylor walked over to where Thompson sat at the other side of the fire, took the Scot's nose between his first two fingers, and twisted it. Thompson roared like a baboon, jerked free, got to his feet, and swung a dynamite-packed roundhouse right at Taylor's head. The kid pulled his chin in and the blow whistled past harmlessly. The next instant Thompson was flat on his prat from a lightning left hook to the jaw. I grabbed Taylor, pushed him back of me, and said:

"Okay. Bare fists, two-minute rounds. Fowler, you second Thompson. I'll handle Taylor."

Thompson said, "I'll kill the bastar-rd."

Taylor grinned.

No grass grew under the acacia trees, and the natives quickly swept away fallen twigs. Thompson and Taylor stripped to their waists and tightened their belts. Thompson was square-shouldered, hairy, heavy-muscled, and straight-backed. Taylor had long, smooth muscles and sloping shoulders. The small of his back was hollow. Thompson was angry and restless. Taylor stood quiet except for a twitching calf muscle.

Fowler, who'd evidently read *Tom Brown's School Days,* knelt and made a knee for Thompson. He said, "Now, lads, shake hands."

"To hell with that," Thompson said. "Get up off your-r bloody knee," and swung a right at Taylor that, had it landed, would have ended the fight right then. Taylor ducked it, and drove a terrific hook to the Scot's floating ribs. Thompson hit the ground doubled up, gasping.

I counted: "One—two—three—four —"

Thompson got to his feet, stared at Taylor with surprise, stuck out his left, dropped his chin into his shoulder, and moved in, jabbing. Taylor backed on his toes, stopped flatfooted, and tempted Thompson with outthrust chin. Thompson's left shot out like a piston. Taylor moved his chin out of the way, and as Thompson's left slid past his ear, crossed it with a solid right to Thompson's cheek. Thompson grunted, and threw a volley of lefts and rights. Taylor back-pedaled smoothly, shooting an occasional left jab.

I glanced at my wrist watch, waited four or five seconds, and said: "Time."

No one paid attention. I said:

"Hey, two minutes!"

Thompson's right cracked high on the side of Taylor's head. The kid went down. Thompson stood over him. Fowler pulled him away. Taylor got to his knees, shook his head, took a deep breath, stood up. Thompson rushed. The kid stopped him with a straight left, then left-jabbed the big guy so fast that Thompson couldn't get off his heels. Taylor's right threatened to shoot, but Thompson's shoulder protected his chin. Taylor dropped his left toward the belly, and Thompson swung—a left, this time. It landed high. Again Taylor went down, and again Fowler pulled Thompson away. I began a count, but at *three* Taylor was up. I said:

"Rules, damn it!"

I might as well have been talking to myself. They went at it again.

Thompson's left landed squarely on Taylor's nose. Blood spurted. Taylor tried to rub it away, and rubbed it into his eyes instead. Half blinded, he slipped, ducked, parried, and danced away from Thompson's swinging fists. But again a solid shot landed— this time on a cheekbone. For the third time Taylor hit the dirt. He was up in a flash, but already his right eye had puffed almost shut.

Thompson immediately laid another right on the same spot, followed it with a left to the belly, and when the kid lowered his guard, Thompson clipped him neatly on the side of the chin. Taylor fell on his face. Thompson drew back, looking relieved. The kid got up, groggy. I said, "That's enough," and clutched his arm.

He shook me off, said, "Stop interfering, please," then wove in close to Thompson, feinted with his left, slipped Thompson's counterleft, pivoted on his toe, and threw all the power in his body into a right to Thompson's short ribs. Thompson was hurt. He gasped, tried to clinch, took an uppercut, stumbled back on his heels—wide open. Taylor drove a hard right under Thompson's heart, and when the big fellow wilted, banged left and right to his jaw. Thompson folded. I didn't bother to count.

Thompson got to his feet wobbly and foggy, held out a hand to Taylor, who suddenly sat on the ground.

"Gr-reat God!" Thompson said, and began rubbing first one, then the other of Taylor's wrists. Taylor said:

"I'm all right."

"It's your-r cir-rculation," Thompson said. "A good r-rubbing will br-ring you r-round."

Taylor laughed and got to his feet without help. "It isn't my circulation, Thompson," he said. "It's relief. From the first punch, I was in a funk."

"Tosh," Thompson said. But from that moment, the Scotsman was Taylor's loyal, admiring friend.

Both still wore bruises the following Wednesday, when an expensively outfitted safari party showed up. First came an old hunter friend of mine, Lennie Gibson. Behind him in single file, boxes and bundles on their heads, came seventy-nine porters. Behind the porters two station-wagonlike cars bumped and jerked across the virgin veld. These were followed by seven 1 ½-ton Ford trucks with specially built, prairie-schoonerlike bodies. Slouching in saddles of hammerhead horses, three other old meat-hunter friends of mine followed the trucks— Jan Cronje, Garnet Smith and Koos Erasmus. At the end of the procession were a camp kitchen and a pantry.

Beyond the acacias Gibson gave a command in Swahili, and the porters formed a hollow square. Another command, and each carrier placed his burden on the ground at his feet. Gibson waved his arm, and the porters moved off about fifty yards and squatted on their haunches. I said:

"What the hell!"

Gibson grinned and said, "I got 'em trained, lad."

The first car pulled up and a graying, heavy-set man stepped to the ground and stood staring at the flower-covered ruins. Then he walked toward them, out of earshot. Gibson said:

"Ostrowski."

"Ostrowski?"

"American moneybags." Gibson nodded toward the ruins. "He owns this place. His grandfather's buried here. Murdered, or something."

Ostrowski walked back, and we shook hands. His eyes were golden-yellow, nose large and solid, handshake firm and confident. He said:

"We'll try to keep out of your way."

"We can move on."

"No. We'll be here only a couple of days." He motioned to his car. An old man, scraggly-bearded, with only one lone, yellow front tooth, stepped out. He was followed by a gangster-type husky. To the old man Ostrowski said:

"All right, Scallon, show us the grave."

Scallon looked about as if dazed. The husky lad, obviously a guard, poked Scallon in the back with a finger. "You heard," he said.

Scallon said vaguely, "It's been a long time." He walked to the ruins, cleared away vines where front steps of the house had been, and stared around. He said:

"Those trees are big now. They were little then," and moved hesitatingly into the growth of wild canna lilies. For a while he kicked about, then stooped and lifted a flat, red rock.

"This is it," he said. "Dig here."

The guard walked Scallon back to the car, opened a door, shoved him inside, and locked the doors. Gibson went to the still-squatting porters and returned with two of them. From one of the trucks Gibson got two shovels and a pick. The two natives began digging.

Cronje, Erasmus, and Smith set porters to unloading supplies and putting up tents. Within half an hour the Ostrowski camp was shipshape and comfortable. The camp kitchen's stovepipe smoked merrily, and canned goods of all descriptions sat on long tables. A white-capped and -aproned chef with long black mustachios was as busy as a bee on a marigold. His name was Jean-Baptiste Flournoy, and he'd once been a chef on an Atlantic liner.

From the trucks natives had unloaded gasoline, kerosene, a five-kilowatt electric plant, two small electric refrigerators, bags of corn meal, tables, chairs, bathtubs, water sterilizers and coolers, a complete folding darkroom, large metal bins of dehydrated fruits and vegetables—everything, in fact, necessary for plushy living.

Fifty or so porters went out after wood for fires. Cronje, Smith, and native hunters took off to look for meat. Then, after everything was in place, a black-haired, blue-eyed girl of about twenty stepped from the second station wagon.

Taylor, Fowler, Thompson, Erasmus, Gibson, and I were chewing the fat about nothing in particular. The girl, in tailored riding breeches and an open-necked khaki shirt, nodded solemnly to us as she walked past. Then she noticed Taylor, and flashed him a smile. Taylor took off his hat, dropped it, picked it up, and fingered his bruised eye. The girl laughed and walked to where her father was watching the natives dig. Gibson said:

"Pamela Ostrowski. Nice girl."

"Struth!" Taylor said, and followed her.

"It's no snap, feeding this mob of natives," Gibson said. "With the drivers and kitchen boys, we've 105 of them. Hungriest Kaffirs I ever saw. Average three pounds of meat each, every day. Ostrowski doesn't shoot animals. Great hand on birds, though. Soon as he locates his grandfather's bones we're going to stage a series of bird drives. If you'd like—"

Gibson stopped as Ostrowski shouted. I followed him to the millionaire's side. The natives had uncovered some bones. Gibson motioned the Kaffirs out of the grave and got in himself. One by one, he lifted out the skeletons of five cats, patches of fur holding their bones together. He next uncovered a human skeleton that had fallen apart. He piled its bones, and a toothless skull, on a blanket. I dropped down into the hole and helped Gibson hoist the macabre bundle to the grave's edge. Ostrowski picked up the skull, examined it, and put it back on the blanket. He said:

"My grandfather was eighty years old. He was murdered because of the cats."

Gibson turned each cat over with a foot. One had been black, one yellow, three gray. Suddenly I thought of Pamela. This was no sight for her. I needn't have worried—she and Taylor were fifty feet away, standing face to face, holding hands. I said to Ostrowski:

"Murdered?"

"Not a finger was laid on the old man," Ostrowski said, "but he was murdered just as surely as if he'd been shot. We'll have Scallon repeat the story later. Scallon helped with the killing. That was forty-five years ago, when Scallon was nineteen."

That night Ostrowski invited Gibson and me to his tent to sit in on his questioning of Scallon. Before the old fellow arrived, Ostrowski said:

"I was a poor man until three years ago, when oil was found on my farm. Scallon, who worked here as gardener for my grandfather, came to my office in New York one day and told me he could prove that Jan Ostrowski, my grandfather, had been murdered. He wanted money for the information, and I bought it.

"I decided to come here and check Scallon's fantastic tale. He refused to accompany me, so I brought him along under guard. He'd told me about burying cats with my grandfather—so that part of his story's been proved.

"Grandfather and his young wife, Hilda, fled Poland because of political antagonism. They settled in Belgium. became prosperous, migrated to the Congo, built this home, and settled down to a peaceful life. Grandmother raised flowers. Grandfather raised cats."

The guard brought Scallon into the tent, pushed him into a folding chair directly under the bare electric bulb that hung at the end of a drop cord. Ostrowski, Gibson, and I sat opposite so we could watch his face as he talked. The guard lay down on a camp cot. Scallon said:

"I won't say another word until I know what you're going to do with me."

"Tell the truth—all of it," Ostrowski said, "and I'll take you to Stanleyville, give you some money, and turn you loose."

The old man talked, his lone tooth sort of jiggling against the darkness of his mouth.

"My father and I," Scallon said, "were hired through an employment agency. Father was to manage the house and do the cooking. I was to help Mrs. Ostrowski in the garden. Everything might have worked out all right if my father hadn't hated cats. He even liked to torture them.

"One day Mr. Ostrowski caught my father poking a sharp stick in one of his cats through the bars of its cage. Mr. Ostrowski hit my father over the head with his walking stick and ordered him to never go near the cats again.

"That night my father told me he was going to kill Mr. Ostrowski. He said he'd figure out a way to do it without leaving any clues.

"A long time passed, but my father didn't forget that blow on his head. Every so often he'd tell me he was still trying to work out a foolproof murder scheme.

"Mr. Ostrowski was old—more than eighty, I guess. He was very fat, and every morning he'd sit sunning himself on a bench at the east side of the house, and there was always a cat in his lap. Even when he was asleep, and snoring a little, he'd be patting the cat. If he'd stop patting, the cat would dig its claws into the old man's leg. Mr. Ostrowski wouldn't open his eyes, but he'd puff out his lips and start patting again.

"Then, Mrs. Ostrowski died, one day, and Mr. Ostrowski collapsed. I went for the doctor. He examined Mr. Ostrowski and said he had a bad heart and might pop off any minute. He told my father not to let the old man have any kind of a shock. 'Humor him,' the doctor said. 'Don't let him get worried or angry.'

"After the doctor had gone, my father told me that he'd kill the cats, and that the shock would probably kill Mr. Ostrowski. But my father liked to torture people, too, so he didn't kill the cats right away. He'd go to Mr. Ostrowski and tell him how good cat-meat pies were, and stories about people who ate rabbit stews that were really cat stews.

"Old Mr. Ostrowski would scream at my father and bang the floor with his stick.

"My father would laugh.

"The older Mr. Ostrowski got, the more he lived with his cats. One big yellow cat slept with him. A black one slept on a chair beside his bed. The others were kept in cages at night because of prowling animals, but they ran loose during the day. Mostly, they hung around old Mr. Ostrowski's feet, rubbing against his legs and mewling up at him. I forgot to say that Mr. Ostrowski raised only male cats. He wouldn't have females on the place, so whenever my father went to town, he'd bring home a female cat and turn it loose behind the house. Sometimes the male cats got in awful fights over a female, and old Mr. Ostrowski would go almost crazy.

"One day Mr. Ostrowski had a bad heart attack. My father sent a native to Stanleyville for the doctor. Mr. Ostrowski's lips were blue and his flesh was cold. We were sure he was going to die, but just in case he didn't, my father decided to help death along. He had me put all the cats in a big basket and carry them out behind the wagons.

"Mr. Ostrowski had some rabbits hanging in the desert cooler. He liked them hung until they were high. When the doctor came, and said Mr. Ostrowski would live, my father decided to have rabbit stew for supper. All the time he was cooking it, he kept laughing and talking to himself.

"When Mr. Ostrowski came to, the first thing he said was: 'My cats. Where's my cats?'

"The doctor came out of the bedroom and told my father to bring the cats in the house. My father answered that he didn't know where the cats were. When the doctor told that to Mr. Ostrowski, the old man began screaming and fighting. The doctor yelled for my father, and they got Mr. Ostrowski calmed down. Then Mr. Ostrowski begged my father to bring him his cats. My father stood there grinning. The doctor said:

" 'Answer, damn it!'

"My father said, 'Well, I thought he'd be dead by now, so...' "

"Mr. Ostrowski began to shake. Tears squeezed out of his eyes and rolled down the wrinkles in his face. He said:

" 'Please, Mr. Scallon, *please!*'

" 'I can't bring them right now,' my father said. 'I've got to watch my stew. I'll bring the cats in later.'

"Mr. Ostrowski sat up in bed, whimpering like a puppy. He held out both hands to my father. My father said:

" 'Rabbit stew burns too easy.'

"Mr. Ostrowski began to choke. His eyes stuck out. Then he fell back. The doctor said:

" 'Where the hell are his cats?'

" 'In their cages,' my father said.

"The doctor bent over Mr. Ostrowski. Pretty soon he straightened up. 'He's dead,' he said.

"A little later while the three of us were eating the rabbit stew the doctor said:

" 'You know, Scallon, back there in the bedroom I thought for a minute that you'd cooked Mr. Ostrowski's cats for supper.'

" 'Mr. Ostrowski thought so too,' my father said."

Miki and Peg Carter, African photographers, with buffalo.

RAW MEAT IN ETHIOPIA

In the summer of 1951 I read a cable dispatch in a New York newspaper that told of the killing of a Reverend Sehemo, a Zulu, during a race riot near Durban, Natal. I believe I am now the only living person who knows that "Sehemo" was not that man's true name, and that he was not a Zulu, but an Abyssinian, named Malikot—a peasant whom Nicobar Jones and I rescued when he was about to be beaten to death by order of his drunken prince, Ras Louis.

With bare fists Jones and I had put twenty whip-wielding Ethiopians to flight, and had hustled Malikot across the Ethiopia-Sudan border. He finally made his way to a Zulu kraal north of Durban, became a member of the tribe, adopted Christianity, and became a wandering missionary. He had no finances; had no backing of any white church. He concentrated his activities in Northern Rhodesia; was persecuted, stoned, beaten with sticks, but persevered, and became the most influential preacher in a vast territory.

I have heard many sensational revivalists, including Billy Sunday and Billy Graham. I've listened to sermons of some of the most publicized ministers of Europe and America, but I've never yet heard one who inspired congregations as Sehemo could.

Our rescue of Malikot took place in 1919, when Lej Yasu, deposed emperor of Ethiopia, was hiding from the wrath of Dajazmach Tafari (now Haile Selassie, King of Kings, Lion of Judah), who'd been appointed regent.

Jones and I had been lured to Gallaland by Ras Kassa, twin brother of Ras Louis, by promise of an order for six hundred lion manes, supposedly to be used as headdresses by officers of an army that the twin brothers were attempting to raise to fight Ras Tafari. Six hundred lion manes at $5.00 each meant $3000—not enough to more than cover expenses of the long trip from Jones's trading post near N'Djolé in French Gaboon. But we were to have been paid in Maria Theresa dollars. We would have traded those for salt, traded the salt for cartridges, the cartridges for more Maria Theresa dollars. The Maria Theresa dollars would have been exchanged for English pounds, and the pounds for American dollars. Thus the original $3000 would have increased to about $48,000.

Rases Louis and Kassa were rascals. They'd not actually wanted lion manes at all, but modern rifles and ammunition, which they'd hoped to persuade us to smuggle in for them. However, we didn't learn this until some time after we'd arrived at their village near Lfeka.

It was April, and the Little Rains had ended. The gentle green slopes of hills surrounding the brothers' village were bestrewed with white blossoms. Upon our arrival Ras Kassa served us curdled milk, great gobs of rancid butter, and a raw, bleeding steak—bleeding because it had just been cut from a flank of a live cow. Two peasants clad in chammas like white nightgowns had herded the skinny cow to where we sat outside the brothers' mud, straw, and galvanized-iron house. One had held the animal's head. The other had drawn a knife, made a large wedge-shaped cut through the hide on the cow's right flank, peeled back the skin, sliced out a triangular steak, then laid the skin back over the wound, plastered the cut with mud, and motioned his fellow to turn the cow loose. The cow had limped away shaking her head.

Jones and I were seated at a rough wooden table. Kassa himself slapped the steak on the boards between us. I said:

"Cook it a bit."

Kassa didn't understand, and looked questioningly at Jones. In pidgin Amharic, Jones said to Kassa:

"He thanked you for a wonderful piece of really fresh meat."

"Nothing is too good for friends of Lej Yasu," said Ras Kassa, then drew a finger across his throat and scowling darkly, added, "And for his enemies. z-z-z-it!"

"Just so," Jones agreed. Jones picked up the steak, stuck a corner of it in his mouth, clamped down his teeth, and with his skinning knife hacked off a hunk close to his lips, then handed the steak to me. I followed Jones's example, chewed, tried to swallow, choked, grabbed up the gourd of curdled milk, swallowed again, and the meat slid down with the milk. Jones said to me:

"Burp."

"What?"

"Burp good and loud. Ya' gotta be polite—show you liked it."

I burped.

We were still eating when Ras Louis entered the yard, said something to Kassa, nodded to us, picked up the remaining piece of steak, and stuffed it into his mouth. He pulled a decanterlike bottle from under his chamma, and took prodigious gulps of evil-smelling liquor. Ras Louis was the image of his brother except that his skin was almost black, while Kassa's was sort of gray-brown. Both men were pig-fat, with sunken eyes and unhealthy-looking jowls; their hair, greasy with butter, stood out around their heads like frightened mops.

When Louis had drunk, he set the bottle on the table and laid beside it a rhino-hide whip sticky with blood. Kassa evidently asked about the whip, for Louis jabbered a reply. Jones interpreted briefly:

"Louis has just given a terrible beating to a peasant named Malikot."

Outside, four donkeys, each attended by two gun-bearing, white-chamma-clad peasants, stood with hanging heads. Kassa motioned us to mount. We moved off with Louis in the lead, Jones and I next, Kassa at the rear. Our attendants strode beside us. Kassa was followed by a mob of about forty servants, each carrying an old Lebel rifle. Incidentally none of the rifles would shoot, and the ammunition was of many calibers. The guns were for show; ammunition was money.

With feet nearly trailing on the ground we rode through a field of *teff* (millet), up a long slope covered with newly planted coffee bushes, into a hilltop forest. Just over the brow we turned off among tall trees, and after an hour or so entered a small meadow in which cattle were grazing. At the far edge of the clearing fourteen of the wildest-looking brown men I'd ever seen stepped into view. Some were tall and thin, some short and fat. All wore white chammas with colored bands around the skirts. Hair and beards of most were plastered with butter.

All were drunk.

The fourteen rushed upon us holding out bottles of *tej,* a ginlike drink that smelled like bad potato whiskey. There were dimpled bottles, square-faced gin bottles, stone ginger-beer bottles, brown glass bottles with lugs, and ordinary whiskey bottles. I took the bottle closest to my nose, tipped it, pushed my tongue against the mouth, and pretended to drink. Jones swallowed his shot, and coughed.

Other bottles were shoved at us with cries of "Yasu! Yasu!" All were shouting and cursing. One long, lean individual slit the throat of a nearby cow. Jones said:

"Trouble, boy. Hold hard."

The mob pushed and pulled us into the trees, where rough planks were lying on wooden horses to make a twenty-foot table. Wooden benches were at the sides, a stool at each end. Jones was given one stool; I the other. Ras Kassa and seven drunks seated themselves at one side of the table; Ras Louis and seven other drunks occupied the opposite bench. At Jones's end of the table was a forty-gallon hogshead of *tej.* Bottles were passed to him, which he filled by immersion in the liquor, then passed back.

A servant placed a bottle before Jones, another before me. Our hosts shouted, slobbered, and burped.

The just-killed cow, skinned and gutted, legs tied over a pole, was carried to the table by two husky peasants. Instantly every man pulled out a knife and held it in readiness. The carcass bearers stopped behind each man just long enough for him to slash off a big hunk of raw meat. The carcass was still warm, and the combined smell of fresh blood and *tej* was nauseating. I hesitated about cutting myself a slice, but Jones's eyes warned me, so I helped myself to a hunk off a foreleg.

Ethiopian teeth were sunk in bloody flesh. Long, sharp knives flashed, and "bites" were severed from hunks so close to noses that I marveled no nose was detipped. Meat was swallowed in noisy gulps. Sometimes an eater choked, and either pulled the meat from his throat with his fingers, or pushed it down. Bottles were emptied, refilled, emptied again.

The cow's carcass was soon a ghastly, pink-ribbed thing with blobs of red meat leeching to it like abnormal growths. Darkness fell, and a fire was lighted so close to the table that its heat melted the rancid butter plastered on the hair of the crapulous crew.

Ras Louis gorged and drank, his skin growing more distended by the minute. Finally with a groan he fell backward off the bench and lay snoring, one hand still clasping his long knife, the other clutching a dollop of partially devoured raw kidney.

One by one others passed out until only Jones, Ras Kassa, and I were left. Kassa was drunk, but not sodden. Jones and I had only pretended to drink. Kassa said:

"We intend to put Yasu back on the throne. We need rifles and ammunition. We have gold. You will get the rifles for us."

"We came to arrange for the sale of lion manes," Jones said.

Kassa looked bewildered.

"Lion manes," Jones said. "You sent for us —"

Kassa laughed. "Lion manes means rifles," he said. "We do not say rifles because our enemies must not know."

Jones was angry, but said pleasantly enough:

"It can be arranged. Where is your gold?"

"At the house of myself and my brother."

"First," Jones said, "I must see the gold."

"You have been greatly honored," Kassa said, and pointed to the sprawled drunkards. "These princes are the great of Gallaland."

"Fine men," Jones said. "They drink well."

"None can drink more," Kassa said. He wobbled, sat down on the stool I'd vacated, lay his head on the blood-smeared table, and slept. Jones said to me:

"We'll pretend to go along with the smuggling deal, but I'll feel a lot better when we're over the border into the Sudan."

Back at the brothers' village the next afternoon, Louis, Kassa, Jones, and I stood under a eucalyptus tree that had been imported from Addis Ababa. That tree was the pride of the brothers' hearts. It was large, and Kassa had just explained that in most of Ethiopia the death penalty was inflicted on anyone who cut down a eucalyptus. "We prune it carefully," he said, "because they fall when they get top-heavy." He pointed up into the branches where a brown-skinned, chammaless peasant sawed on a limb. "That is Malikot," he said, "whose responsibility is the pruning of this tree."

Malikot! The bloody whip! The fellow who'd been beaten by Ras Louis!

Kassa and I stood directly below Malikot, and I took a closer look at him as he stood on a limb about twenty feet above the ground. He seemed sick as he used a rusted handsaw on a branch at his waist.

Louis and Jones were talking a few feet away. Some sawdust trickled down on Kassa's head. He looked up and cursed. Malikot, his saw halfway through the branch, clutched at another branch, then fell. I jumped clear. Kassa tried to duck, stumbled, and Malikot crashed squarely on Kassa's head. Both hit the ground hard. Malikot got up, cringing with terror. Kassa, head twisted to one side, didn't move. I started to lift him by the shoulders. His neck was broken.

Malikot went to his knees, crossed his arms on his chest, and bowed his head. Louis bent over Kassa, cried something in Amharic, straightened up, and kicked Malikot in the side. Malikot curled up in a ball, arms protecting his head. Louis kicked him again. I started a punch, but Jones grabbed my shoulder and hurled me on my backside. Then he pushed Louis, who was foaming at the mouth, away from his victim.

I helped Malikot to his feet. The kicks had hurt him badly and he gasped as if ribs were broken. It was then that I noticed his back was cries-crossed with purple whip welts, some of them crusted with blood. He sat huddled beside the eucalyptus tree—little more than skin and bone—while Jones and Louis carried Kassa's body to the house.

Thirty other peasants, in frightened groups, back a little distance, began murmuring among themselves and staring at something behind me. It was an ancient, gray-haired man shuffling beside a tiny donkey. The old man paused to watch Kassa carried through the door, then came on, greeted me, and stopped beside Malikot. They spoke a few words. The old man looked sad, shook his head, took a folded quilt from the donkey's back, spread it on the ground, and sat himself in the middle of it. The peasants timidly drew closer. When they were about thirty feet from the old man, he spoke one word. The peasants squatted silently on their haunches.

Jones and Louis returned from the house, and Jones greeted the old man gravely; Ras Louis spoke gruffly. The old man talked, pointing to Malikot from time to time. The peasants inched closer. Jones said to me:

"Looks like they're going to try Malikot under the 'law of the old men.' The old man will be judge, and render a decision."

"Try Malikot for what? That was an accident."

"Louis is charging Malikot with murder. Now, be quiet."

It seemed a long time that the old man sat there studying us. His eyes seemed young in his old face—he stared at me for a full minute. When he withdrew his gaze and turned his attention to Jones, I sighed with relief.

Finally Louis began to talk. He accused Malikot of deliberately jumping down on Kassa's head. "Revenge for a beating I gave him the other day," Louis said.

The old man motioned to Malikot, who crawled close on hands and knees, and, kneeling, said:

"I have been sick with fever, and therefore could not do my full share of work. Therefore, Rases Louis and Kassa withheld meal for my pot. Being hungry, I could do less work, so I was given less meal. My wife is dead, and the child is but recently off the breast. Therefore, I took no food myself that the child might eat. When there was no more meal in my hut, I went to Ras Louis and threw myself at his feet and clutched his knees. I said, 'Give me food for my child, or she will die.' Ras Louis beat me with his whip—and the child has died.

"I fell from the tree because I have not eaten for five days, and also because I have no heart now that my child is dead. I fell because blackness covered my mind. I fell on Ras Kassa, and he has died."

Louis began to speak again, but the old man held up a hand, and said:

"A life for a life. Your brother was killed when this worker fell upon him from the tree. Therefore, you will kill this man in like manner. You will climb to the very same limb of the tree and fall upon this man in like manner. If this man dies, he has paid the debt he owes you. If he does not die yet, he has paid the debt—and you may not try again. It is the law."

Malikot whimpered. Louis cursed, protested, was silenced. Angrily he went to his house, returned with a bottle, drank deeply, hurled the bottle at Malikot and began to climb the tree. He couldn't quite straddle the first branch, so peasants boosted him until he got his feet on a low branch, hands on a higher. Grunting and puffing, he mounted to the limb in which Malikot's saw was still wedged.

Four peasants pushed Malikot to a spot directly below Louis, then scurried to safety. Louis hesitated to jump. Malikot stood with bowed head—trembling. There was a sudden, loud crack as the limb on which Louis leaned broke at the saw cut. Louis screamed as he fell head-first. Malikot slumped in a faint. Louis hit the ground on one shoulder, beside Malikot. I heard a bone crack. He sat up, screeching and spitting foam. He yelled something to the peasants. They scattered to huts and came running back, each with a rhino-hide whip.

Louis pointed to the prostrate Malikot, then stood aside, nursing his shoulder.

About twenty peasants rushed at Malikot—whips raised.

I hit Louis's chin so hard that his heels came up and he lit on the back of his head. He didn't even groan. I drove a left into the belly of a peasant who'd just brought his whip down on Malikot. The peasant turned a complete somersault and landed across Louis, his chamma up around his shoulders, bare buttocks exposed.

Someone banged me on the head from behind, and for a moment I was too dizzy to do anything but hang on to a guy who was trying to cut me across the face with his whip. My head cleared suddenly and I knocked my assailant down. For a few minutes all was bedlam—peasants yelling, whips swishing, Jones banging away with rights and lefts, laying a peasant low with each punch. I jerked a whip from a raised hand and lay about me among screaming blacks. Two or three broke and ran. Within seconds the whole mob was high-tailing across a field, chammas tucked high, bare flanks gleaming.

Louis was still out. The "old man" still sat patiently on his quilt. Jones and I had left our wagons and natives at a Sudan village east of Piborpost, and had foot-slogged over the mountains to Kassa's. Now we helped Malikot to where donkeys were corralled, threw on our packs, sat Malikot on the largest beast, and with rifles in one hand, led the string toward western hills.

Inside the Sudan we turned south, picked up our outfits, crossed a corner of Uganda, entered the Congo and pushed steadily on until over the Aruwimi River. We left Malikot with a missionary named Johnson, near Kilo.

Years later, I happened to be at a kraal in Northern Rhodesia when the Zulu minister, Sehemo, arrived. I recognized him at once as Malikot. He was then a fine-looking man, bearded, with large, kindly eyes. He knew me at once also, but we didn't get a chance to talk privately until the next morning.

He told me of his conversion, his call to preach to the sick and unfortunate, and some of the tribulations he'd undergone. He'd been well educated since I'd last seen him, yet the learning had made him more humble.

On the Sunday morning following, he preached. There was not enough room in the little church for the throng that came to hear, so he preached in the open, a packing case for pulpit, thorn trees for background.

Here is the sermon I heard that day. I have translated it from notes. Malikot spoke in Shangaan:

"Some of you, my children, tell me that you pray, but get no answers. You tell me that you ask and ask, but that God turns away His ear. You tell me that you have great faith, because you are good men, but still, God does not hear you.

"You tell me that you refrain from swearing, from stealing, from committing adultery, from coveting your neighbors' belongings.

"I tell you that your prayers are not answered because the Love of God is not in them. You tell God how good you are. Then, you lie around the *mealie* pots waiting for Him to give you things as *bansela*—a reward. You obey the Old Testament commandments, but you forget that Jesus gave us two new commandments. They tower above all others, as yonder mountain towers above the veld. Listen:

"And thou shalt love the Lord thy God with all thy heart, and with all thy soul, and with all thy mind, and with all thy strength: this is the first commandment.

"And the second is like, namely this. Thou shalt love thy neighbor as thyself. There are none other commandments greater than these.

"Hear me, my children! You are like oxen. God is your driver. The road is rutty, stony, winding, scored. It climbs steeply toward the distant peak of the wind-tortured mountain. It dips into mudholes. The oxen slip. Their hooves make grooves in the mud. The road hangs on the edge of a cliff. To fall means death on the rocks far below. The wagon skids, and slides toward the edge of the *krans.* It stops. The oxen tremble. The driver speaks to them, calling each by name. He speaks gently, encouragingly. He talks them into leaning against their yokes... all together... all as one.

"The driver says, 'Pull, my sons. We must reach the summit and get down into the warm valley on the other side before the night comes with its purple thunders; before the winds rise shrieking, and the rain makes our road a torrent. Pull, my sons, with all your hearts, with all your souls, with all your minds, with all your strength.'

"The oxen strain. They bow their backs. The wagon creaks. It moves. It rolls. The driver walks up and down beside the span. He pats an ox here, and another there. He encourages all. He praises their sturdy efforts.

"At last he lets the span pause to rest beside a road that winds off to the left. It has an easy grade, and the grass that grows along it seems green and moist. In the span is a young ox, a gray one. He turns toward the left-hand road. He tries to pull his yoke mate with him. The driver tries to soothe him. But the young ox sees only the easy way. He tries to break from the span. He jerks at his yoke chain. He falls. He struggles to rise, and his long horns tangle in his neighbor's yoke strap. All is confusion.

"Gently the driver pats the wayward ox. He says, 'You have not learned to obey—to trust me to know the best way to go. Until you learn, we must get along without you, for the night comes, and we must get to the fruitful valley.'

"He unyokes the gray ox, and says, 'Follow us, or remain behind, as you choose. We can let you delay us no longer.'

"The gray ox turns down the easy road, but the wagon, drawn by the faithful oxen, creaks steadily up the hill. The gray ox bawls in protest at being left alone. There is no answer. He turns, and follows the wagon, still bellowing.

"The summit is reached just as darkness falls upon the eastern slopes. But westward through the pass shines the copper-red sun, spreading his comfort over the wide, grassy valley far below. The driver sets the wagon brakes, and the load rolls easily down, down into the valley floor with its knee-high grass, and clear, cooling waters.

"The oxen graze until shadows fall, and are then driven into a thorn *boma* that has been prepared for their protection against night-prowling lions and hyenas. The gate is shut, and the faithful oxen lie down to rest, scratching their backs with the points of their long horns. But the gray ox stands with his head over the *boma* gate. He sees the darkness creeping across the plain. He sees the shadows blacken beneath the thorn trees. But the grass is high, and he bawls to be let out. He pushes at the gate. Again he stands bawling, entreating his master to let him go forth into the danger.

"The driver hears him bellowing, but he does not answer.

"It comes to me, O Foolish Ones, that you have been bawling for the Master to let you out among the lions."

Nicobar Jones was a shrewd but honest trader. Until he was twelve years old he'd lived on a farm near Alliance, Ohio, had run away from home to join a circus, had become fascinated by its elephants and lions, had worked his way to Africa, and within ten years had established trading areas in Northern Rhodesia, Angola, German East Africa, German West Africa, Uganda, Congo, and Cameroons. I've known many of Africa's best traders, but none with the imagination and ingenuity of Jones.

Now at Kilo, where we'd left Malikot, Jones said to me:

"Take one wagon, follow the Aruwimi to Basoko, then trade along the Congo to Brazzaville. This Ethiopian business has set us back $3000."

"Wagons are practically empty," I said. "What'll I use for trade goods?"

"That Number Two Brownie camera," Jones said.

I must have shown resentment, for Jones said:

"There ain't no easier or quicker way to make a dollar. You couldn't make a shilling by hunting across that stretch."

"All right," I said, sighing. That battered, old Number Two Brownie had earned Jones thousands of dollars. In one four-week trip alone I'd picked up four hundred goats with it. Of all the jobs I've ever done those snapshot-taking safaris stand out in my memory as most galling.

Into my wagon Jones loaded a roll of blueprint paper—three feet long and five inches in diameter. He said:

"There's 26,000 square inches of paper here. That'll make about 3200 pictures. Figuring 'em at five to a goat means 640 goats. You trade seven goats for an ox. That's ninety oxen. Sell 'em to construction crews for $30 each. That's mighty close to $3000. You're carrying a thousand yards of calico, too. All in all, you ought to hit Brazzaville with $4000."

He handed me a waterproof box containing the Brownie camera that took 2 1/2 x 3 1/2-inch pictures, a small developing tank, 200 rolls of film, 200 tubes of developing powders, several pounds of hypo, a pair of scissors, a 4 x 6-inch printing frame, and three small hard-rubber trays. I said:

"Nothing to it—just take six or seven hundred pictures, and make three or four thousand prints."

Jones bristled his eyebrows at me. Hastily I said, "All right. All right."

This happened more than thirty years ago, yet some of those darned blue-and-white snapshots I took on that trip are still to be found in kraals all across Congo Belge. Incidentally we used blueprint paper because it could be printed in daylight, and "fixed" with plain water.

One of the most delightful pictures I've ever taken I took on that trip. It was a bright, golden morning with no breeze. The veld was not quite brassy, for tinges of green remained in the drying grass. I was out after meat, and toward noon approached a group of anthills—some as large as native huts. As I rounded an anthill I saw a goat, ears forward, tail perked, head on one side, eying with intense interest something outside my vision.

I stepped softly, and peeked around the anthill. A few feet away a little black boy about eight years old was urinating in a high, silvery arc. The stream was falling a few inches from the goat's nose. I snapped the picture. The boy heard the click of the camera, turned, saw me, and, still holding his penis, stared at me with absolute horror. I turned the film and got that picture, too. Then I gave the lad a shilling. He snatched it and ran as if devils were after him—the goat galloping behind him.

Well, I took pictures of natives for four months—men, women, and kids—fat ones, thin ones, short ones, tall ones, clean ones, dirty ones, mean ones, pleasant ones. I put the films in the little developer tank, turned the handle for several minutes, opened the tank in dark, smelly huts, ran the films through hypo baths, washed them in water, hung them to dry, and next day scissored 2¼ x 3¼-inch pieces out of the blueprint roll, put them under the film in the printing frame, set the frame in the sunlight, watched the pictures transfer with beautiful, purple-bronze shadows, washed the prints in water, saw them turn to cold blues and whites, dried the prints, and gave five of them to natives in exchange for one goat.

Herd boys, accepting their wages in pictures, drove the goats to cattle-raising kraals where other herders, also accepting pictures for wages, drove the oxen, for which I'd traded the goats, to construction stations.

Determined to show Jones that I was as good a trader as he, I worked out a meat-trading system that added considerably to my take. I'd trade a rhino for three oxen, a giraffe for two, a zebra for four goats, a hartebeest for two, an impala for one.

I traded calico for bangles, leopard hides, ivory, native musical instruments, drums, and weapons.

On arrival at Brazzaville I handed Jones $4100 in cash, and pointed to my wagonload of miscellaneous junk. He held the bag of money, patted the wagon affectionately, and with eyebrows working like mad, said:

"You done good."

I felt pleased—that was the highest praise that Jones could bestow.

It was on that same trip that I first met Frederick Schlick, now a Hollywood playwright—and a leading authority on baboons. As with the little boy who'd been amusing the goat, I took Schlick's picture before he was aware of me. I'd stepped out of the brush, and there he was on a camp stool, holding a fishing rod with a banana dangling at the end of the line in place of hooks. A big baboon, torn between hunger and caution, danced uncertainly several yards beyond the banana. Schlick held a camera in his lap. He was attempting to lure the baboon close enough for a picture.

At sound of my camera shutter Schlick looked up, grinned, and said:

"Suspicious devils, baboons."

"Watch," I said, and stepped behind Schlick and grunted the baboon word for "okay"— "Oog-WAH."

The baboon stopped his nervous shuffling, looked beyond Schlick and me, seemed puzzled, circled around us and back to his place near the banana. Again I grunted, "Oog-WAH."

The baboon looked at me from the side of his eye. I said:

"Oog-WAH, oog-WAH, oog-WAH."

With almost no hesitation he sidled to the banana, picked it up, tore it from the line, peeled it, stuffed it into a cheek pouch, and sat down expectantly.

Schlick tied another banana on the line and cast it to the baboon. At my word "Oog-WAH" the baboon grabbed that banana, peeled and stuffed it into his other cheek.

I grunted, "Jorgoom." The baboon tensed. I barked:

"Jor-GWAUFF." The baboon streaked for the bushes. Schlick said:

"He understood you!"

"I'm the only white man living who can speak Baboon," I said, and added, "Well, four words, anyway."

"You mean men speak Baboon?"

"Well, some natives 'converse' with baboons. I learned two words from baboons themselves, when studying them in the Magaliesberg district in the Transvaal. My other two words were taught me by a black boy who'd lived with baboons, as a baboon, for about twelve years."

This baboon boy, later known as Lucas Smith, was stolen by a mother baboon, from a Xhosa kraal, when an infant. For twelve years he lived with the baboon troop on the *kopjes* northeast of Grahamstown, Cape Colony.

One day two mounted policemen saw the troop invading a field, and frightened them away. Unable to keep up with his terrified mates, Lucas was run down and caught. It required some believing, but the policemen became convinced that they'd captured a boy —not a young baboon.

Authorities put him in the Grahamstown Mental Hospital, where he prowled the corridors, snarling and threatening to bite. Finally turned out of the hospital, Lucas was "adopted" by a nurse. He tore up his clothes, killed the woman's cats, chased her dogs, rode her oxen into declines.

Authorities took the boy to his mother, but she refused to have anything to do with him. A kindly farmer, named George Smith, decided to try his hand with the boy.

It required months for the boy to learn even his name. Meanwhile, however, he insisted on tearing up the garden in search of insects for food. Smith tried keeping the lad in the house, but he wouldn't housebreak, so at night he was kept in a locked hut. Sometimes he would break out, and go roaming through the hills. Smith would hunt him down and bring him back.

Lucas finally learned to leave small animals alone, but for years he couldn't be broken of riding oxen at every opportunity. It was many years before the boy gave up his diet of insects and rodents, but in time he became a reasonably reliable farm hand, and was devoted to George Smith.

I visited Lucas when I was about nineteen. He'd been with Smith only a few years, and was still more baboon than human. He hid from all visitors, and hid from me, but when he heard my "Oog-WAH" two or three times, he lost his fear. I think he had the impression that I too was a baboon who'd somehow got mixed up with humans, as he had.

Using his very limited vocabulary, he told of many incidents in his early life. He'd received the long scar on his face when an ostrich kicked him while he was robbing its nest. He said all baboons listen for their sentries' call: "Jorgoom!" which means:

"Be alert." "Jorgoom" is usually followed by the cry: "Jor-GWAUFF!" meaning: "Run! Danger!"

Another word the boy taught me was a throaty, gurgling "Zhooooo," used by young males when attempting to persuade females to dally with them.

On my last African trip I went to visit Lucas again, but he had died. I was shown his grave on the slope of the *kopje* that had been his childhood home. The headstone reads:

LUCAS, THE BABOON BOY

RHINO HORNS FOR ROMANCE

Writing only of the exciting adventures in a hunter's life is like crossing a wide, level plain by leaping from high anthill to high anthill. There are smaller anthills on the veld, and, although less dramatic, I like them better. Miki Carter and the lion that climbed trees, for instance.

Most lion pictures one sees in Europe and America were taken on the Serengeti Plain in Tanganyika, where lions are tame to the point of absurdity. Serengeti lions even climb trees. So fearless are some prides that they permit humans to approach within a few feet. Martin and Osa Johnson once came upon a family of Serengeti lions devouring a kill. The lions ignored the Johnsons completely, so Martin decided to join them at dinner. He and Osa set up a small folding table, laid plates on it, placed folding chairs, seated themselves, and had their picture taken while enjoying a spot of tea less than twenty yards from the feeding cats.

Another time, taking a close-up of a feeding lion, Martin became so impatient with the big beast's benign expression that he drove the animal off, sprinkled the kill with red pepper, and photographed the lion as it spat, sneezed, and snorted over the tongue-stinging flesh.

On Miki Carter's first African trip every penny he owned was invested in his cameras, and he was so concerned about their safety that he instructed me that in case it came to a choice of protecting the cameras or himself I was to protect the cameras.

One morning we left camp in a wobbly, battered Ford flat-bed, and headed for two large, low-forked trees that stood alone in the center of a vast, grass-grown prairie. The grass was only inches high, and it didn't seem possible that anything larger than a rabbit could hide in it. The morning was hot, and the partial shade afforded by the two trees was so welcome that we decided to move camp to the shelter of their flat-topped, umbrellalike branches.

A few small birds were the only living things abroad. They were hopping about on a sun-dried zebra carcass that lay partially overgrown with grass, about fifty yards beyond the trees. While I drove back to pick up our meager outfit and Kamgwara, our only native, Miki stayed beneath the trees to tinker with a camera.

About an hour later, as Kamgwara and I chugged and bumped toward the two trees, Kamgwara, beside me on the cushionless seat, began grunting. I said:

"Don't keep making like a pig."

Kamgwara was not a smart native. I doubt he had the intelligence of an aardvark. But he was big and strong, and willingly did the work of three ordinary Kaffirs. He weighed at least 225 pounds, and every pound was tough muscle. His grunting grew so persistent that I stopped the flat-bed and asked him if he were sick. He pointed to the two trees, and said in Chingoni:

"*Ngwenyama.*"

"Lion? Where?"

"In tree."

I shaded my eyes. Sure enough, there was a large, dark lump in each of the low-forked trees. I dug my glasses out of the gear on the truck, focused, and saw that the lump in the tree to the left was Carter, and the lump in the other tree a lion. At the base of Carter's tree his camera lay, one leg of the tripod sticking up as if pointing.

I headed for the trees, honking the horn, bouncing equipment off the truck at every bump. The lion leaped to the ground, bounded over the zebra carcass, then disappeared. Carter stayed in his tree until I stopped the truck a few yards away. Then he dropped to his feet beside the overturned camera, and fussed over it like a mother over a baby with colic. When he found his camera wasn't hurt, he said:

"After you'd gone, I took off the lens, polished it, set the camera on the tripod, and focused it on that dead zebra. That's all it was—an old, dried-up, dead zebra. But when I peeked at the focusing glass, there were two lions staring at me from behind the carcass. Automatically I began taking pictures. All of a sudden it struck me that I was in a hell of a spot. Next thing I knew I was up in that tree, one of the lions stretched out like a cat after a bird, stalking toward my camera. I yelled, and the other lion took off across the plain, but that first one, a big, dark-maned fellow, kept right on stalking the camera. When he got close, he put out a paw and slapped at a leg of the tripod. The camera fell over, one leg flying up, hitting the lion under the chin. He growled, and leaped to the fork of the other tree. He's been squatting there ever since, eying the camera, and making nasty noises."

"He disappeared back of the zebra," I said. "Must be a big hollow in the ground back there. I'll go see."

"Wait," Carter said. "That lion hates my camera. I'll get a rope from the truck, tie it to the camera, put Kamgwara up in the tree with the other end of the rope, and if the lion charges, Kamgwara can pull my camera up out of danger."

"Okay," I said. While Carter got the rope, then sent Kamgwara up the tree with one end and fastened the other to the tripod, I checked my rifle and moved so I could come at the zebra carcass from the side.

When Carter felt sure that Kamgwara knew what to do, he took his stand beside the camera, grasped the crank, and said:

"Let's go."

I'd taken only a few steps when Kamgwara yelled a warning. I turned to see a light-maned lion coming at me from behind. My bullet hit him as he struck the ground at the end of a jump. He rolled over two or three times, and lay kicking. Kamgwara yelled again. Carter's lion was stalking the camera again, Carter grinding away like mad.

Twenty yards away the lion stopped, lay flat on his belly, drew his hind legs under him, lifted his rump, and with head still on the ground began switching his tail.

Kamgwara, panicky, hauled up frantically on the rope. But in his excitement Kamgwara had left the rope so slack that it'd formed a loop in the grass beside the camera. Unknowingly Carter had put one foot inside the loop. As the lion leaped, Carter suddenly dangled upside down by one foot, the camera twisting and spinning in the air just below him. Evidently nonplussed by Carter's shrieks and Kamgwara's roars, the lion skidded to a stop just as Carter, his foot free of the rope, fell with a thump a yard from the lion's nose.

In a single bound the lion was back in his tree, out the other side, and bounding across the plain as fast as he could go.

Looking dazed, Carter got to his feet, motioned Kamgwara to lower the camera, examined it, sighed with relief that it was undamaged, then said:

"Whew!"

And the adventure of Captain Wilson, Ubusuku, and the punchdrunk rhino. It started because the girls of Italian Somaliland are trained for love. Many of them are beautiful, ranging in color from black to cream. Adept at lovemaking, they're the most praised prostitutes in East Africa, and many a wealthy playboy pays large sums to acquire a lighter-colored Somali girl as a mistress.

Captain Butler Wilson, once of the British Army, Ubusuku, and I were hunting along the Guaso Nyiro, west of Lorian Swamp. Wilson, about sixty, limped badly because of old leg wounds, and, although in considerable pain at times, he never complained. He was after big tusks, and big crocodiles. He was not interested in rhino.

One stuffy, airless afternoon we were sitting beneath a dom palm on the north bank of the river, eating figs out of cans. The only greenery in sight was the fringe of trees along the river. The plain to the north was flat and dry, not a blade of grass to be seen. Here and there were dusty, gray thorn bushes. Downstream a six-foot crocodile lay, snout out of water, watching a thin Boran cow stepping down to drink. Through a gap in the palm trees I saw the back end of a herd of slowly moving zebras. Directly across from us a rhino walked to the river's edge and began to drink. Wilson said:

"I've heard that powdered rhino horn's an aphrodisiac."

"At your age!"

"No, no," Wilson said, flushing, "not for me. I've a friend who's just taken a Somali girl as his mistress. I was thinking it might be a good rag to send him a rhino horn, er, I mean to say, he'd get the significance, don't you think?"

"Powdered rhino horn isn't really an aphrodisiac," I said. "I've sold a lot of them for that purpose, though—to a dealer in Mombasa. He ships them to India."

"Damn it! I know they're not an aphrodisiac. I merely want to have a game with this chap. The Somali girl, y'know... I mean, I've heard ..."

I looked at the rhino, estimated the distance at 350 yards, and suggested that Wilson try to pot it from where we sat. He got his .505 from

Corel Professional Photos CD-ROM

Black rhino with tickbirds.

the wagon, set the sights, and knelt for the shot. Before he could press the trigger, the rhino wheeled and trotted away.

There were two gerenuks waiting behind the wagons to be skinned, and I wanted the job done before they got too high. I said:

"You and Ubusuku go get the rhino, Captain. You won't need me along. Rhinos aren't particularly dangerous in open country. If this fellow should charge, remember that a shot anywhere in the foreparts will turn him."

With the help of two Boran boys I got the hides off the gerenuks, and got to wondering about Wilson. He'd been gone almost an hour, and I'd heard no shot. I got my .303 and took out after him.

I walked for a good half hour. The sun was so hot I didn't dare touch the rifle barrel. Sweat soaked my boots and came through the leather in salty-white streaks. Once I stopped to try to cool off in the shade of a thorn bush, but as soon as I sat, sweat seemed to pour from me. I got up and plodded on.

As I approached a small clump of brush, a rhino rose to its feet, walked into the open, turned, and stood moving his head nervously from side to side, occasionally tilting his horn so he could peer past it. From a grass clump about seventy yards beyond the rhino Wilson rose, aimed and fired. The rhino staggered a few paces, then began trotting in a tight circle. Wilson limped closer, fired again. The rhino stopped circling and took after Wilson at a gallop. Wilson turned to run, his game leg collapsed, and he sprawled in the grass, his rifle hurtling off.

Ubusuku bounded out of the brush. I threw up my rifle, but lowered it as the rhino went to its knees and flopped over on its side—dead. As a second rhino came full-tilt out of the brush at Wilson, he got up, clutched his game leg, then fell writhing to the ground. Running to pick up Wilson's rifle, Ubusuku got between me and the rhino. Then he spoiled my shot again by running to the rhino and, with Wilson's heavy .505 in his hands, racing along beside the brute.

Wilson got to his feet again, but fell. The rhino had lowered his head for the thrust when Ubusuku, clubbing the rifle, banged the beast's horn with a tremendous swipe. The rhino went down. The butt broke from the barrel and whirled off by itself. The rhino got up. Ubusuku banged the horn again. Again the rhino went down. Wilson, less than twenty feet away, tried hopping on one foot. The rhino struggled to rise, but went flat again as, for the third time, Ubusuku crashed the rifle barrel against the front horn.

I came up running, put the muzzle of my .303 against the side of the rhino's head just under the rear horn.

"Don't shoot," Wilson said.

I stepped back from the rhino as it got groggily to its feet.

"He's a game old boy," Wilson said. "Let him go."

"What about your friend's love life?" I asked.

"One Somali girl—one rhino, eh?" Wilson said.

The rhino, still punchdrunk, ambled into the brush.

I've seen rhinos knock themselves out by barging horn-on into trees, and I've seen them knocked cold when a bullet tipped the front horn, but that was the first and last time I've seen a rhino knocked stiff with a club.

Sharif was a camel. Most camels are stupid, sullen, and vicious. Sharif was all that, and cross-grained, insolent, malicious, dirty, and dangerous to boot. He hated me with awesome intensity. Yet he worked well after he'd received his daily morning beating.

I don't approve of beating animals, but camels are different. No amount of sweet talk will get the average camel to his feet once his load has been strapped on. Even while loading is going on, he'll spit, cry, howl, sputter, and bite. Some are worse than others, of course, but almost all refuse to move until given several hard bangs with a stout stick.

Sharif began shenanigans the moment he got the idea he was to be loaded. He'd kneel, all right, then roll a cud up his throat the size of a cricket ball, and hold it in his mouth. Then he'd moan and mutter, groan and splutter until you forgot yourself and stepped too close to his head, whereupon he'd spit that nauseating, soft green cud smack into your face and spray your clothes with a mouthful of stomach juices. If you weren't careful, he'd then bite you for good measure.

While Sharif moaned and cried, we'd place his "saddle pads." On them would go rugs, then a wicker frame. Next, four red wooden waterpots would be hung from the "saddle," two on each side. On the frame would go the load, and over that my folded tent, strapped on like a tarpaulin. When all was snug, I'd yell:

"Goom [Rise]!"

Sharif would howl like a banshee.

"*Goom! Goom!*"

More howls, and Ahmed, my camel boy, would rush up waving a stick, shouting:

"Goom, you son of a dog! Goom!"

Sharif would stop howling and begin to whine. A blow on the flank. Sharif would cry. Another blow. Sharif would groan. A blow. Sharif would howl again—this time loud enough to shatter the heavens. Then he'd heave to his feet to stand sputtering and blubbering. If you didn't know it was only a pose, you'd have felt sorry for him. I felt sorry the first time I loaded him. While he stood so apparently heartbroken, I stepped close to pat him. He kicked me in the stomach. I've been kicked by horses, but. none ever dumped me so violently as Sharif did that day. As kickers, horses are sissies compared to camels.

And that wasn't the end of Sharif's insults that morning. When I got my breath back, I got to my feet, grabbed Ahmed's stick, and with fire in my eye, approached Sharif from behind. He put out the fire by immediately reversing his penis and urinating on me from between his back legs. That's how male camels always urinate. I'd forgotten, but I never forgot again.

Having thus established our future relationship, Sharif and I got along well. He spat on me, kicked, or bit me whenever he got the chance. I added to his load until he was carrying 550 pounds, and, once under way, carrying it more or less cheerfully. Sharif could outwork any other camel in the caravan. He'd do thirty miles a day across the hottest, driest sands, and do it without food or water for eighteen days before commencing his thirst cry. After a prolonged waterless spell he'd drink fifteen gallons without lifting his head, lie down for an hour, then come back to the pan and drink another ten gallons.

Camels don't store water in their humps—those humps are pure fat. Water is stored in the muscles. During semi-starvation periods the hump fat is used as food, and as it's absorbed, the muscles release water. When Sharif's hump got soft and thin, he'd replenish it with only three weeks' grazing. Most other camels require at least three months.

I owned Sharif only during a two-month trip I took through the country between Marsabit and Buna. I was with a British army officer named Closset, who was making a survey of Northern Frontier District resins and woods. When the job was done, I sold Sharif to Aly, an East Indian friend of mine who ran a little trading post at Buna. But that wasn't the end of my association with Sharif.

A few months later I stopped at Buna en route south to Archers Post. While I stood near the well, watching the watering of cattle, camels, and goats, and half hypnotized by the chanting of the bucketpassers, Ahmed, my former camel boy, rushed up, and after shaking my thumb hurriedly, began to weep. I said:

"Now, now, Ahmed," then realized that he was thin and weak. I asked:

"Have you tick fever, Ahmed?" Almost everyone gets tick fever at Buna sooner or later. He said:

"My camels, my goats, my wives and my children are dying of thirst near the yellow-sand pan. A bandit sheik—a French Somali —will not let them drink until I pay him money—and I have no money. I came to Buna to find police, but there are no police— and my children die."

"Come with me," I said, and led the way to Aly's store.

Water-hole bandits—usually Somalis who prey on their own people— are the meanest robbers on earth. Nomad Somalis with families and flocks wander through brush so hot that white men find breathing difficult. The Somalis wander across almost grassless red, gray, and yellow soils in country so hot that only the hardiest of them travel during the day. It is at night that the caravans move, searching for grass so sparse that it sometimes seems that if one less blade grew, a beast would die. Somali camels, particularly during long, dry spells, are always thirsty. They drink, rest, and plod away on their eternal hunt for grass. Seldom do they get more than seven days away from pan or well, for fourteen days is the average camel's limit without water.

At Buna there is only one well, and day and night water is passed up from underground in camel-hide buckets, passed from hand to hand, poured in a trough while camels, goats, and cattle drink in relays. Day and night bleating, bawling, howling, and crying are continuous—as caravans arrive and depart.

Almost always, when a family arrives at water, It is touch and go. Often one additional day would be one day too many. Robber sheiks wait at outlying pans for caravans in such straits, and extort the last possible farthing for permission to drink.

"Lend me a fast camel, Aly," I said.

Aly grinned, and pointed inside a wire enclosure where Sharif lay on folded legs, his long-lashed eyes shut, his jaw working rhythmically.

I walked close, and said:

"Hi, Sharif!"

Sharif opened his eyes, saw me, and howled like a coyote. Then he broke off his howl, rolled his cud up his throat, and spat it at me. I ducked.

Aly handed Ahmed Sharif's pads and frame. Sharif howled and cried all the time he was being loaded, and when I crawled atop the load, almost broke his snakelike neck trying to bite my legs. An unusually hard beating was required to get him to his feet, but once up, he moved off swaying, head moving from side to side.

The pan was eighteen miles out. Its water was dirty, and warm. Lolling under a tree was a lone Somali, his eyes shifting from me to Ahmed's animals farther back in the brush. I said:

"Have you rested?"

He glared without answering.

"You will be late at Wajir," I said. "You had better go."

He sneered.

I said: "Get out of the way, so Ahmed's cattle can drink. They do not like your smell."

Several of Ahmed's smaller children, all boys, all naked, moved close with wide, frightened eyes. The Somali pulled at his beard, got to his feet, and in a quiet, almost polite voice, damned the children, their forebears, and future offspring to hell. Forgetting dignity as his anger mounted, he began waving his arms just as Ahmed, who'd followed me on foot, came up. Ahmed yelled something. Four teenage boys came to his side. The Somali's arm-waving grew violent. Sharif, who'd been eying the robber with increasing distaste, now opened his lips and shot sprays of spit in the Somali's face.

Ahmed said something to his sons, and the five of them began pummeling the Somali. I turned Sharif and for a few minutes watched the melee from a little distance. As I rode away, the bandit was skirting the pan in a frenzied lope, and Ahmed's cattle, goats, camels, and children were all drinking from the pan together.

It was dark when, back at Aly's, Sharif knelt to let me dismount. A camel boy unsaddled him. I turned to loosen the wire gate.

Sharif kicked me hard, between the shoulders.

I stood alone in the Congo dusk, one degree north, twenty-five degrees east. Pink-and-copper clouds, deserted by the sun, were losing their colors like dying fish. The moon, full-bellied and pumpkin-yellow, floated upward from behind a purple hill. Scattered thorn trees turned from gray to black. A lone antelope, knee-deep in darkening grass, for a few moments was pink in the fading light.

The heart of Africa—and Christmas Eve.

I gathered twigs and dry grass into a mound, and placed five dry-rotted logs on top. I put a match to the leaves, and a ribbon of flame wriggled snakelike through the kindling. I went to a nearby tree, took down a young zebra haunch, cut off a thick steak, speared it with a stick, held it close to the blossoming fire. A toad hopped onto my foot, then into the flames. One of the logs began steaming. A scorpion, angry tail held above its back, rushed out from one end of the log, scurried to the cooler end, then tumbled off into burning twigs.

The moon, now almost white, seemed to be drawing farther and farther away, but millions of stars that had seemed distant and feeble now came closer, as if being let down on strings.

As so often when loneliness came, I had a weird feeling I'd drifted from America to Africa like a toy balloon that escapes the hand of a child. There seemed no logical reason why I should be out here in tropical Africa's moody silences—and alone.

The zebra steak sizzled, but I was no longer hungry. I dropped meat and stick into the fire, watched the resulting bomb-burst of sparks, moved back a bit from the heat, sat on my folded blanket, and thought of men in the world's distant places—alone on Christmas Eve.

I remembered an army campfire in Southwest Africa and a young lieutenant reading bits from *A Shropshire Lad* to his platoon. And another night in the Cameroons when another young Britisher, who'd been brooding for hours, got abruptly to his feet, and quoted:

> *"Name me no names for my disease,*
> *With informing breath,*
> *I tell you I am none of these,*
> *But homesick unto death."*

I remembered Benny Cashmore, onetime corporal in the Tenth Royal Grenadiers, who one night in Angola, delirious and dying, stopped tossing and moaning, to sing:

> *"I remember Polly, hanging up the holly, and*
> *the..."*

Benny paused, listened, whispered hoarsely:

"Give me a thousand yards of barbed wire, and six Mills bombs, and I'll take the Western front," then fell back—dead.

The immensity of Africa around me aroused strange emotions. I felt growing resentment toward Nicobar Jones, who'd taken the wagons and Kaffirs and gone off to Murchison Falls, leaving me to guard some gear and await his return. I dug a stub of a pencil from a pocket and began writing a verse beginning: "Alone! Alone?"—having a fine time feeling sorry for myself—when I noticed that night noises had ceased. I listened.

Faintly, but clearly, I heard a voice raised in song—a Scottish voice, a drunken voice—an *American* song.

Excited and startled, I got to my feet and yelled:

"Ahoy!"

"What-ho! What-ho! What-ho!" came the answer.

The singing continued, words garbled by a liquor-thick tongue:

" 'On the banksh of the Washbank far-r away.' —"

Abruptly the singer was within the circle of firelight. A little man with a big nose, a rolled pack low on his back, and a bottle of whiskey, one-half full, in his hand. He took off his pack, offered me the bottle, and said:

"If you've a wee bit of meat not too well done ..."

"Banks of the Wabash," I said, "not Washbank."

"R-richt, y' ar-re. Washbank it is. You'r-re an Amur-rican. So was Louis. That bit of meat now?"

I cut another steak from the zebra haunch and began to broil it on a stick. The stranger said:

"Louis taught me that song. My name's David Roger, and I'm dr-rinkin' my way acr-ross Afr-rica. I could see your-r fir-re."

"It's Christmas Eve," I said.

Roger looked at me strangely, then said:

"It is. It is. Ah, me! Louis'll be home by now. He always wanted to be home. Place called Detr-roit. Poor-r Louis. Ah, well, hand me the meat. I like it dr-rippin' r-reddish."

He ate with gusto, taking frequent small nips from his bottle. When he'd finished the steak, he wiped his mouth on his sleeve and said:

"I'm just fr-rom Bangassou on the Mbomu R-river-r. Know the place?"

"Yes—at the Equatorial Africa border."

"I'm on my way back to Elizabethville, and doin' a bit of dr-rinkin' as I go."

"Still seven or eight hundred miles to go," I said. "A half quart won't take you far."

"Half quar-rt? Hoot! I've dr-runk four-r quar-rts in the last two hundr-red miles, and I've yet twenty quar-rts waitin' for-r me along my way. Half quar-rt? Na, na!"

Then he told me that several months before, at Elizabethville, he'd been hired to guard a twenty-wagon freight outfit en route to a mining development near Bangassou. A long-time friend of his, Louis Weimer, had also been hired as mine foreman. The first day out Roger had discovered that one of the wagons carried ten cases of bottled whiskey. About every fifty miles thereafter he'd stolen a bottle and hidden it along the way. He said:

"I'm now dr-rinkin' my way back to civilization."

"And Louis?" I asked.

He sighed. "Louis is home safe by now, I tr-rust. He never-r could save enough money to go home. But I'm the saving kind, and when I'd saved enough, I paid his passage. He'd a ver-ra pr-retty wife back ther-re. He showed me her-r pictur-re often enough." He sighed again, and added:

"It r-requir-red five year-rs of savin' my odd shillin's. Or-rdinarrily I don't make much money, being a tinker-r, y'see. Mend pots, and the like."

Little by little, Louis's story came out. Six years ago Louis had married a "lovely, r-rosy-cheeked" Dutch girl at Johannesburg. At that time he'd been working in the Robinson Deep mine, and making good money. His wife became pregnant, and he shipped her off to Detroit, promising to be with her by the following Christmas. He'd gotten as far as Cape Town that year, gone on a bender while waiting for his ship, spent all his money, so returned to Johannesburg and his job. For four more years he'd done the same thing, growing sadder each year. "For-r," Roger said, "he loved that wee wife desper-rately."

"And you finally bought his ticket," I said. "You're a good sort, Roger."

"Aye. I bought his ticket."

"Well, he's home for Christmas this year, then," I said.

"Aye. Home for-r Chr-ristmas."

"You'll be hearing from him one of these days. Drink up."

Roger drank. "No," he said, "I won't be hear-rin' fr-rom him. He got dr-runk up ther-re at Bangassou, for-rgot to boil his dr-rinkin' water-r, and got the fever-r. I shipped Louis home, all r-richt, but he was dead."

I threw more wood on the fire. For a long while neither of us felt like talking, so we just sat, staring into the flames. At last Roger killed the bottle, got to his feet, and said:

"I was within thr-ree or-r four-r miles of another-r bottle when I saw your-r fir-rt. Let us get it and celebr-rate one mor-re Chr-ristmas."

It took some sleuthing, but Roger finally located the bottle in a brush clump. He uncorked it by thumping its bottom with the heel of his hand. We drank. We sang all the way back to my fire. We pulled my blanket nearer the heat, spread it out, sat down, and sang some more. We nipped from time to time, and tried harmonizing. It sounded good, so we put our heads close together, shut our eyes, and really made the welkin ring.

We sang *It's a Grand Old Flag, Scots Were Nae When Wallace Bled, On the Banks of the Wabash, Comin' through the Rye, Any Old Place in Yankeeland Is Good Enough for Me, Braw Bricht Nicht,* and Lord knows what else. Then each began singing a different song at the same time. Finally we got mixed up and thought we were celebrating New Year's Eve, so we joined hands and sang *Auld Lang Syne.*

Then it was morning. I looked up from where I lay in the grass beneath a thorn tree to see Roger dry-shaving with an old-fashioned straight razor. I was too headachy to talk, so lay watching. He wiped his razor, wrapped it in a piece of flannel, got out a canvas "housewife," mended a tear in his trousers, put the housewife away, picked up the almost empty bottle, shook his head, put the bottle near me, strapped on his pack, and started away. I sat up and said:

"Hey!"

Roger turned, smiled, and said:

"I've left you a dr-rink. Y'll need it, for-r 'tis plain you'r-re no a dr-rinkin' man."

And without a backward look he walked away, singing.

KILLERS IN AFRICA

The truth about animals lying in wait and hunters lying in print

Alexander Lake

series editor: Mike Resnick

RESNICK'S LIBRARY OF AFRICAN ADVENTURE

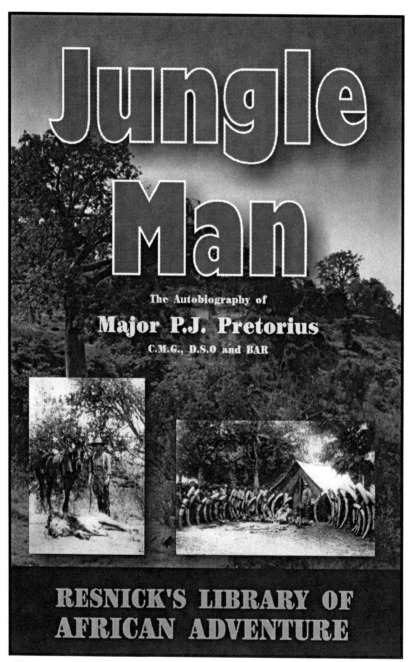

Jungle Man

The Autobiography of

Major P.J. Pretorius
C.M.G., D.S.O and BAR

RESNICK'S LIBRARY OF AFRICAN ADVENTURE

Printed in the United Kingdom by
Lightning Source UK Ltd., Milton Keynes
138424UK00002B/99/A